SIKHISM AND INDIAN CIVILIZATION

CULTURE AND CIVILIZATION SERIES

SIKHISM AND INDIAN CIVILIZATION

Edited by

Dr. R.K. Pruthi

DISCOVERY PUBLISHING HOUSE PVT. LTD.
NEW DELHI-110 002

First Published - 2004

Reprinted - 2015

ISBN: 978-81-7141-879-4

Published by:

DISCOVERY PUBLISHING HOUSE PVT. LTD.

4383/4B, Ansari Road, Darya Ganj

New Delhi-110 002 (India)

Phone: +91-11-23279245, 43596064-65

Fax: +91-11-23253475

E-mail: discoverypublishinghouse@gmail.com

sales@discoverypublishinggroup.com

web: www.discoverypublishinggroup.com

Printed at:

Infinity Imaging Systems

Delhi

Contents

PREFACE

Arnold Toynbee while writing forward for the UNESCO's project selections from the sacred writings of the sikhs held that Adi Granth is part of mankind's common spiritual treasure. He hailed its publication as an important event in the history of the rapidly increasing contact between different peoples and civilizations.

Aim of this exercise is to describe the teaching, philosophy, the great *gurus* and saints whose message have influence our civilization through the ages.

Needless to say how grateful we are to the authorities on the subject who have influenced us and whose works we have found very much worth including in preparing this work.

We are thankful to our scholar friends like Mohinder Singh, Sangat Singh, Avtar Singh Sohal and many others for their help and guidance.

Last but not the least we thank our publisher and his staff members for their hard work in its prompt publication.

R.K. Pruthi

Introduction

The sudden widening of the spatial horizon has widened at the same time the horizons of the mind. There is an eagerness to know the ideas and beliefs by which other people live. This translation of a few selections from the *Ādi Granth* is a small attempt towards the better understanding of other peoples' ideas and convictions.

The *Ādi Granth,* which is regarded as the greatest work of Punjabi literature, is largely the work of Guru Arjan, the fifth of the ten Sikh Gurus.[1] He brought together the writings of the first four Gurus and those of the Hindus and Muslim saints from different parts of India. Guru Arjan's successors made a few additions and the tenth Guru, Gobind Singh, said that there would be no more Gurus and the *Granth* should be regarded as the living voice of all the prophets: *Guru-Vāṇī*. William Penn says: 'There is something nearer to us than scriptures, to wit, the word in the heart from which all scriptures come'. Japji says: '*gurmukh nādaṁ gurmukh vedaṁ,'* 'the Word of the Guru is the music which the seers hear in their moments of ecstasy; the Word of the Guru is the highest scripture. By communion with the Word we attain the vision unattainable'. Guru Arjan says that the book is the abode of God: '*pothī paramesvar kā thān*'. The hymns are set to music. We find in *Ādi Granth* a wide range of mystical emotion, intimate expressions of the personal realization of God and rapturous hymns of divine love. The Sikh creed includes belief in the ten Gurus and the *Ādi Granth*.

A remarkable feature of the *Ādi Granth* is that it contains the writings of the religious teachers of Hinduism, Islam, etc[2].

This is in consistency with the tradition of India which respects all religious and believes in the freedom of the human spirit. Indian spiritual tradition is not content with mere toleration. There can be no goodwill or fellowship when we only tolerate each other. Lessing, in his *Nathan the Wise*, rebuked the habit of condescending toleration. We must appreciate other faiths, recognize that they offer rich spiritual experiences and encourage sacrificial living and inspire their followers to a noble way of life.

The Sikh Gurus who compiled the *Ādi Granth* had this noble quality of appreciation of whatever was valuable in other religious traditions. The saints belong to the whole world. They are universal men, who free our minds from bigotry and superstition, dogma and ritual, and emphasize the central simplicities of religion. The great seers of the world are the guardians of the inner values who correct the fanaticism of their superstitious followers.

The Hindu leaders neglected to teach the spiritual realities to the people at large who were sunk in superstition and materialism. Religion became confused with caste distinctions and taboos about eating and drinking. The Muslims were also victims of superstition and some of their leaders were afflicted with the disease of intolérance[3].

Saints arose in different parts of the country, intent on correcting the injustices and cruelties of society and redeeming it: Jnānesvar, Nāmdev, and Eknāth in Mahārāṣṭra, Narsingh Mehta in Gujerat, Caitanya in Bengal, Kabīr in Uttar Pradesh, Vallabhācārya in Āndhra and others.

All these stirred the people with a new feeling of devotion, love and humanity. They stressed that one's religion was tested not by one's beliefs but by one's conduct. No heart which shuts out truth and love can be the abode of God.

At a time when men were conscious of failure, Nānak appeared to renovate the spirit of religion and humanity. He did not found a new faith or organise a new community. That was done by his successors, notably the fifth Guru. Nānak tried to build a nation of self-respecting men and women, devoted to God and their leaders, filled with a sense of equality and brotherhood for all.

The Gurus are the light-bearers to mankind. They are the messengers of the timeless. They do not claim to teach a new doctrine but only to renew the eternal wisdom. Nānak elaborated the views of the Vaiṣṇava saints. His best known work is *Jap Sahib* or *Japji*, the morning prayer. Guru Arjan's popular composition is *Sukhmaṇi*.

The Sikh Gurus transcend the opposition between the personal and impersonal, between the transcendent and the immanent. God is not an abstraction but an actuality. He is truth, formless nirguṇa, absolute, eternal, infinite, beyond human comprehension. He is yet revealed through creation and through grace to anyone who seeks him through devotion. He is given to us as a Presence in worship. The ideas we form of Him are intellectualizations of that presence.

A great Muslim saint observed: 'Who beholds me formulates it not and who formulates me beholds me not. A man who beholds and then formulates is veiled from me by the formulation'. It is the vice of theology to define rather than to express, to formulate rather than to image or symbolize the indefinable.

Silence is the only adequate expression of that which envelopes and embraces us. No word, however noble, no symbol, however significant, can communicate the ineffable experience of being absorbed in the dazzling light of the Divine.

Light is the primal symbol we use, of a consciousness ineffably beyond the power of the human mind to define or limit. The unveiled radiance of the sun would be darkness to the eye that strives to look into it. We can know it only by reflection, for we are ourselves a part of its infinite awareness.

Muhammad adopted the rigid monotheism from Judaism. Thou shalt not make unto thee a graven image, nor any manner of likeness of anything that is in the heaven above or that is in the earth beneath, or that is in the water under the earth[4].

Rāmānanda was hostile to the worship of images. If God is a stone I will worship a mountain. Kabir says:

> The images are all lifeless, they cannot speak:
> I know, for I have cried aloud to them.
> The Purāṇa and the Qurān are mere words:
> Lifting up the curtain, I have seen[5].

Nānak was greatly impressed by the monotheism of Islam and denounced image worship. One God who is just, loving righteous, who is formless and yet the creator of the universe, who desires to be worshipped through love and righteousness that is the belief that has dominated Sikhism. When at the temple of Jagannāth, Nānak saw the worship in which lights were waved before the image and flowers and incense were presented on gold salvers studded with pearls, he burst into song:

> The sun and moon, O Lord, and Thy lamps; the firmament
> The salver and the oils of the stars the pearls set therein.
> The perfume of the sandal tree is Thy incense; the wind
> Is Thy fan, all the forests are Thy flowers, O Lord of light.

God is not limited to any one incarnation but sends His messengers from time to time, to lead struggling humanity towards him. It is the law of the spiritual world that whenever evil and ignorance darken human affairs, morality and wisdom will come to our rescue[6].

The Guru is the indwelling Divine who teaches all through the gentle voice of conscience. He appears outside in human form to those who crave for a visible guide. The enlightener is the inner self.

Nānak is, for the Sikhs, the voice of God arousing the soul to spiritual effort. Faith in the Guru is adopted by both the Hindus and the Muslim sufis. The latter emphasize the need of a religious teacher, Pir, to guide the initiate in prayer and meditation.

The Gurus are human and not divine. They are not to be worshipped. Guru Govind Singh says: 'Whosoever regards me as Lord shall be demned and destoyed…I am but the servant of God'.

God alone is real. The world is real because God animates it and is found through it. The created world is not in an absolute sense. It arises from God and dissolves into Him. How came the Changeless to create a world of change? How did the one go forth into the many?

If the one is compelled to create, it suffers from imperfection and insufficiency. But total perfection cannot have this insufficiency. The question assumes that the Eternal at one moment of time began the task of creation. But Eternity has no beginning and no end. If its nature is to create, it eternally creates.

The idea of a God absorbed in self-contemplation and then for some unknown reason rousing himself to create a universe is but a reflection of our human state. We alternate between activity and rest, between inertia and excitement.

Divine beatitude consists in a simultaneous union of contemplation and of act of self-awareness and of self-giving. A static perfection is another name for death. Nānak looks upon the creative power of the Supreme as māyā. It is integral to the Supreme Being.

The way to the knowledge of God is through self-surrender. It is not ceremonial piety; it is something inward in the soul. Those who, in the humanity of a perfect self-surrender, have ceased to cling to their own petty egos are taken over by the superhuman reality, in the wonder of an indescribable love.

The soul rapt in the vision and possession of a great loveliness grows to its likeness. Surrender to God becomes easy in the company of a saintly teacher, a Guru.

Man is a child of God. He is mortal when he identifies himself with the perishable world and body. He can become immortal through union with God; until then he wanders in the darkness of the world.

He is like a spark from the fire or a wave of the ocean. The individual comes forth from God, is always in Him as a partial expression of His will and at last, when he become as perfect, manifests God's will perfectly.

We have to tread the path which saints have trodden to direct union with the divine. We have to tread the interior way, to pass through crises, through dark nights and ordeals of patience.

Nānak says: 'Yoga is not the smearing of ashes, is not the ear-rings and shaven beard, not the blowing of conches but it is remaining unspotted amidst impurity, thus is the contact with Yoga gained'.

Nānak was critical of the formalism of both the Hindus and the Muslims. He went to bathe in the Ganges as is usual with devout Hindus. When the Hindus threw water towards the rising sun as an offering to their dead ancestors, Nānak threw water in the opposite direction. When questioned, he said: 'I am watering my fields in the Punjab. If you can throw water to the dead in heaven, it should be easier to send it to a place on earth.

On another occasion, he fell asleep with his feet towards Mecca. An outraged Mulla drew his attention to it. Nānak answered: 'If you think I show disrespect by having my feet towards the house of God, turn them in some other direction where God does not dwell'.

Nānak says: 'To worship an image, to make a pilgrimage to a shrine, to remain in a desert, and yet have the mind impure is all in vain; to be served, worship only the truth'.

Nānak tells as: 'keep no feeling of enmity for anyone. God is contained in every bosom. Forgiveness is love at its highest power'.

Nānak says: 'where there is forgiveness there is God Himself.

When Ajita Randhava asked Guru Nānak about ahiṁsä, Nānak replied:

1. Do not wish evil for anyone. This is ahiṁsä of thought.
2. Do not speak harshly of anyone. This is ahiṁsä of speech.
3. Do not obstruct anyone's work. This is ahiṁsä of action.
4. If a man speaks ill of you, forgive him.
5. Practise physical, mental and spiritual endurance.
6. Help the suffering even at the cost of your life.

Belief in a separate self and its sufficiency is the original sin. Self-noughting is the teaching of the seers of all religions. Jesus says: 'If any man would follow me, let him deny himself'.

Meister Eckhart declared that the kingdom of God is for none but the thoroughly dead. We should aim to escape from the prison of our selfhood and not to escape from the body which is the temple of God. Until we reach the end we will have other lives to pass through. No failure is final. An eventual awakening for all is certain.

Nānak and his followers believe in the doctrine of karma and rebirth. We are born with different temperaments. Some are greedy and possessive, others fretful and passionate. We come into the world bearing the impress of our past karma. Circumstances may stimulate these qualities. We may by our effort weaken the evil dispositions and strengthen the good ones.

True happiness cannot be found in perishable things. It is found only in union with the Supreme.

We are caught in the world of saṁsāra or change, in the wheel of births and deaths because we identify ourselves with the physical organism and the environment. We can be freed from the rotating wheel of saṁsāra by union with God attained through devotion.

We must accept God as the guiding principle of our life. It is not necessary to the renounce the world and becomes an ascetic. God is everywhere, in the field and the factory as in the cell and the monastery.

The Sikhs, like some other Vaiṣṇava devotees who preceded them, denounce caste distinctions. Rāmānanda said:

Jāti panthi pūcchai nahī koi
hari ko bhaje so hari kā hoi.

Let no one ask of caste or sect; if anyone worships God then he is God's. As God dwells in all creatures none is to be despised. When we become one with God through wholehearted surrender, we live our lives on earth as instruments of the divine.

The aim of liberation is not to escape from the world of space and time but to be enlighten, wherever we may be. It is to live in this world knowing that it is divinely informed. To experience a timeless reality we need not run away from the world.

For those who are no longer bound to the wheel of saṁsāra, life on earth is centred in the bliss of eternity. Their life is joy and where joy is, there is creation. They have no other country here below except the world itself. They owe their loyalty and love to the whole of humanity.

God is universal. He is not the God of this race or that nation. He is the God of all human beings. They are all equal in His sight and can approach Him directly. We must, therefore, have regard for other peoples and other religions.

Nānak strove to bring Hindus and Muslims together. His life and teaching were a symbol of the harmony between the two communities. A popular verse describes him as a Guru for the Hindus and a Pir for the Muslims.

Guru Nanak shah Fakir
Hindu kā Guru, Mussulman kā pīr.

The transformation of the peaceful followers of Nānak into a militant sect was the work of the sixth Guru, Har Gobind and of Guru Gobind Singh, the tenth and last Guru. The tenth Guru converted the young community of disciples (Sikhs, śiṣyas) into a semi-military brotherhood with special symbols and sacraments for protecting them. When his father Guru Teg Bahadur was summoned by Emperor Aurangzeb who faced him with the alternative of conversion to Islam or death, he preferred death and left a message: I gave my head but not my faith.

sirr dīyā purr sirrar nā dīyā.

His four sons also gave their lives in defence of their faith.

On the New Year Day in 1669, Guru Gobind initiated five of his followers known as Panj Pyārās (five beloved ones), into a new fraternity called the Khalsa or the Pure. Of these five one was a Brahmin, one a Kṣatriya and the others belonged to the lower castes.

He thus stressed social equality. They all drank out of the same bowl and were given new names with the suffix Singh (Lion) attached to them.

They resolved to observe the five K's, to wear their hair and beard unshorn (Keś),[7] to carry a comb in the hair (Kangha), to wear a steel bangle on the right wrist (Kara), to wear a pair of shorts (Kaccha), and to carry a sword (Kirpan).

They were also enjoined to observe four rules of conduct (rahat), not to cut their hair, to abstain from smoking tobacco and avoid intoxicants, not to eat meat unless the animal has been slaughtered in the manner prescribed, and to refrain from adultery.

A new script, a new scripture, new centres of worship, new symbols and ceremonies made Sikhism into a new sect, if not a new religion. What started as a movement of Hindu dissenters has now become a new creed.

It is, however, unfortunate that the barriers which the Sikh Guru laboured to cast down are again being recreated. Many pernicious practices against which they revolted are creeping into Sikh society. Worldly considerations are corrupting the great ideals.

Religion which lives in the outer threshold of consciousness without conviction in the mind or love in the heart is utterly inadequate. It must enter into the structure of our life, become a part of our being.

The Upaniṣad says: He alone knows the truth who knows all living creatures as himself. The barriers of seas and mountains will give way before the call of eternal truth which is set forth with freshness of feeling and fervour of devotion in the *Ādi Granth*.

—S. Radhakrishnan

REFERENCES

1. *(i)* Guru Nānak, 1469-1539.
   (ii) Guru Angad, 1504-1552.
   (iii) Guru Amar Dās, 1479-1574.
   (iv) Guru Ram Dās, 1534-1581.
   (v) Guru Arjan, 1563-1606.
   (vi) Guru Har Govind, 1595-1644.
   (vii) Guru Har Rai, 1630-1661.
   (viii) Guru Harkishan, 1656-1664.
   (ix) Guru Tegh Bahadur, 1621-1675.
   (x) Guru Gobind Singh, 1666-1708.
2. The *Ādi Granth* includes hymns by Farid (twelfth century), Beni (twelfth century), Jaideva (twelfth century), Sadhna (thirteenth century), Trilochan (b. 1267), Nāmdeva (thirteenth century), Rāmānand (1360-1450), Sain (1390-1440), Pipa (b. 1425), Kabir (1440-1518), Ravidas (fifteenth century); Dhanna (early sixteenth century), Bhikan (d. 1573), Sūrdas (b. 1528); Parmānanda, a discipline of Ramanand.
3. Nanak wrote: 'The age is a knife. Kings are butchers. They dispense justice when their palms are filled. Decency and laws have vanished, falsehood stalks abroad. Then came Babar to Hinduism. Death disguised as a Moghul made war on us. There was slaughter and lamentation. Did not thou, O Lord, feel the pain'?
4. Exodus xx. 3-4.
5. Rabindranath Tagore's English translation.
6. See *Bhagavadgita* iv. 7-8. (With Sanskrit text, translation and commentary by S. Radhakrishnan; Allen and Unwin, London, 1948).
7. Some Hindu ascetics do not cut their hair and beards.

Sikhism

While both Buddhism and Jainism were inspired by religious and social ideas that grew out of an entirely Hindu background, Sikhism is a comparatively recent development which has much to do with Islamic ideals. The conquest of India by Muslims brought Hinduism into close contact with Islam, and the simplicity of Muslim worship and its theology began to attract many enlightened Hindus. The incessant quarrels between Hindus and Muslims which at times resulted in bloodshed also made intelligent men recognize the need for an understanding between the followers of the two religions. The astute Akbar realized the political advantage of a union between Hinduism and Islam, and wished to found a national Indian religion with himself as the prophet of the new faith. He failed in his attempt. Guru Nanak who approached the problem from a purely religious angle succeeded in funding Sikhism.

Nanak was born at Talvandi, near Lahore, in 1469 A.D. He belonged to the Khatri caste of the Punjab, well-known for their fine physique and martial spirit. The boy Nanak was of a religious turn of mind. He neglected his secular duties and kept company with holy men, spending most of his time in discussing and brooding over subjects which had no bearing on farming or trade and the villagers pronounced him mad. At last the call came, and Nanak left his home and wandered all over India in the manner of Hindu saints. Religious music profoundly moved him, and he himself was the composer of many hymns. In the course of his wanderings he was accompanied by Mardana, a Muslim musician who played on the Rebek for Nanak.

This was the time when the great saint Kabir was wandering from Bukhara to Kalighat preaching his revolutionary ideals, and Nanak came under his influence. A few words about Kabir will not be out of place here. Kabir was a remarkable man and both Hindus and Muslims, to this day, claim him as their own. The Hindus say that Kabir was really a Hindu brought up by a family of Muslim weavers whereas the Muslims say that he was born a Muslim. Whatever his origin, at an early age he showed great interest in religion and became a disciple of the Vaishnava saint Ramananda who was a follower of Ramanuja, the founder of the Vishishta Advaita philosophy and of the Bhakti cult. Ramananda was persecuted it, South India for his extreme views on caste and migrated to Benares. Here he preached the Bhakti cult, and "among his twelve disciples were a Rajput, a cuurier, a barber and a Mussalman weaver named Kabir".

Kabir excelled the master himself. He was blessed with a keen wit and in his 'sayings' and songs poured ridicule on all formalists. All ceremonials and formal worship, those endless repetition of sacred texts and words, circumbulations round idols and the numerous prayers addressed to gods as a matter of form were, according to Kabir, mere waste of time and energy. "The beads are wood; the gods are stone; Ganges and Jumna are water; Rama and Krishna are dead and gone, and the Vedas are empty words". The ascetic with his matted locks and unkempt beard struck him as resembling a goat. The shaven priest with his long face and lengthy religious discourses was a babbler who did not understand what he was teaching others. Those who wished to worship God were asked to flee from the temple and the mosque, and seek Him in the fields, in the weaver's shop and the happy home. Only fools would try to find God in stones and structures. "God is one, whether we worship Him as Allah or as Rama. The Hindu worships Him on the eleventh day; the Muhammaden fasts at Ramzan; but God made all the days and all the months. The Hindu God live at Benares; the Muhammaden God at Mecca; but He who made the world lives not in a city made by hands.

Buddhism, Jainism, Sikhism, Brahmo Samaj and Arya Samaj

There is one father of Hindu and Mussalman, one god in all matter: He is the lord of all the earth, my guardian, and my priest". Again,

> "Oh servant, where dost thou seek Me? Lo, I am beside thee.
>
> I am neither in temple or in mosque: I am neither in Kaaba or Kailas[1].

Neither am in rites and ceremonies, nor in yoga or renunciation.

If thou art a true seeker, thou shalt at once seek me:

Thou shalt meet me in a moment of time.

Kabir says: 'O Sadhu! God is the breath of all breath"[2].

Such revolutionary teachings, a saintly life and a ready wit made Kabir the most popular figure of his time. But, for obvious reasons, organised society could not tolerate him for long. He was persecuted by the ruling classes and exiled from Benares. He wandered all over India with a band of followers. Wherever he preached the people applauded him. Even in distant Afghanistan, which place he visited, Kabir became the pet of the people. This great wandering saint of India died in 1518, and on his death both the Muslims and the Hindus claimed the body, the former to bury it according to Muslim rites and the latter to burn it. A legend says that while the disciples were thus violently disputing for the possession of the dead body, a celestial voice was heard commanding them to remove the wrapper of the coffin and look inside. On this being done, no corpse was found but the coffin contained only a heap of fresh flowers. Even this miracle could not settle the dispute. It is said the heap of flowers were equally divided among the Hindus and Muslims, the former taking away their share for burning and the latter for burying.

Although Kabir founded no organised sect, he is considered by Indians as one of the greatest saints India has ever produced and his followers, known as Kabirpanthis, number more than a million souls.

The life and teachings of Kabir profoundly influenced Nanak. After some years of wanderings, the call came to Nanak to teach and he preached before Jain and Hindu temples and Muslim mosques, and collected a number of Sikhs or disciples. Religion, he thought, was a bond to unite men, but in practice he found it setting men against men. The antagonism between Hinduism and Islam he particularly regretted and his lifelong attempt was to weld them into one. That he actually succeeded only in founding a new religion, is unfortunately true; but Nanak was the first Indian saint who devoted his life to this cause. One of the familiar sayings of Nanak is: "There is no Hindu and no Mussalman". Nanak rejected caste and the racial pride of the Hindus. "God has said", says Nanak, "that man shall be saved by his works alone. God will not ask a man his tribe or sect, but what he has done".

Like Kabir, Nanak vigorously attacked all formalism. He told the Muslims:

Make love thy mosque; sincerity thy prayer-carpet; justice thy Koran;

"Modesty thy circumcision; courtesy thy Kabba; truth thy Guru; charity thy creed and prayer;

Nanak's definition of caste is this:

"Evil-mindedness is the low-caste woman; cruelty is the butcher's wife; a slanderous heart the sweeper-woman; wrath the pariah woman.

What availeth it to have drawn lines round thy cooking place, when these four sit ever with thee?

Make truth, self-restraint and good acts thy lines, and the utterness of the name thine ablutions.

Nanak, in the next world, he is best who walketh not in the way of sin"[3].

Nanak is believed to have performed the Haj (pilgrimage to Mecca) like a good Muslim, but he got into trouble with the keepers of the Kaaba. The story goes that he went to sleep in the holy city with his feet towards the sacred stone. He was censored for this disrespect towards the Kaaba and was taken before the authorities. Nanak maintained the omnipresence of the Kabba and asked them to drag his feet to a direction where the Kabba was not.

Shortly before his death, Nanak appointed one of his disciples as the Guru or pontiff of his followers who was to be their spiritual head and guide. This institution of Gurus is a distinguishing feature of Sikhism. The Sikhs recognize ten such Gurus and pay extraordinary reverence to them. The institution was abolished by Guru Gobind Singh, the tenth Guru, was substituted the *Granth* or Bible for a Guru.

Sikhism was a peaceful religion under the first four Gurus and was pervaded by the spirit of Kabir and Nanak. The fourth Guru Ramdas lived in the time of Akbar and received from that generous monarch the grant of a piece of land at Amritsar (pool of immortality), so called because of a tank supposed to possess healing properties. The shrine that Ramdas built on the bank of this tank was rebuilt into the golden temples by the Sikh monarch Ranjit Singh and is at present the most sacred stronghold of Sikhism. It was in the time of the fifth Guru, Arjun, that the Sikhs for the first time, began to show political ambition. Arjun was drawn to the side of Khusru, Jahangir's son, who rebelled against his father, and when the revolt was suppressed Jahangir imposed a heavy fine on the whole community of Sikhs. Arjun refused to pay the fine and was tortured to death.

The martyrdom of Arjun made the Sikhs realize the need for a military organisation for their self-preservation and for promoting their political interests. During the peaceful reign of Shah Jehan, the Sikhs, however, did not fall foul of the Mogul power, but Aurangzeb saw in them an obstacle to his scheme for converting all India to Islam. The emperor summoned to Delhi Tej Bahadur, the ninth Guru; the during his stay at Delhi the venerable pontiff was charged with "presuming to gaze from the roof of his abode upon the apartments of the ladies of the royal harem", and put to death. Before his departure to Delhi Tej Bahadur had taken the precaution of investing his son Gobind with his sword. On hearing of the massacre of his father, Gobind swore undying vengeance on the Moguls. Militarist ideals, originated by the Sixth Guru Hargobind, Arjun's son, were perfected by Gobind. Gobind instituted the Baptism of the Sword, and every Sikh, on his initiation, had to drink water stirred by a dagger and partake of cakes made of consecrated flour. After this ceremony, a Sikh was to be known as the Khalsa or elect and adopt the affix Singh or lion to his name. The Khalsa was to be distinguished by the five K's, Kes (uncut hair), Kaccha (short drawers), Kankan (comb), Kirpan (a dagger), and Kangha (a steel bangle). The use of tobacco and wine was prohibited to the Khalsa. Valour and physical virility became the essential qualities of the Khalsa and everything else was made subordinate to them. To infuse the proper martial spirit in his followers, Gobind Singh introduced the worship of Durga, the war goddess of the Hindu pantheon, among the Sikhs.

Gobind Singh abolished the institution of Gurus. He was the tenth and the last Guru and the Khalsa, after him, were to be guided by the *Granth* or the Bible. The *Granth* is, more or less, a revised edition by him of the *Adi Granth* (the original Granth) compiled by Guru Arjan from the inspired sayings of Kabir, Nanak and other saints.

Gobind Singh was murdered by a Pathan, but the spirit he infused thrived among the Sikhs. War became the God of the Sikhs and the more bigoted among them styled themselves as the Akalis or deathless. The Akali was contemptuous of death and was feared even by the Sikhs themselves. The sword was accepted as the last word in every dispute. This religious militarism eminently suited the genius of the hardly races of the Punjab to whom war, from the very beginning of Indian history, was a natural state of human relationship. Every Sikh had to discard caste, and the sacred thread had to be cut on undergoing the Baptism of the Sword. This made the higher castes fight shy of joining Sikhism; but it attracted a large number of lower classes from the peasantry who proved to be the bulwark and mainstay of Sikhism.

Thus the quietist religion preached by the meek Nanak was turned into one of the most powerful forces of aggression by Gobind singh. Soon after Gobind Singh's death, the Mogul empire collapsed and the Sikhs became the terror of the Punjab. The Afghan prince Ahmad Shah Durrani, who invaded India at this time, destroyed the temple at Amritsar and temporarily broke the Sikh power. But when Durrani went back to Afghanistan, the Sikhs appeared in the Punjab again; but these Sikhs had forgotten the teachings of Kabir, Nanak and even of Gobind Singh and had degenerated into disorganised gangs of bandits who robbed, looted and terrorized the peaceful population. The decay of the central power and the state of anarchy the country had fallen into at that time, suited the ambitions of these Sikhs, and they took a terrible toll of the Muslim population of the Punjab for the sins of the Moguls and of Ahmad Shah Durrani. At this time, there arose a great leader among the Sikhs. He was Ranjit Singh, "short, deformed and blind in one eye, illiterate, but a born leader of men". He organised the Sikhs into a powerful fighting force and soon become the master of the Punjab. He extended his influence into Kashmir and Afghanistan, and the Mirs of Sind lived in fear of him. He had his army trained by famous French generals, and some of his most trusted generals were Europeans.

The Sikhs reached the zenith of their political power under Ranjit Singh. He built the Golden Temple at Amritsar, and had his capital in the ancient city of Lahore. The British and the Sikhs under Ranjit had a profound respect for each other's power and had managed to get on without a conflict. But Ranjit Singh passed away in 1839, and the leadership of the community fell into less able hands. Internal dissensions and intrigues started, and in their folly the Sikhs discarded the wary policy of Ranjit Singh and declared war on the British. A fierce and bloody conflict ensued which ended the suzerainty of the Sikhs in the Punjab. In the battle of Sabraon, fought on the 21st February 1849, the Sikhs were finally defeated and the Punjab passed into British hands.

The Sikhs at present number about five million souls, and the Punjab is still the noted stronghold of Sikhism. It is worthy of note that even so recent a religion as Sikhism has produced sects which differ from one another. We have already mentioned the Akalis, the extreme militarists among the Sikhs. The Nanakpanthis or Sahidharis (easy-going) do not believe in all the teachings of Gobind Singh, but follow the peaceful religion of Nanak. They do not wear their hair long and are not distinguishable from other Hindus. The Keshdhari Sikhs, on the other hand, believe in all the five K's and are distinguished by their uncut hair. The prohibition regarding smoking is observed by most of the Sikhs, especially the Keshdharis, but there are few Sikhs who abjure intoxicants.

Nanak, the founder of Sikhism, was a breaker of systems and forms, and hence it is difficult to say what exactly are the doctrines and dogmas of Sikhism. Nanak accepted the Hindus doctrine of metempsychosis, but rejected caste, polytheism and the authority of the *Vedas*. The theism of Nanak was combination of Islam and the Vishishta Advaita doctrine of Ramanuja. Idolatry was prohibited, but the extraordinary position given to the *Granth* or the bible by Guru Gobind Singh who installed it as his successor has made his followers pay exceptional reverence to it. In every Sikh temple a *Granth* is placed on an alter and devotees offer flowers to it. A person stands behind the sacred book and fans it with a yak tail fan day and night. When the *Granth* is taken out, it is accompanied by a procession and much music. Some of the Sikh temples began to adopt Hindu practices and installed idols in them, but the Akali revival that started early in the 19th century, made vigorous efforts to combat all tendencies that were at work to degenerate Sikhism into a Hindu sect.

Because of the long persecution of the Sikhs by the Moguls, in social matters the Sikhs lean more towards the Hindus than to the Muslims. Though intermarriages between Sikhs and Hindus are rare, the Sikhs freely dine with non-vegetarian Hindus. The Sikhs burn their dead like the Hindus. The custom of burning windows was prevalent among the Sikhs, though prohibited by the Gurus, and four queens, we are told, died with Ranjit Singh. The cruel practice was stopped all over India by William Bentinck in 1829. The Sikhs consider killing of cows a sacrilege and abstain from beef.

Guru Nanak and, later, Gobind Singh freed the Sikhs from many of the tiresome restrictions imposed by caste rules on eating, drinking and social intercourse. Asceticism was condemned and every Sikh had to bear in mind Kabir's saying that "a hungry man is not in the proper mood to worship the Almighty". So every true worshipper of God should first work for a living, and religion was not to be made an excuse for indolence or laziness. Exceptions were permitted in cases of certain individuals who were allowed to leave their profession for a higher calling. As a rule, every man is to stick to his trade and his sword, and realize that work itself is worship.

This manly philosophy, and its practice have made the Sikhs one of the most enterprising communities of India. Nor have they lost any of the martial spirit. War is still the delight of the Sikh, and in valour and physique the Sikhs are second to none among the several races of India.

—P. Thomas

REFERENCES

1. Kailas is the abode of Shiva.
2. Quoted from Rawlinson's *India*.
3. *India*, Rawlinson.

The Development of Sikhism As a Distinct Religion

Tolerance, a belief that there are many roads to God, is a feature of Hinduism. The Bhakti and Sufi movements both subordinated doctrine to the establishment of a direct communion with God. Akbar attempted an eclectic, approach; Dārā Shikōh argued that nothing separated Muslim and Hindu but terminological differences. Kabīr or Dādu called God indifferently Allāh, Rāma, Karīm. For his part Nānak probably sought neither to fuse Islam and Hinduism, nor to found a new religion of his own. He did allow that the Muslim or Hindu who lived up to the best in his creed achieved something—but of incomparably less value than the worship of the True Name. God was within—the externals of Islam or Hinduism could not lead man to him. On the other hand, as far as the records go, he did little or nothing to organise those whose spirit he had quickened, to prescribe for them a distinctive way of life, or a distinctive form or ritual of worship.

Yet Nānak's personal influence did not die away; Sikhism emerged as a distinct religion. Nanak's personal rejection of the ascetic life, and of his son Sri Chand because he had formed a quietist sect, may have been one factor, along with his stress on living the good life in this world, which contributed to a distinctive Sikh way of life. His unusual decision, to appoint a successor, whom he regarded as the guru for his followers, certainly was another, for it made possible the emergence of the Sikhs as a separate body.

The guruships of Nānak's first four successors—Angad (1539-1552), Amar Dās (1552-1574), Rām Dās (1574-1581), and Arjun (1581-1606)—passed in peaceful development. Akbar admired their saintly lives and there was no quarrel with Islam or the State. But each added something to the separate identity of Sikhism.

Angad elaborated a distinctive script, Gurmukhi, based on that of the Punjab moneylenders, in which to write down Nānak's life and teaching. He also made the institution of the *langar*, or free kitchen, more important. Under Amar Dās the self-conscious organisation of Sikhism went further. It may have been in his day that "the active and domestic Sikhs" were set apart from the ascetic Udasis who followed Sri Chand[1]. By thus barring the ascetic, Sikhism acquired a distinctive social character. Amar Dās, by even greater stress upon the *langar*, possibly weakened caste feeling among those who shared the common meal. He certainly provided a common purpose for the Sikhs who contributed to support of the *langar,* as he did when the great step-well (bawli) was built at Goindwal, the fist Sikh place of pilgrimage. His appointment of three days in the year on which Sikhs should foregather, his provision of specifically Sikh funeral and marriage ceremonies, his discouragement of sati and indulgence in wine all served further to separate the Sikhs from their fellow Punjabis, Hindu or Muslim. Moreover there were so many recruits, from both communities, as to require the setting up of some twenty-two *manjas* or circles, each under a pious Sikhs, where the Sikhs assembled for worship and whence missionaries were sent out. (This congregational worship is perhaps another Islamic contribution).

Rām Dās completed the most famous shrine of Sikhism, the *amritsār*, tank of nectar, from which the town takes its name, and began the Golden Temple in its midst. He took the significant step of sending out agents (*masands*) to collect funds for this. His successor, Guru Arjun, was still more active in organising the circles (*manjas*) and the collection of the tithe levied on the faithful through his agents. Amritsar in his day became a centre for all Sikhs. His greatest contribution, however, was the compilation of the *Ādi Granth* (first book), the official collection of the hymns and sayings of Nānak and his successors, together with a very large selection from Kābir and other Bhaktas and Sufis whose message was consonant with that of Nānak. Sikhism now had its book, which was to receive the reverence among Sikhs given by Muslims to the Qur'ān. By Arjun's day Sikhism had a distinctive language, scripture, ritual, communal life, and centre. He himself emphasised this fact:

I have broken with the Hindu and the Muslim,

I will not worship with the Hindu, nor like the Muslim go to Mecca.

I shall serve Him and no other[2].

This claim, however, conceals the fact that Sikhism was turning more strongly against Islam than Hinduism. Angad and Amar Dās had been zealous Hindus before their conversion, and the writings of Amar Dās, Rām Dās, and Arjun are very Hindu in tone. There were some Muslim but many more Hindu converts. Moreover since the Sikhs were now emerging as an organised community under gurus with great temporal power, there was more likelihood of friction and conflict developing between them and their Muslim rulers. In 1606, Arjun was involved in the unsuccessful rebellion of Prince Khusrau against his father, the Emperor Jahāngīr. Punished with a fine, Arjun refused to pay and was executed. Though Jahāngīr, once secure on his throne, was almost as tolerant in religious matters as his father, Akbar, nevertheless in the eyes of the Sikhs Arjun became a martyr and the Muslims their enemies.

Harboind (1606-1645) succeeded Arjun at the age of eleven, and obeying his last injunction, assembled a military force about him. There were several clashes with Mughal troops during his guruship, notably in 1628, 1631 and 1634, and conflicts also with the rājas of the Himālayan foothills. The guru had become a military as well as spiritual leader. Later the ninth guru, Tegh Bahādur (1664-1675)—who had served with the Mughals in Assam—was called to Aurangzib's court and offered the choice of conversion to Islam or death. He chose martyrdom.

It was his son, Gobind Singh (1675-1708), who completed the final transformation of the Sikhs into a militant community[3]. His father, he said had died "to protect the frontal marks and the sacred threads of the Hindus"[4]. Now he would uproot tyranny from the land, Gobind Singh's life is a record of continuous warfare, largely unsuccessful against the Mughals, more successful against the hill rājas. But if he failed as a soldier, he succeeded as a Sikh. In 1699 he inaugurated the khāsls, the sworn brotherhood of fighting Sikhs. At baptism into the khālsa, Sikhs were given five signs marking them off from Hindu or Muslim—notably the uncut hair and beard—and received the name of Singh. Their joint drinking from one bowl of baptismal nectar cut at caste within Sikhism. Association with Hindu or Muslim was declared sinful. Paradise was promised to those who died in the Sikh cause.

In the fighting with the Mughals Gobind Singh lost all his sons. He provided in two ways for the succession to the guruship, first, by making his obeisance and offering to the *Granth Sahib* (he had added a considerable body of his own writings to the *Ādi Granth*), with the instruction, "Obey the *Granth Sāhib*. It is the visible body of the guru";[5] and second, by making the khālsa likewise an embodiment of the guru: "Wherever there are five Sikhs assembled who abide by the guru's teaching know that I am in the midst of them. Henceforth the guru shall be the khalsa and the khālsa the guru"[6].

In the institutions of Gobind Singh may be seen the coming together of three distinctive strands in Sikhism, the idea of the guru, of the *Granth Sāhib*, and of the Brotherhood of the Sikhs. Nānak had said, "Through the guru, man obtaineth real life,"[7] and the same stress is laid upon the guruship's importance by the succeeding gurus. This was no more than Kabīr had done, however. What gave the guruship such importance was the practice of the guru choosing his successor, to whom he made an offering and obeisance. That choice was made, in the case of Angad and Amar Dās, from among the disciples, on the grounds that these two excelled all others in the completeness of their surrender to the guru's will. Rām Dās, the fourth guru, was the son-in-law of Amar Dās, but even so it was stressed that he excelled in submission and humility. Here was emphasized for all Sikhs, the merit of absolute obedience to the guru. There was also developed the theory that the gurus were in fact one spirit, passing from one body to another. Since from Rām Dās the guruship passed by hereditary succession, it was easy for the Sikh to think of the gurus as somehow divine. The gurus, notably Gobind Singh, denounced any such idea as sacrilegious, but it persisted. Indeed when boys of five or nine (Har Kishan and Gobind Singh) were recognised as spiritual leaders, it is clear that the idea of incarnation had superseded that of the human teacher.

Something of the same process is seen in the Sikh attitude to the *Granth Sāhib*. To the concept of a book were added to overtones associated with Nānak's mystical use of the words *The Name,* or *The Word*, until the book itself became sacred and an object of worship.

The third basic concept was that of the Sikh brotherhood (compare this with the brotherhood of Islam). The union of Sikhs in cooperative efforts—sometimes opposed by Muslims or Hindus—gave a practical sense of corporate life. To this was added a sense of being elect. Rām

Dās cursed those who left the community, and promised the faithful sure salvation, "God himself is the protector of the True Guru, and will save all who follow him"[8]. The true Sikh was not merely saved himself, he could save others[9]. The fellowship of these saints was likewise given a peculiar sanctity, until gobind Singh could equate any five of the khālsa gathered together with the guru himself. These ideas, and the practical organisation achieved under the gurus, served to preserve Sikhism and the Sikh community in the very difficult years after the death of the last of the gurus.

ANGAD

The Succession to the Guruship

Little from Angad has survived, but these lines from the Coronation Ode by the ministerial Balwand reflect the growing *mystique* of guruship and the importance of obedience as the prime qualification for it. Here "Lahina" refers to Angad (1539-1552).

[From Macauliffe, *The Sikh Religion*, II 25, 26]

Guru Nānak proclaimed the accession of Lahina as the reward of service. He had the same light, the same ways; the king merely changed his own body. [p. 25]

The divine umbrella waved over him; he obtained possession of the throne in the place of Guru Nānak…

Lahina obeyed what the guru had ordered him, and earned the reward of his acts. [p. 26]

AMAR DĀS

The third guru, Amar Dās (1552-1574), was a powerful preacher, who to Nānak's teaching added ever greater stress upon the guru—the *human* guru—together with a sharper disdain of Brāhmans and those who reject Sikhism.

[From Macauliffe, *The Sikh Religion*, II, 166-67, 22, 238]

They who turn their faces from the guru, shall find no house or home.

They shall wander from door to door like divorced women of bad character and evil reputation.

Nānak,[10] they who are pardoned through the guru's instruction shall be blended with God. [p. 221]

Let none be proud of his caste.

He who knoweth God is a Brāhman.

O stupid fool, be not proud of thy caste;

From such pride many sins result.

Everybody saith there are for castes,

But they all proceed from God's seed.

The world is all made out of one clay,

But the Potter fashioned in into vessels of many sorts.

The body is formed from the union of five elements;

Let anyone consider if he hath less or more in his composition.

Saith Nānak, the soul is fettered by its acts.

Without meeting the true guru salvation is not obtained. [p. 238]

If the perverse by admonished, will they ever heed the admonition?

If the perverse meet the good, these will not associate with them; they are doomed to transmigration.

There are two ways—one the love of God, the other of mammon; the way man treadeth dependeth on God's will.

The believer chasteneth his heart and applieth to it the touchstone of the Word.

It is with his heart he quarreleth, with is heart he struggleth, he is engaged with his heart.

Whoever loveth the true Word shall receive what his heart desireth.

He shall ever eat the ambrosia of the name, and act according to the guru's instruction.

They who quarrel with others, instead of quarreling with their own hearts, waste their lives.

The perverse are ruined by obstinacy and by the practice of falsehood and deception.

He who by the guru's instruction subdueth his heart, shall fix his affection on God.

Nānak, the believer practiceth truth; the perverse suffer transmigration, [pp. 166-67].

RĀM DĀS

Rām Dās (1574-1581), the fourth guru, gave further form to Sikh religion by his teaching and direction of the Sikh community.

[From Macauliffe, *The Sikh Religion*, II, 264].

Let him who calleth himself a Sikh of the true guru, rise early and meditate on God;

Let him exert himself in the early morning, bathe in the tank of nectar. Repeat God's name under the guru's instruction, and all his sins and transgressions shall be erased.

Let him at sunrise sing the guru's hymns, and whether sitting or standing meditate on God's name.

The disciple who at every breath meditateth on God, will please the guru's heart.

The guru communicateth instruction to that disciple of his to whom may lord is merciful.

The slave Nānak prayeth for the dust of the feet of that guru's disciple who himself repeateth God's name and causeth others to do so.

ARJUN

Guru Arjun (1581-1606) wrote a great deal and, unlike the second, third, and fourth gurus, addressed Hindus and Muslims alike.

[From Macauliffe, *The Sikh Religion*, III, 13, 28-29, 64, 311, 422]

I practice not fasting, nor observe the [month of] Ramazan:

I serve Him who will preserve me at the last hour.

The one Lord of the earth is my God,

Who judgeth both Hindus and Muslims.

I go not on a pilgrimage to Mecca, nor worship at Hindu places of pilgrimage.

I serve the one God and no other.

I neither worship as the Hindus, nor pray as the Muslims.

I take the formless God into my heart, and there make obeisance unto Him.

I am neither a Hindu nor a Muslim.

The soul and the body belong to God whether. He be called Allāh or Rām.

Kābir hath delivered this lecture.

When I meet a true guru or pīr, I recognize my own master. [p. 422].

Without the society of the saints, man, ever wavering, suffereth great misery:

By love of the one supreme God the profit of God's essence is earned. [p. 311].

. . . .

To the word and the name are now added an instruments of salvation bathing in the Amritsar tank, and the *Ādi Granth* compiled by the guru.

By bathing in the tank of Rām Das
All the sins that man commiteth shall be done away,
And he shall become pure by his ablutions.
The perfect Guru hath given us this boon.
When we meditate on the Guru's instructions,
God bestoweth all comfort and happiness,
And causeth the whole cargo to cross over safely.
In the association of the saints uncleanness departeth,
And the supreme being abideth with us.
Nānak by meditating on the Name
Hath found God the primal Being. [p. 13].

. . . .

Three things have been put into the vessel [the *Ādi Granth*]—truth, patience, and meditation.

The ambrosial name of God, the support of all, hath also been put therein. He who eateth and enjoyeth it shall be saved.

This provision should never be abandoned; ever clasp it to your hearts.

By embracing God's feet we cross the ocean of darnkess; Nānak, everything is an extension of God. [p. 64].

. . . .

O my soul grasp the shelter of the Supreme and Omnipotent God.

Repeat the name of God who supporteth the regions of the earth and the universe.

O saint of God, abandon thine intellectual pride, understand the will of God, and thou shalt be happy.

Accept the act of God as good: in weal and woe meditate on Him.

The Creator saveth in a moment millions of fallen ones, and in this there is no delay.

The Lord is the destroyer of the pain and sorrow of the poor; He rewardeth whom He pleaseth;

He is mother and father, cherisher of life and soul, and a sea of comfort for all.

There is no deficiency in the Creator's gifts; He is omnipresent, and a mine of jewels.

The beggar beggeth Thy name, O Lord; Thou abidest in every heart.

The slave Nānak hath entered the sanctuary of Him from whom nobody departeth empty. [pp. 28-29].

GOBIND SINGH

The tenth guru, Gobind Singh (1675-1708), was founder of the khālsa, the sworn brotherhood of fighting Sikhs. His hymns sound a warlike note.

[From macauliffe, *The Sikh Religion*, V. 117, 261-62, 286].

May we have the protection of the immortal Being!

May we have the protection of All-steel!

May we have the protection of All-death!

May we have the protection of All-steel! [pp. 261-62]

. . . .

Thou art the Subduer of countries, the Destroyer of the armies of the wicked, in the battle-field Thou greatly adornest the brave.

Thine arm is infrangible, Thy brightness refulgent, Thy radiance and splendor dazzle like the sun.

Thou bestowest happiness on the good, Thou terrifiest the evil, Thou scatterest sinners, I seek thy protection.

Hail! hail to the creator of the world, the Savior of creation, my Cherisher, hail to Thee, O Sword! [p. 286].

Finally, as an example of how far Sikhism had travelled since Guru Nānak's day, here is part of Guru Gobind's instructions on the means of salvation.

Have dealings with every one, but consider yourselves distinct. Your faith and daily duties are distinct from theirs. Bathe every morning before repast. If your bodies endure not cold water then heat it. Ever abstain from tobacco. Remember the one immortal God. Repeat the Rahirās in the evening and the Sohila at bedtime. Receive the baptism and teaching of the guru, and act according to the *Granth Sāhib*. Cling to the boat in which thou hast embarked. Wander not in search of another religion. Repeat the guru's hymns day and night. Marry only into the house of a Sikh. Preserve thy wife and thy children from evil company. Covet not money offered for religious purposes. Habitually attend a Sikh temple and eat a little sacred food therefrom. [p. 117]

LATER DEVELOPMENTS IN SIKHISM

It is evident that in Gobind Singh's day there were many among the Sikhs who clung to Hindu ways, despite the elaboration of a distinctive pattern for Sikh life by the gurus. The years of Mughal proscription, from the days of Aurangzib's attack upon both Hindus and Sikhs, threw the Sikhs into the arms of the Hindus, to whose civil usages and customs they largely adhered. At the death of Ranjīt, founder of the Sikh kingdom in the Punjab, the Hindu rite of satī was observed. Veneration of the cow, never taught by the gurus, led to rigid prevention of cow slaughter. Malcolm stresses the tremendous strength of caste within Sikhism, ruling absolutely over marriage, but also affecting commensality.

This continued drift away from the teaching of the gurus called forth a series of reform movements. First was that of Dyāl Dās (1783-1855), the *Nirankāris* (the formless), who attacked the worship of idols—even images of the gurus. He also attacked the adoption of Hindu marriage ceremonies and pilgrimage. His son Bhāi Dārā did win back the Sikhs to ceremonial conforming to the scriptures. There was also an antimilitarist element in the movement. The *Nāmdhari* movement of Sāīn Sāhib (d. 1862) attacked the introduction of caste distinctions and taboos, satī, and idol worship. Later in the nineteenth century, when Hindu and Christian missionaries were active, the *Singh Sabhā* (or Association) was formed. Its influence was marked in fostering Sikh education, with particular emphasis on the teaching of Gurmukhi and the Scriptures.

Missionaries were appointed and the Khālsa tract society formed to distribute religious literature.

One unexpected aid to the reformers was provided by the attitude of the British military authorities. Impressed by Sikh fighting capacity and grateful for Sikh aid during the Mutiny, they freely recruited Sikhs into the Indian army. The army insisted, however, on recruiting Khālsa Sikhs; an order of the commander-in-chief read, "Every countenance and encouragement is to be given to their comparative freedom from the bigoted prejudices of caste, every means adopted to preserve intact the distinctive characteristics of their race, their peculiar conventions and social customs".

In the twentieth century the most powerful reformist movement was the Akāli, whose greatest achievement was the Sikh Gurdwāras Bill, passed in 1925, which restored to the Sikh community control of the gurudwāras (temples), which had in many cases fallen into the hands of mahants (priests) who were far more Hindu than Sikh but who exercised a hereditary control. With the intensification of the Indian struggle for independence, the Akāli movement took up increasingly the political cause of the community, the latest aspect of which is the demand for the separate Sikh state in East Punjab[11].

REFERENCES

1. Sir J. Malcolm, *Sketch of the Sikhs*, p. 27. (Nānak, Angad, and Amir Dās were all married, family men).
2. Cf. Macauliffe, *The Sikh Religion*, III, 422.
3. Not all the Sikhs had approved of this conflict with the Mughal authority, either in Hargobind's day or in Gobind Singh's.
4. Macauliffe, *The Sikh Religion*, IV, 392.
5. Macauliffe, *The Sikh Religion*, V. 244.
6. *Ibid.*, V, 243-44.
7. *Ibid.*, I, 149.
8. Macauliffe, *The Sikh Religion*, II, 301.
9. "He had saved himself and his family, and he shall save twenty one generations, yea the whole world". *Ibid.*, II. 292.
10. As may be judged from the preceding examples, it was a poetic convention for the poet's name to appear in the last lines. Use of the name Nānak by later gurus reflects the belief that his spirit spoke through them.
11. For a full account of the reform movements, see Khushwant Singh, *The Sikhs* (London, 1953).

Sikh Tradition: Competing Organisations and Ideology

The continuing debate among Sikhs over the nature of their religious, political and social tradition involves concerns and intellectual issues that have been surfacing intermittently over a century. The attempts to define "who is a Sikh", orthodoxy, and basic rituals and practice are not new. To the contrary, these questions, and the underlying process of formulating and then transmitting Sikh tradition, lay at the heart of an extraordinary burst of dynamism and intellectual fervor during the Singh Sabha of recent Sikh history, c. 1875-1925.

In the first decades of the movement, individual Singh Sabhas wrestled with ideological and institutional problems. Their efforts usually reflected the social and political circumstances of local groups, as well as the priorities of individual leaders who shaped the development and application of community resources. Initially there were two primary circles of Sikh activists, tied to the Lahore and Amritsar Singh Sabhas and their networks. Recent research on this beginning phase underlines the diversity and conflict among Sikhs over critical matters such as doctrine, festivals, historical events, and Hindu-Sikh relations. Despite differences, however, by 1900 there had emerged a fresh formulation of Sikh tradition, often referred to at the time as the "Tat Khalsa", increasingly seen by many Sikhs as an accurate reflection of the essence of Sikhism.

This essay briefly reviews the emerging conflict over ideology and control of institutions among Sikhs at the turn of the century, and then focusses on the struggles among specific Sikh organisations, most notably the Chief Khalsa Diwan and the Bhasaur Singh Sabha headed by Teja Singh, to influence Sikh identity and practice both within and beyond the Punjab. The period 1900-1920 was a critical juncture in the evolution of modern Sikhism, a time when rapid economic and political change shaped new alignments and distribution of power. The gradual transfer of authority from the colonial power created particular problems for Sikhs. As a minority community, they felt under attack, lagging in the race for jobs and education, allegedly persecuted by Hindus, and in general, uncertain about how to survive and prosper in a changing world. The Chief Khalsa Diwan saw its mission essentially as consolidating and expanding resources, broadening the numbers of Sikhs while at the same time insuring that the community as a whole agreed on principles and priorities. Compromise and averting conflict that might threaten fragile Sikh unity were hallmarks of the CKD. The Bhasaur Singh Sabha, later calling itself the Panch Khalsa Diwan, had a different agenda, a radical vision of Sikhism that emphasized purity of ideology and practice. Survival meant adhering to fundamental values and daily practice, not numbers. For the Bhasaur group, the only real Sikhs were *Amritdhari* men and women who adhered to discipline and who worked firmly to clean Sikhism of any accretions of Hindu influence incompatible with the message of the Gurus. Although, the Sabha and the CKD disagreed on strategy and some basic premises, they used the same techniques to mobilize support and disseminate their view of the world. These included public meetings, conferences, rapid transmission of ideas by post, rail and telegraph, and most importantly, through use of the new print media. After the early 1920s, both organisations ceased to be a vital part of Sikh daily life. A review of their efforts to disseminate a vision of Sikhism in the modern world, both their successes and failures, tell us much about the conflicts and dilemmas facing Sikhs at a crucial point, and suggests patterns and continuities that continue today.

Between the founding of the first Singh Sabha in Amritsar in 1873 and appearance of the Chief Khalsa Diwan in October, 1902, Sikhs engaged in a very public and often bitter debate over Sikh tradition, practice, and the future of the community. Two loose constellations existed among the hundred or so Singh Sabhas spread across the Punjab, and occasionally in outlying areas. As a definitive work on this period by Harjot Oberoi has demonstrated, the Amritsar Sabha was led by a group of leaders that included religious teachers and aristocrats. Known as the "Sanatan" Sikhs, the Amritsar network recognised a diversity of traditions within contemporary Sikhism and defended the role of custom in defining who were Sikhs and what they should believe. Initially dominating Sikh public life and controlling major shrines and institutions, the Sanatanists held decedents of the Gurus in particular respect, and included within Sikhism both Udasis, followers of Guru Nanak often dressed as Hindu mendicants, and *Sahajdharis*, Sikhs who were shaven and who had not adopted the *rahit*, the discipline maintained by the *Amritdhari* and *Kesdhari* Sikhs who accepted the outward symbols and conduct associated with Guru Gobind Singh.

The Sikhs linked to the Lahore Singh Sabha, referred to frequently as the "Tat Khalsa", had a quite different perspective. Coming from a variety of classes and castes, including aristocrats, lawyers, teachers, publicists, businessmen, educationists and minor officials, these Sikhs were joined by a shared experience in anglo-vernacular education and a commitment to strengthening a 'true' Sikhism devoid of popular custom and clearly separate from Hinduism. The Tat Khalsa attacked caste and other social customs that seemed to undermine Sikh brotherhood, and called on Sikhs to quit worshipping "living gurus" such as pirs, local saints, and descendents of the ten Gurus. A return to original Sikh values also involved a renewal of attention to the *Guru Granth Sahib* as the source of theology and authority, the promulgation of rituals devoid of Brahmin and Hindu influence, and a cleansing of sacred space such as gurdwaras and shrines[1].

After almost three decades of virtual warfare between the two groups of Sikhs and their allies, the Tat Khalsa became ascendant in Sikh public life. Three related processes help account for their success. First, as Harjot Oberoi notes, there existed a fundamental historical legacy from the past, emphasizing a separate Sikh identity, that provided a foundation of social and intellectual support. Secondly, the British government and its institutions contributed to a homogeneous Sikh religion. The British helped shape how Sikhs and other Punjabis looked at themselves. Censuses, British ideas about administrative categories, and support for the Khalsa tradition as a critical element for Sikh soldiers reinforced the identity of those supporting the Lahore Singh Sabha[2]. Except for the Tat

Khalsa's ability to respond creatively to challenges and to build new institutions and networks, however, Sikh history might have taken a somewhat different direction. The more Westernized leaders of the Lahore Singh Sabha and their followers quickly realized the value of developing new means of communalism and education. They set up tract societies, newspapers, schools and eventually Khalsa College, which trained generations of new Sikh intelligentia not only in specific skills but also with a strong sense of community service and identity. The Tat Khalsa gained control of the new print culture and used it effectively to promulage their ideas and to collect funds. They reinforced their information network with a mixture of specialized preaching teams (trained in special schools) and a regularized system of district and regional meetings (*diwans*).[3]

The Singh Sabhas affiliated with the aggressive Lahore group fought for their programme in the press, social organisations, and in sacred space controlled by Sanatan Sikhs, especially the *takhts* (the four major centres of Sikh authority), historical gurdwaras and the Golden Temple in Amritsar. Sanatan Sikhs, aligned with traditional leaders and religious figures who shared some of the Tat Khalsa concern with education and revitalization but who rejected its insistence on defining Sikh identity, countered with their own tracts and social ostracism. Leading Tat Khalsa Sikhs such as Gurmukh Singh and Teja Singh Bhasaur were ejected from shrines and gurdwaras, and the courts became a battlefield for libel suits and attempts to alter administration of gurdwaras and other holy spots. *Hukamnamas*, edicts from the *takhts*, occasionally were issued against the Tat Khalsa reformers, as for example in 1905 when that group successfully removed icons from the Golden Temple. Religious administrators also occasionally prevented worship in shrines by Tat Khalsa advocates, or in one instance, participants from the 1910 Sikh Education Conference which supported lower caste reclamation were banned from attending the Golden Temple.

Despite over two decades of conflict and hard-won victories, the Singh Sabha reformers still struggled with many internal divisions and a range of activities that tended to mirror local concerns but which remained uncoordinated. The Khalsa College had been established but its finances remained shaky. The preaching teams were reaching some rural areas although growing resistance from peasants created problems[4]. Influence of Sanatan Sikhs and their Hindu allies remained in key pockets of public life, most notably in the shrines and also in several educational institutions.

In 1901, the lingering divisions among Sikhs and the ongoing conflict between Lahore and Amritsar finally led Sikhs to hold a large meeting in Amritsar to form a unitary body that would carry on and expand the work of the Singh Sabhas. The ascendancy of the Tat Khalsa as the voice of the Sikhs therefore became institutionalized with the founding of the Chief Khalsa Diwan. Amritsar, on October 30, 1992. A total of 29 Singh Sabhas initially joined the Diwan, rising quickly to over a 100 within five years. The CKD coordinated Singh Sabha activities and consolidated gains. Its leadership came from a small group of men, led by Bhai Jodh Singh, Trilochan Singh, Bhai Arjan Singh, and Sundar Singh Majithia who became in essence its permanent secretary. Governance came from an executive committee that met monthly, with members elected by a much larger general committee representing Sabhas, representatives from the states, individuals who met specific financial and service criteria, and the *takhts*. The executive body relied upon sub-committees who handled finances and historical and religious issues[5]. The announced aims of the CKD included strengthening the Khalsa Panth, spreading the teachings of the Gurus, providing accurate information on traditional and contemporary issues, and in general, safeguarding the culture and political rights of Sikhs, As a central organisation representing a variety of interests, however, much of its programme tended to reflect the programme and influence of the most active sabhas. Leaders such as Vir Singh, Mohan Singh Vaid, Takht Singh, and Teja Singh Bhasaur initially were active. These leaders consulted with member associations and guided the ogranisation through both public meetings and private discussions on controversial issues[6].

The special strategies and policies of the CKD changed in light of immediate crisis or perceived long-term needs of the community as a whole. A consistent emphasis involved building a base of ideology and institutions to which most if not all Sikhs could adhere. This involved focus on strengthening Sikh, cultural boundaries, such as festivals and distinct rituals, and widening the public debate over issues ranging from doctrine to historical fact and emergent problems involving the correct printing of the *Guru Granth Sahib*, maintaining the finances of local and central organisations, and developing human resources (e.g., the training of preachers, missionary activists, and educationalist). A problem that demanded constant attention was rampant factionalism and conflict among Sikhs. In 1908, for example, the CKD helped form the Khalsa Biradari, a group dealing with Sikh attitudes toward untouchables.

Similarly, the Diwan attempted to mediate in controversies between Malwa and Majha Sikhs, and to do whatever possible to unify the panth.

Within a decade, the Diwan had remarkable success in fostering Sikh identity and building institutions. A new Sikh Educational Conference provided an ongoing forum for fund-raising and public attention to education at all levels, while a network of hospitals, orphanages, and other self-help units provided services for Sikhs and prevented intrusion by other competing groups including missionaries and Arya Samajists. Behind this achievement lay much hard work and an overall strategy of controlling public forums for the purposes of unifying and at times indoctrinating sikhs around the world. Through local and provincial meetings, public appeals (*benati*), and reliance on tracts, journals and newspapers, the CKD excelled in fund-raising and at the same time utilizing the new print culture in the Punjab[7].

The Diwan also had some success in improving the political situation of Sikhs as the British began to transfer power to the Indian population. Appreciating the permanent minority status of Sikhs, the leaders pursued a dual policy of cooperating with the government in order to insure or expand patronage as well as defending Sikh interests in public matters and constitutional discussions. Examples included having more Sikh holidays on the Punjab official calender, the expansion of Punjabi in educational and bureaucratic networks, the acceptance of turbans and kirpans in many public arenas, and most notably, the passage of the Anand Marriage Bill in 1907. The Diwan came to be seen as a major if not the most important Sikh organisation by Sikhs and British rulers alike[8].

Challenges to the CKD came from many sides. Some Sikhs involved in revolutionary or extremist politics questioned the strategy of working with the British and chose instead developing mass anti-colonial movements such as the attacks on colonial irrigation policies in 1907, the Ghadar party in America, or open defiance of British authority over emotional issues such as damage to Rikabganj Gurdwara in New Delhi, 1913. The Diwan managed temporarily to neutralize these opponents through public appeals and conciliatory responses from the British, who relied upon Sikhs and the Diwan for assistance in recruitment and publicity during the First World War[9].

The most persistent and troublesome opposition came not from Sikh politicians but individuals and organisations who did not share the Diwan's approach to Sikh tradition and culture. Although no longer able to control centre stage in Sikh public life, the earlier foes of the Tat Khalsa, the Sanatanists, persisted in denouncing the CKD and occasionally sided with Hindus in regional organisations or in battles over the removal of idols from the Golden Temple in 1905 and afterward. The son of Khem Singh Bedi, Gurbaksh Singh, and their allies among *Sahajdhari* Sikhs, such as Harkishen Lal (owner of the Lahore *Tribune*) had great influence over Sikh shrines and used them as a basis to embarrass and attempt to isolate CKD advocates. The *udasi* managers of the Golden Temple complex, for example, prevented Sikh reformers from attending worship services during the Educational Conference of 1910. Similarly, sympathetic *jathedars* (head officials) of the centres of Sikh authority, the Tikhts, occasionally issued *hukamnamas* (religiously sanctioned commands or instructions) against CKD activists[10].

An increasingly vocal attack on the Chief Khalsa Diwan, and one that tended to focus attention on controversy and matters that were divisive came from a splinter group within the Tat Khalsa movement, radicals such as Teja Singh and the Bhasaur Singh Sabha, whose agenda differed sharply from that of the Diwan. Bhasaur, a small village near Patiala, had a reputation for advocating a more literal, fundamentalists approach to Tat Khalsa principles. At least three individuals shaped its programme. Sant Attar Singh Maustana, a prominent saint and activist, served as the *jathedar* for the Bhasaur Singh Sabha and its successor, the Panch Khalsa Diwan. Much of the intellectual prowess came from Kahan Singh Nabha, a leading Sikh thinker who attended meetings and provided guidance in the preparation of documents and the evolution of ideology. The controversial secretary of the Sabha and PKD, Teja Singh Bhasaur, was a totally committed public figure known for his prickly oratory and frequent bull-headed attacks on opponents. One story demonstrating Teja Singh's personality involved his leaving an accident in which his son had been injured in order to continue a preaching schedule. He supposedly replied to yells about his son being in pain with the retort that while the boy was only one person, "many people are crying for baptism"[11].

Founded in 1893, the Sri Guru Singh Sabha Bhasaur quickly came to be known for its commitment to revitalizing Sikhism by eliminating perceived non-Sikh elements. Fanatically attempting to covert or undercut opponents, Teja Singh and his associates called for a return to the principles of the Khalsa, a small but pure Sikh community. No compromise was possible. The numerous tracts and proceedings of the

Diwan were dotted with provocative words such as *milgobhi* (mixed up doctrine, filled with hot air), *dhillaur* (lazy, back-sliding), *patit* (fallen, sinner), and *tankhahia* (literally a person fined because of a breach of religious principles, but in PKD parlance, a reprobate to be cast out by pure Sikhs). Virtually every printed page contained a judgement as to whether an action or idea was *gurmat* or *manmat* (according to the Gurus, truth, or arrogant, self-willed, against the Gurus). A major goal involved removing any taint of Hindu or Muslim influence from custom, ritual and theology. Special criticism was reserved for those claiming to be gurus or leaders without meeting criteria of purity and total commitment. Marriage and social custom based on caste or class was seen as total *manmat*.

The Bhasaur group's relations with the larger Sikh community and Punjab culture in general went through three phases. Between 1893 and approximately 1905, it tended to be accepted as a radical but necessary part of the Tat Khalsa cause. Its annual diwans attracted large crowds and Sikh leaders for extended debate, up to five days. Issues received full discussion, and consensus was the rule. Often the Sabha and its successor the Panch Khalsa Diwan (formed in 1907) did not take up a position because all attending did not agree. Some of its actions were highly controversial but seen as necessary at the time. In 1894, for example, the organisation initiated several low caste Hindus and converted Muslims to the Sikh faith, and baptized and renamed a Sikh who had been living with a Muslim woman. A decade later, in a special diwan at the village of Bakapur near Phillaur, Teja Singh brought together leading Singh Sabha activists from across Punjab and had a mass conversion of 35 "fallen" Sikhs and Muslims, part of a larger Sikh effort of *shuddhi* (reclaiming Sikhs who had "apostatized" themselves by living with or marrying Muslims)[12]. In addition the Bhasaur Sikhs also proved to be masters of propaganda and aggressive pamphleteering. Print runs of tracts sometimes exceeded 10,000, supported by local patrons and also through special appeals for grants to a "Pustak Fund". Financial accounts suggests a sizable network of support and communication stretching from Southeast and East Asia to North America. Proceedings and leaflets usually were printed at the Sri Gurmat Press, Amritsar (Budh Singh proprietor). Despite its outreach, however, the Bhasaur Sabha often worked in isolation. Teja Singh distrusted large organisations and felt keenly that city life tended to corrupt morals and purpose[13].

Leading in public confrontation and challenging existing mores, the Bhasaur Sabha evoked threats or reprisal from more conservative Sikh elements. That only reinforced Teja Singh's sense of duty and commitment to ensuring that true Sikhs, those who had undergone baptism and took on the discipline demanded by Guru Gobind Singh, controlled Sikh public life. The organisation sponsored *anand* Sikh marriages stripped of Hindu influence and railed incessantly against Hindu festivals and control of shrines by those labelled apostates, only Hindus in disguise. Adopting a literalist approach to the *Guru Granth Sahib* and later religious texts, the Diwan demanded full equality within the panth, encouraged female education, banned ornaments, and demanded a central role for women in worship. Baptism of women was only with the *khanda*, the two-edged sword hitherto reserved for men, and not a small dagger currently used in many ceremonies. Since all Sikhs should keep long hair and wear turbans, girls at PKD schools and women in the congregation wore turbans rather than scarves[14].

In essence, Teja Singh and his followers provided some of the front-line or shock troops for the Tat Khalsa movement. From approximately 1905 onward, however, the radical ideas of the Bhasaur contingent became less acceptable to many Sikhs. The Sabha and the PKD became alienated intellectually and organisationally from the network of Singh Sabhas aligned with the CKD. Although many of Teja Singh's associates were prominent in the central Diwan, he felt that they had sold out and become lazy, tainted with power and too willing to compromise, to accept *milgobhi* ideas. His alienation surfaced as early as 1902 when he tried unsuccessfully to convert Muslims. Teja Singh attributed the initial failure to a lack of commitment of Tat Khalsa Sikhs, and even when finally the large meeting was organised at Bakapur in June 1903, he argued that many leading Sikhs had neither the will not the courage to act on principle and mix socially with new *Amritdhari* Sikhs of a lower social class. Despite frequent invitations to join various CKD committees and working groups, Teja Singh remained outside and threw darts at the Diwan in a series of harsh challenges[15].

Three sets of issues separated Bhasaur from Teja Singh's former colleagues. First, from his perspective, the CKD misused its authority to resolve details on Sikh *rahit* and practice. For example, in 1908 the CKD circulated a draft document outlining "orthodox" Sikh practices in worship and other public activities, a *rahit maryada*. Attacking the draft mercilessly, the PKD pointed out inconsistencies and "non-Sikh" elements in the document. Especially offensive were differential roles for women in ceremonies, a tendency to blend different perspectives on authority and underlying principles, and specifies about ritual, matters concerning the *Guru Granth Sahib*, and family life. Unable to forge a consensus, the CKD typically backed away from the divisive controversy[16].

In addition, the Bhasauris highlighted a persistent problem for Sikhs, the relationship between *Sahajdhari* and *Amritdhari* Sikhs. Although CKD leaders were all *Amritdhari*, in order to broaden the Diwan's influence and include a variety of interests, provisions were made for clean-shaven Sikhs to be advisers and even to have their separate meetings at the annual conferences. Given the diversity existing among Sikhs, the Diwan argued those who worshipped in gurdwaras and accepted that Sikhism was a separate religion should be part of the larger Sikh community. Always aware of the permanent minority status of Sikhs (approximately 10-13 per cent of the Punjab population), and also realizing the devotion of many *Sahajdharis*, the CKD tried to accommodate and be tolerant of diversity. Although having a long-term goal of seeing all Sikhs maintain common rituals and symbols, the official paper of the CKD, the *Khalsa Advocate*, noted that even shorn Sikhs were on the path of religious searching and should be encouraged to remain within the panth (July 15, 1904). Community interest required such toleration. In the past, *Sahajdharis* such as Sewa Ram Singh and Teja Singh, M.A., had eventually been baptized and contributed notably to Sikhism[17].

Such a position infuriated Teja Singh. Only *Sahajdharis* who clearly intended at some point to become real Sikhs by undergoing baptism and accepting the Khalsa discipline should play any role in panthic affairs. Intermarriage and social contacts with *Sahajdharis* was judged as adulterating the purity of mind and action of other Sikhs and must be rejected. Only true believers, the Khalsa, should act together even if that meant rejecting help from those who nominally thought of themselves as Sikhs[18].

The last and most basic differences involved a correct understanding of Sikh history, the Gurus, and scripture. The PKD absolutely rejected any suggestion of Hindu influence. Dramas on the lives of the Gurus, for example, mirrored Hindu practice and should be avoided, as also pictures of the Gurus since that could lead to idolatry. The spread of the printing press had led to wide circulation of popular Sikh art, a development viewed as sacrilege by the PKD[19]. Not only should Sikhs attend festivals only at the time of the birthdays, the *gurpurabs*, of the Gurus, but such occasions had to be celebrated in very specific, pristine ways and generally only at major shrines.

The PKD addressed the tension between Sikhism as a set of theological precepts and requirements of an orthodox lifestyle with set rituals and symbols. It increasingly highlighted the primacy of Guru Gobind Singh's call to arms and sacrifice. While acknowledging that the Dasam Granth, the collection of the Tenth Guru's writings, was not equivalent to the *Guru Granth Sahib*, the Diwan tried to incorporate sections of Guru Gobind Singh's message in services. Care was taken, however, to remove any references to goddesses or Puranic themes. Moreover, the Diwan advocated rules about the presentation and place of the scriptures in all circumstances. Any writing such as the detailed commentary, the Faridkot Tika, should be clearly relegated to a secondary role and not be associated with any aspect of worship because it might be viewed as having authority similar to the *Granth*. Similarly, all historical writing and reference to the secondary literature emerging from the late eighteenth and early nineteenth century had to be evaluated critically to prevent pro-Hindu or confusing ideas from undermining the panth[20].

Consumed with isolating and destroying non-Sikh elements, the PKD debated whether parts of the *Granth* in fact had been mistakingly included at a later date. One especially vexing question involved the Ragmala, a short piece associated with a Muslim poet Alam. As early as 1905, a Diwan at Bhasaur discussed the Ragmala at a large meeting and urged that this portion of the scripture be eliminated from printed volumes as "non-Sikh". The debate continued for a decade, during which time, according to PKD documents, some members of the CKD sought a compromise by organising a committee (including Vir Singh, Giani Thakur Singh, Pandit Variam Singh, and Gaini Sher Singh) to consider publishing the Granth in tract form. When these efforts did not moderate Teja Singh's insistence on doctrinal purity, the committee disbanded, and in 1916, the PKD published a version of the *Granth* without the controversial section.

There are two versions as to what happened next. The Bhasaur group claimed that the CKD launched a massive campaign to discredit their group, using the issue as a means of undercutting support for its rival and casting doubts on its claim to represent one segment of the Sikh community[21]. The Amritsar Diwan on the other hand claimed that the PKD overstepped reasonable boundaries and had to be kept from further sacrilege[22]. For whatever reason, the Ragmala issue further worsened relations between the two organisations, and between Budh Singh and his paper, the *Panth Sweak* (a supporter of Teja Singh), and the CKD mouthpiece, the *Khalsa Samachar*.

The fiery editorials and a series of meetings and counter meetings, organised by groups in Punjab and by supporters in Southeast Asia and beyond, finally set the stage for intervention by the Maharaja of Patiala. The Sikh ruler, with whom the PKD had been struggling for years, promulgated an order in the spring of 1918 that the Bhasaur organisation must turn in all copies of the controversial volumes and send printed pages of the Ragmala section to those who had bought the truncated edition. Patiala declined to become involved in whether or not Ragmala was *gurbani*, the authentic teachings of the Gurus, and instead acted for the announced reason that the state had to stop Teja Singh from spreading enmity and disrupting law and order[23].

When Teja Singh did not back down and refused to heed orders from Patiala, nothing happened. What accounts for the resulting stalemate that lasted for half a decade? First, Sikhs were caught up in massive debate over the implications of fresh constitutional changes for their minority community. The forthcoming 1919 Government of India Act would transfer substantial power at the provincial level to those who could organise political parties and win voter approval. Under these circumstances, Sikhs fully engaged in meetings, preparing petitions, and worrying about the future. Finding a way to muzzle Teja Singh was far less a priority than dealing with new political challenges[24]. Too, the PKD still had some residual respect because of its strident confrontation with pujaris and managers of shrines who challenged the Tat Khalsa programme. The PKD was engaged in several legal battles and even direct action against gurdwara administrators.

Ultimately, however, the radical Bhasaur action went unchecked because no central Sikh body had the authority or the will to tackle Teja Singh. One traditional source of authority, the four *takhts*, had issued resolutions over the Ragmala incident, but they were seen as being under the primary influence of anti-Tat Khalsa forces, and these resolutions, along with earlier ones on a range of subjects, had never been implemented[25]. Patiala was caught up in the war effort and was not prepared to be an enforcer of sarcedotal resolutions against the Diwan. Similarly, the CKD was in an increasingly precarious position by 1918. Its efforts to defend the community while at the same time assisting the British came under heavy fire, particularly with military over-recruitment beginning to cause rural discontent. Facing internal divisions and new opposition from militant Sikhs who criticized the Diwan and held public demonstrations challenging its legitimacy, the Amritsar body kept trying to moderate Teja Singh's actions and did not lead in launching a more strident campaign over the open challenge to current Sikh practices.

The turbulent events after the 1919 Punjab disturbances overtook both the Chief Khalsa and Panch Khalsa Diwans, and initiated a new phase of Sikhs politics and religious debate that left each on the periphery of public life. The Punjab riots, British repression, and massive upheaval helped erode the leadership of the CKD, which characteristically tried to find a middle ground between supporting the government and joining militant Sikhs and other Punjabis in denouncing official *zulum*. Despite having led the fight to win control of gurdwaras from pro-British and Hindu elements, the Diwan refused to align with activists who used aggressive and sometimes unlawful tactics to complete the task. Amidst charges that the CKD was old-fashioned and out of step with the times, the mantle of authority moved swiftly from that organisations to those prominent in the Akali movement and eventually the Shiromani Gurdwara Parbandak Committee[26].

For a brief period, the Panch Khalsa Diwan had a revival and improved its position among Sikhs by participating fully in confrontations, marches and *jathas*. The Bhasaur group already had been fighting with the manager of the Akal Takht, who labelled Teja Singh and his followers "*chuhras*", outcastes, because of their repeated association with low-caste converts. Pujaris refused to let PKD members worship in the Golden Temple and later did the same with others. This led eventually to the takeover of the complex[27]. There is abundant evidence that Bhasaur militants also were prominent in several *jathas* and intensified their call for true followers of Guru Gobind Singh to take up the sword against repression.

With the growing ascendancy of the Akali leadership, however, Teja Singh began to argue that these new leaders were self-serving and probably more irreligious than the CKD. Labelling the SGPC a *manmat* organisation, the Bhasaur party noted that many Akalis still respected caste differences and pursued personal gain and prestige. To a large extent, the Akali Dal heads were portrayed as representative of urban and commercial interests who had neither to courage or the support to lead the community[28]. The crescendo of personal attacks and outcry against the Akalis continued until 1925, when discussion of the Sikh Gurdwaras Bill made matters much worse. The proposed legislation stipulated that anyone signing an oath that he or she was a Sikh would be considered a Sikh for the purposes of elections and administration. This compromise position aimed at maximizing the size and influence of the Sikh population, and at the same time avoided a major division, and possible negative vote, over the bill. Furious at the definition, Teja Singh and his band labelled Akali leaders as cowards who only wanted to get out of jail and curry favour with the British. Since only *Amritdharis* were real Sikhs, any vague or loose definition undermined tradition[29].

The PKD struck out sharply against many major organisations and centres of authority. The SGPC's programme for converting untouchables, for example, came under fire because Teja Singh insisted that all brought into the Sikh fold must undergo *amrit* and then be treated as social and religious equals. Numbers meant nothing, *amrit* meant everything. The Diwan made fun of Akalis who waffled on the issue, challenging even their marriages in instances when the couple had not taken *amrit* prior to the final ceremony[30]. The *takhts* came in for even harsher criticism. Diwans at Bhasaur challenged the jathedars to give up their positions, insisting that all gurdwaras belonged to the community. Jathedars should be elected democratically and not appointed for political reasons. The PKD expressed particular concern about the close relationship between these religious leaders and the SGPC, which had either direct or indirect influence over the *takhats*.[31]

The PKD's escalating attacks eventually managed to alienate almost everyone. Fighting with the Maharaja of Patiala over titles led to an embarrassing incident in which Teja Singh instructed those in charge of a worship service not to give *karah parshad* to the Raja because he was impure and a sinner. Patiala retaliated by cutting off all funds to Bhasaur and then imprisoning Teja Singh for a year, 1922-23, on charges of "sacrilege" and creating disturbances. After returning home, Teja Singh kept up his assaults on Patiala and prominent Sikhs. He renewed publication of gurmukhi lessons consisting of sections of the Granth with deletions and commentary interspersed, changing words and raising questions about specific passages. This incitment coincided in 1927 with another printing of the Granth minus the Ragmala[32].

On July 15, 1928, the *takhts* and the SGPC issued a joint communique that suspended Teja Singh and his wife from the Khalsa Panth, banned members of the PKD from all gurdwaras, and called for a total boycott of Bhasaur. The SGPC also declared the manager of the Sri Gurmat Press, Bodh Singh, *tankhahia*, but he later appeared before the Akal Takht and received a pardon after agreeing not to publish literature judged sacrilegious[33].

Teja Singh met the challenges with characteristics fervour. He questioned the authority of the *takhts*, claiming that the heads had not been elected according to *gurmat* customs and therefore were illegitimate. Either appointed or pressured by the SGPC, he claimed, the jathedars had issued rulings for political and not religious reasons without serious deliberation and consultations with the community[34]. Nevertheless, this time the sanctions took hold. The flow of outside support disappeared although occasional funds trinkled in from Malaysia and Singapore. Balasore came to be seen as a polluted and blasphemous spot, and a series of challenges and public accusations, even threats, further cut off Bhasaur from its former allies. Kahan Singh Nabha, for example, received a death notice because of his connection with Teja Singh, and at least publicly avoided any assistance for individuals and positions associated with Bhasaur[35].

The Bhasaur Diwan continued to issue edicts, including its own set of rules about daily practice and worship, *rahit*. However, the intellectual vitality of the organisation diminished sharply after 1928. When Teja Singh died in 1933, a former secretary, Lal Singh, became the new leader, but the Sabha gradually sank into obscurity. Just as in the case of the Chief Khalsa Diwan, which survived only in truncated fashion, an organisation once at the cutting edge of the Tat Khalsa activism lost support and became irrelevant, rising only sporadically to write its own history or to pass resolutions in annual meetings, now attended by just a handful of supporters. The issues and resolutions continued to project the Bhasaur view of Sikh tradition: *amrit pahul* for both women and men, turbans for women, celebration of only distinctly Sikh festivals, a stringent social code devoid of caste or clan distinctions, and most importantly, the sole legitimacy of *Amritdhari* Sikh. Conversely, all contact with *Udasis, Nirankaris*, and *Sahajdharis* must cease[36].

What can be learned from the experiences of the Chief Khalsa Diwan and the Panch Khalsa Diwan? First, the history of the two organisations throws light on how Sikhs viewed their tradition, religious ideals, and practice in the pre-Akali period. There was substantial disagreement over ritual, the role of women, the importance of caste in social relations and worship, and both historical fact and theological issues. Exemplifying the tenacity and energy of the Tat Khalsa movement, Teja Singh and his associates made many Sikhs uncomfortable by raising awkward questions and then providing unpopular answers. For a brief period, Bhasaur helped focus the debate through innovations in organisations (five-day diwans) and publicity, and then used reports and tracts, along with sending out preaching teams and missionaries, to transmit its views effectively. Nevertheless, those views increasingly came to be seen as irrelevant or even dangerous. The Chief Khalsa Diwan was aware of the differing interpretations and usually tried to smooth over or reconcile differences by using committees, deflecting debate to less controversial matters such as education, and in general, to expand the institutional base of Sikhism.

Secondly, the reaction to the Bhasur's radical ideas suggests that by early in this century, the Singh Sabhas had fostered a general consensus about the boundaries of Sikhism and the Sikh understanding of their past. Bhasaur was only one of numerous associations attempting to develop resources and influence attitudes and values through traditional and more modern means. The PKD's major rival, the CKD, had a world-wide network of communication involving correspondents, newspapers and organisations. The CKD perspective tended to dominate and left a lasting legacy. Although not overly concerned with theological or academic aspects of some of the arguments relating to Ragmala, ritual, and the role of women in ceremonies, many Sikhs had an increasingly specific understanding of the basic tenets and boundaries of their faith[37]. The sacred nature of the *Granth* was well understood and accepted, for example, and any attempt to edit or raise questions about its authenticity evoked a strong reaction. At the same time, a popular culture disseminated by the new print media, including pictures, dramatizations of the lives of the Gurus, martyrs, folk heroes, was beginning to be established in the urban areas, while traditional bards and wandering musical groups played a similar role in the countryside[38]. The PKD's charge that these trends were anti-Sikh and resembled Hindu practice fell on deaf ears. Similarly, the persistence of typical Punjab values relating to women, family, marriage patterns, and caste was so strong that the Bhasaur attempts to change the social basis of daily life of Sikhs proved ineffectual. The CKD and most Sikh organisations did not even address the challenges of the PKD in matters such as inter-marriage, the role of women in ceremonies, and related issues[39].

Most important, this review of a turning point in the evolution of modern Sikhism highlights the confusion and conflict over authority and decision-making that existed then and persists even today. Unlike Catholicism and some Protestant sects, since the time of the Gurus, Sikhism has never had an organisational church with generally accepted leaders who could resolve religious or political issues. The *takhts* made pronouncements, but those tended to reflect the attitudes of the period (for example, pro-British edicts in the nineteenth century, or statements attacking Tat Khalsa programmes in 1905, or support for the war effort and the British during the First World War). Teja Singh was accurate in claiming that the leadership of the *takhts* reached decisions at least partially influenced by the political balance within the community. Only when specific organisations, such as the SGPC, or individuals with power such as the Maharaja of Patiala, enforced decisions did they become seen as legitimate. The hesitation to publish a *rahit maryada* until the second quarter of this century, for example, suggests the uncertainty about doctrine and practice that existed. The contemporary questions about the nature of the *Granth*, the correct interpretation of historical events, and even the Ragmala, also involves institutional conflict and often political struggle between groups vying for legitimacy[40]. This is not to suggest that there are not accepted traditions and boundaries associated with modern Sikhism. To the contrary, the recent experience of Sikhs from the Singh Sabha period onward mirrors the variety of arguments and self-examination that one necessarily finds in any vibrant religious tradition that legitimately claims to have universal appeal. Sikhism is an accepted world religion, and with that comes the type of challenges and programmes associated with the Chief Khalsa Diwan and the Panch Khalsa Diwan, and continuing now in the intellectual debate over the Gurus, history, and the nature of tradition. As in the Singh Sabha days, the battle involves not just intellectual argument, but who controls institutions and dominates the communication network linking-Sikhs throughout the world[41].

—N.Gerald Barrier

REFERENCES

1. The most recent and thorough study of the issues and the Singh Sabha movement in general include the essays and new book by Harjot Oberoi. *The Construction or Religious Boundaries: Culture, Identity and Diversity in the Sikh Tradition* (Delhi: Oxford University Press, 1994), and the sources and historiographic discussion in N.G. Barrier. *The Sikhs and Their Literature* (Delhi: Manohar, 1970).

2. Richard Fox's *Lions of the Punjab* (Berkeley: University of California Press, 1985) over-emphasizes the British role. For useful criticism, Oberoi discussion, *Construction*, pp. 370-76; Ian Kerr, "Fox and the Lions: The Akali Movement Revisited", in Joseph O'Connell, ed. *Sikh History and Religion in the Twentieth Century* (Toronto: University of Toronto South Asia Centre, 1988), pp. 211-225.

3. Background in Barrier, "Sikh Emigrants and their Homeland", in Barrier and Van Dusenbery, eds., *The Sikh Diaspora* (Delhi: Chanakya, 1989), pp. 49-89. Also Oberoi, *Construction*, pp. 263, 273-4. On the information infrastructure and its product, see Barrier, *Sikhs*.

4. On present reaction, and the continued existence of local culture and popular religion, see Oberoi, *Construction*, pp. 397-401.

5. Background in Barrier, "Sikh Politics in British Punjab Prior to the Gurudwara Reform Movement", in O'Connell, *Sikh History*, pp. 159-90.

6. A readable survey on the CKD is in Harbans Singh, ed., *The Encyclopaedia of Sikhism* (Patiala: Punjabi University, 1992), v. 1, 461-65. Also detailed treatment in Barrier. "Sikh Politics in British Punjab Prior to the Gurdwara Reform Movement", in O'Connell, *Sikh History*; Barrier, "The Singh Sabhas and the Evolution of Modern Sikhism, 1875-1925", in Robert Baird, *Religion in Modern India* (Delhi Manohar, rev. ed. 1989), pp. 189-220.

7. On the functioning of the CKD, see Surjit Singh Narang, "Chief Khalsa Diwan", *Journalism of Sikh Studies*, 12 (1981), 97-108. The primary sources of the CKD include sporadic reports, the minute of Executive Committee meeting (hitherto referred to as *CKD*, available in mss with the CKD, Amritsar and the author), and two newspapers, *Khalsa Samachar (KS)* and *Khalsa Advocate (KA)*. On the climate of pamphleteering and tract literature, Barrier, "Vernacular Publishing and Sikh Public Life in the Punjab, 1880-1910", in Kenneth Jones, ed., *Religious Controversy in British India* (Albany: SUNY Press, 1992), pp. 200-226.

8. For example, the brief overview in the *Encyclopaedia of Sikkim* essay, and arguments in Barrier, "Sikh politics".

9. Reviewed in Barrier, "Singh Sabhas", 209-10. On the Rikabganj agitation and its aftermath, see Harjot Oberoi, "From Gurdwara Rikabganj to the Viceregal Palace", *Punjab Past and Present*, 14 (1980), 182-98. On the First World War and Sikh assistance, Barrier, "Ruling India: Coercion and Propaganda in British India During the First World War", in De Witt Ellinwod, *India and World War one* (Delhi: Manohar, 1978), pp. 74-108. On constitutional issues, Gurdarshan Singh, "Sikh Politics in the Punjab", *Punjab Past and Present*, 3 (1970), 67-78. Also overview in Rajiv Kapur, *Sikh Separatism* (London: Allen and Unwin, 1986).

10. Background in Teja Singh, *The Gurdwara Reform Movement and the Sikh Awakening* (Jullundur: Desh Sewak Book Company, 1922); also the writing in Mohan Singh Vaid and his diaries reproduced in Munsha Singh Dukhi, *Jivan Bhai Sahib Bhai Mohan Singhji Vaid* (Amritsar: pub. by author, n.d.). A useful study on authority and the Akal Takht is Harijnder Singh Dilgeer, *The Akal Takht* (Amritsar: Punjabi Book Company, 1980).

11. *Aduti Jivan Britant Panth Ratan Babu Teja Singh Observer* (Amritsar: n.d), p. 76. On Teja Singh's life and work as a publicist, Barrier, "Vernacular", pp. 217-19. Also correspondence between Bhai Takht Singh and Teja Singh in Lal Singh, ed. *Kalmi Taswir* (Chandigarh: privately pub., 1965). Standard works on the Bhasaur Singh Sabha and the PKD include its official history, *Itihas Panch Khalsa Diwan* (henceforth PKD; Bhasaur: PKD, 1967).

12. Background in Harbans Singh, "The Bakapur Diwan and Babu Teja Singh Bhasaur" in *Punjab Past and Present*, 9 (1975), 322-32; "Bakapur Diwan" in Harbans Singh, ed., *Encyclopaedia Sikhism*, v. 1, 259-61.

13. Letters in *Kalmi Taswir*, pp. 42-66, and discussions with Nahar Singh, M.A., who knew Babu Teja Singh just prior to his death.

14. Detailed if somewhat disjointed review of Bhasaur history in PKD. Also tracts and reports described in Barrier, *Sikh Literature*.

15. On the controversied surrounding Banakpur, *Vir Sudhar Patter* (Bhasaur: no pub. 1903), scattered comments, PKD.

16. Details in *Salana Diwan* (Bhasaur: PKD, c. 1916) *and Gurmat Sanskar Bhag* (Bhasaur: PKD, 1908). Numerous references to the events in KS and KA, 1908-1916.

17. For examples, stories in KS. April 29, 1908, p. 2; CKD, 1902, 1906, especially Oct. 1, 1916; *KA* comments, July 15, 1904, p. 3. Background on Teja Singh in *KS*, 1908-1911. Lala Sewa Ram had participated in the Khalsa Youngmens Association and took *amrit* in 1908, *KS*, March 23, 1904, pp. 2-3, *KS*, July 15, 1908, p. 4. He played a major role in the Rikabganj negotiations and later CKD matters.

18. PKD, pp. 52-59.

19. Harjot Oberoi evaluates the centrality of the new print culture in his various writings. Also especially useful is a recently completed study on views toward Sikh martyrdom, a dissertation by Louis Emanuel Fenech, "Playing the Game of Love: The Sikh Tradition of Martyrdom" (unpub, Ph.D. diss., University of Toronto, 1994). On Sikh art and its representation, W.H. McLeod, *Popular Sikh Art* (Delhi: Oxford University Press, 1991). Relevant, PKD resolutions in *Gurmat-i-Prakash* (Bhasaur: PKD, 1914).

20. PKD, pp. 54-59.

21. Discussion in *Sambodh Pattar* (Bhasaur: PKD, 1917) and *Ragmala Nirnaya* (Bhasaur: PKD, n.d.).

22. CKD resolutions, 1917-18, *KS, KA* stories and editorials. October 1917-May 1918. Useful notes on the issue in Surindar Singh Kohli, *A Critical Study of Adi Granth* (Delhi: Motilal, rep. 1976), pp. 93, 105-11.

23. Background in *Ragmala Niarnaya* and PKD, p. 30.

24. On politics of the new legislation, discussions in Barrier, "Sikh Politics", pp. 187-9; Gurdarshan Singh, "Sikh Politics".

25. Several KS editorials noted this point, questioning the relationship between edicts and their acceptance by members of the panth. The CKD effort to include the PKD are reflected in CKD minutes, 1905-7. These include resolutions and debate about how to involve Teja Singh in review of issues and the nature of *rahit*.

26. On the transition, Barrier, "Sikh Politics", and Mohinder Singh, *The Akali Movement* (Delhi: Macmillan India, 1978).

27. PKD, pp. 77-78.

28. For example, resolutions about Sardar Sadhu Singh who allegedly did not act according to *gurmat* by permitting his son to marry a Hindu, and then having the ceremony with non-Sikh rituals. He also was charged with sending family ashes to Hardwar. *Sambodh Pattar*, pp. 7-8.

29. PKD, pp. 34, 83.

30. PKD, pp. 32-33. The Diwan also attacked Patiala for having a Hindu, Pandit Kishan Kaul, as Prime Minister.

31. These charges are also found in letters to the *Tribune* and other Punjab newspapers in the period 1924-1928.

32. *Shiromani Gurdwara Parbandhak Committee De Alian No. 82* (Amritsar: n.d., c. August 1928). Edicts from Hazur Sahib, the Akal Takht and Sri Patna Sahib and reprinted in the SGPC document. Background on issues in *Tribune*, May-August 1928.

33. *Kalmi Taswir*, pp. 79-80. p. 90. Also PKD, 157-58.

34. PKD, pp. 118-121. Also correspondence with Takht Singh in *Kalmi Taswir*.

35. PKD, pp. 118-122. Kahan Singh repeatedly had come under attack as a primary intellectual source for Bhasaur from the early 1990s onward.

36. Cumulative resolutions reprinted in PKD, pp. 190-195.

37. Oberoi and McLeod discuss the generally accepted tenets and also some of the basic disagreements in their articles and books.

38. This theme receives new and important exploration in the French dissertation.

39. See, for example, the result of the rural survey by Clearance McMullen, *Religious Beliefs and Practices of the Sikhs in Rural Punjab* (Delhi: Manohar, 1989).

40. For example, the struggles among Sikhs after Operation Blue Star led to a variety of *hukamnamas*, special assemblies at the Akal Takht, and forced changes in Akal Takht management. An interesting overview is in Gurmit Singh, *History of Sikh Struggles,* v. 4 (Delhi: Atlantic Publishers, 1992), 35-93. The continuing discussion of Ragmala and *rahit maryada* is a theme often reflected in conflict over control of Sikhs institutions, or in disturbances over management of gurdwaras in Canada, California, New York and the Washington, D.C. area. Background in the *World Sikh News*, summer and fall 1993. Also see the Pashaura Singh chapter, in this volume.

41. There are a variety of journals, newspapers, and occasional papers that are published by local, national or international organisations. The most prominent is the *World Sikh News*, associated with the World Sikh Organisation; many associated with that group also have produced a variety of scholarly and polemical works on historical, religious and political issues. Some of the variety of opinion and a reasoned assessment of where Sikhs stand at this juncture are found in the essay by I.J. Singh, *Sikhs and Sikhism* (Columbia, Mo.: South Asia Publications, 1994).

The Sikh Gurus

The Palace of the Lord God is so beautiful. Within it, there are gems, rubies, pearls and flawless diamonds. A fortress of gold surrounds this source of nectar. How can I climb up to the Fortress without a ladder? By meditating on the Lord, through the Guru, I am blessed and exalted. The Guru is the Ladder, the Guru is the Boat, and the Guru is the Raft to take me to the Lord's Name. The Guru is the Boat to carry me across the world-ocean; the Guru is the Sacred Shrine of Pilgrimage, the Guru is the Holy River. If it pleases him, I bathe in the Pool of Truth, and become radiant and pure". (Guru Nanak, Sri Rag, pg. 17).

The word "Guru" is a Sanskrit word meaning teacher, honoured person, religious person of saint Sikhism though has a very specific definition of the word guru. It means the descent of divine guidance to mankind provided through ten Enlightened Masters. This honour of being called a Sikh Guru applies only to the ten Gurus who funded the religion starting with Guru Nanak in 1469 and ending with Guru Gobind Singh in 1708, thereafter it refers to the Sikh Holy Scriptures the Guru Granth Sahib. The divine spirit was passed from one Guru to the next as "The light of a lamp which lights another does not abate. Similarly a spiritual leader and his disciple become equal, Nanak says the truth".

They distinguish and separate one Guru from the other. And rare is the one who knows that they indeed, were one. They who realised this in their hearts, attained Realisation of God" (Guru Gobind Singh, Dohira, Vachitra Natak)

Pictures of the Gurus

Sikhism rejects any form of idol worship including worship of pictures of the Gurus. Although some of the Gurus did pose for paintings, unfortunately none of these historical paintings have survived. Artists renditions are for inspirational purposes only and should not be regarded as objects of worship themselves.

The Great Masters of Sikhism

The first master:	Guru Nanak Dev	(1469 to 1539)
The second master:	Guru Angad Dev	(1504 to 1552)
The third master:	Guru Amar Das	(1479 to 1574)
The fourth master:	Guru Ram Das	(1534 to 1581)
The fifth master:	Guru Arjan Dev	(1563 to 1606)
The sixth master:	Guru Hargobind	(1595 to 1644)
The seventh master:	Guru Har Rai	(1630 to 1661)
The eighth master:	Guru Harkrishan	(1656 to 1664)
The ninth master:	Guru Teg Bahadur	(1621 to 1675)
The tenth master:	Guru Gobind Singh	(1666 to 1708)

The First Master Guru Nanak Dev (1469-1539)

Me, the bard out of work, the Lord has applied to His service. In the very beginning He gave me the order to sing His praises night and day. The Master summoned the minstrel to His True Court. He clothed me with the robe of His true honour and eulogy. Since then the True Name had become my ambrosial food. They, who under the Guru's instruction, eat this food to their satisfaction, obtain peace. By signing the Guru's hymns, I, the minstrel spread the Lord's glory. Nanak, by praising the True Name I have obtained the perfect Lord" (Guru Nanak, Pauri, pg. 150).

The founder of the Sikh religion, Guru Nanak was born on April 15, 1469 in the Western Punjab village of Talwandi. He was born to a simple Hindu family. His father Mehta Kalian Das was an accountant in the employment of the local Muslim authorities. From an early age Guru Nanak made friends with both Hindu and Muslim children and was very inquisitive about the meaning of life. At the age of six he was sent to the village school teacher for schooling in reading and writing in Hindi and mathematics. He was then schooled in the study of Muslim literature and learned Persian and Arabic. He was an unusually gifted child who learned quickly and often question his teachers. At age 13 it was time for Guru Nanak to be invested with the sacred thread according to the traditional Hindu custom. At the ceremony which was attended by family and friends and to the disappointment of his family Guru Nanak refused to accept the sacred cotton thread from the Hindu priest. He sang the following poem:

"Let mercy be the cotton, contentment the thread, continence the knot and truth the twist. O priest! If you have such a thread. Do give it to me. It'll not wear out, not get soiled, nor burnt, nor lost. Says Nanak, blessed are those who go about wearing such a thread" (Rag Asa)

As a young man herding the family cattle, Guru Nanak would spend long hours absorbed in meditation and in religious discussions with Muslim and Hindu, holy men who lived in the forests surrounding the village. Thinking that if bound in marriage Guru Nanak might start taking interest in household affairs a suitable match was found for him. At age 16 he was married to Sulakhani daughter of a pious merchant. Guru Nanak did not object as he felt that married life did not conflict with spiritual pursuits. Guru Nanak was happily married, he loved his wife and eventually had two sons Sri Chand in 1494 and Lakshmi Chand three years later. Now that he had a family of his own Guru Nanak was persuaded by his parents to take a job as an accountant in charge of the stores of the Muslim governor of Sultanpur Daulat Khan Lodi. Guru Nanak agreed and was joined by his family and an old Muslim childhood friend Mardana, a musician by profession. Guru Nanak would work during the days, but early in the mornings and late at nights, he would meditate and sing hymns accompanied by Mardana on the rabab (a string instrument). These sessions attracted a lot of attention and many people starting joining the two.

Early one morning accompanied by Mardana, Guru Nanak went to the river Bain for his bath. After plunging into the river, Guru Nanak did not surface and it was reported that he must have drowned. The villagers searched everywhere, but their was no trace of him. Guru Nanak was in holy communion with God. The Lord God revealed himself to Guru Nanak and enlightened him. In praise of the Lord, Guru Nanak uttered;

"There is but one God, His name is Truth. He is a Creator, He fears none, He is without hate, He never dies, He is beyond the cycle of births and death. He is self illuminated. He is realized by the kindness of the True Guru. He was True in the beginning. He was True when the ages commenced and has ever been True. He is also true now". (Japji).

These words are enshrined at the beginning of the Sikh Holy scriptures, the Guru Granth Sahib. Guru Nanak did not believe in a Trinity of Gods, or the belief that God can be born into human form.

After three days Guru Nanak appeared at the same spot from where he had disappeared. He was no longer the same person he had been, there was a divine light in his eyes and his face was resplendent. He remained in a trance and said nothing. He gave up his job and distributed all of his belongings to the poor. When he finally broke his silence he uttered "There is no Hindu, no Muslim". Daulat Khan asked what he meant when he said to Guru Nanak, "Perhaps the Hindus were no longer Hindus but the Muslims remain devout to their faith". Guru Nanak replied,

"Let God's grace be the mosque, and devotion the prayer mat. Let the Quran be the good conduct. Let modesty be compassion, good manners fasting, you should be a Muslim the like of this. Let good deeds be your Kaaba and truth be your mentor. Your Kalma be your creed and prayer. God would then vindicate your honour". (Majh)

Guru Nanak was thirty years old at this time in 1499. The next stage of his life began with extensive travels to spread the message of God. Accompanied by his Muslim rabab player Mardana for company, Guru Nanak undertook long journeys to convey his message to the people in the form of musical hymns. Guru Nanak choose this medium to propagate his message because it was easily understood by the population of the time. Wherever he traveled he used the local language to convey his message to the people. He traveled throughout the Indian Subcontinent and further east, west, and north to spread his mission. Wherever he went he set up local cells called manjis, where his followers could gather to recite hymns and meditate.

Once when Guru Nanak came to the small town of Saidpur in West Punjab he choose to stay there with Lalo, a low caste carpenter. At the same time the local chief of the town Malik Bhago, who was quite wealthy and a very proud man was holding a feast to which all holy men were invited. When Malik Bhago found out that Guru Nanak would not attend his feast but instead partook of the simple fare of his host Lalo, he was quite angry and had the Guru brought to him for questioning. When asked why he didn't join in the feast, the Guru sent for the meal served by Malik Bhago and also some of the simple meal served by Lalo. Holding these in separate hands he squeezed them, blood appeared out of the rich food of Malik Bhago, while milk oozed out of Lalos simple fare. Malik Bhago was put to shame and realized that his riches had been amassed by exploiting the poor, while what Lalo offered was the milk of hard earned honest work.

Another time while camped out at a town during the rainy season, several devotees would come to the Guru on a regular basis. One of them while on the way to see the Guru, came across a prostitute and was allured by her. Thereafter he would leave home on the pretext of going to see the Guru, but insisted visited the prostitute. A few days later his friend who daily came to pay homage to the Guru was picked by a thorn, while his neighbour, who visited the prostitute, found a gold coin in the street. The incident bewildered the Guru's devotee who came every day religiously. He mentioned it in the morning prayer meeting where Guru Nanak heard it and was amused. He told the Sikh;

"Your friend was destined to come across a treasure but due to his evil ways, it has been reduced to a single coin. While on the account of your past karma you were to have been impaled with a stake, but having reformed yourself, you have been let off with the mere prick of a thorn". (Janamsakhi).

When the Guru visited Kurukshetra in Haryana, a big fair was being held at the holy tank to celebrate the solar eclipse. There were a large number of pilgrims all over the country. On his arrival at the fair, Guru Nanak had Mardana cook them a meat dish of a deer presented to them by one of his followers. Upon finding that meat was being cooked on the holy premises, a large angry crowd gathered in anger to attack the Guru for what they thought amounted to sacrilege *(Bhai Mani Singh, Gyan Ratnavali, pg. 123)*. Upon hearing the angry crowd Guru Nanak responded;

"Only fools argue wheth to eat meat or not. They don't understand truth nor do they meditate on it. Who can definite what is meat and what is plant? Who knows where the sin lies, being a vegetarian or a non-vegetarian?" (Malhar)

When Guru Nanak stopped at Hardwar a pilgrimage centre on the Ganges river he found a large gat ring of devotees. They were taking ritual baths in the holy river and offering water to the sun. When the Guru asked "Why do you throw water like that?" The pilgrims replied that they were offering it to their ancestors. Guru Nanak upon hearing this started throwing water in the opposite direction towards the west. When the pilgrims asked him what he was doing? Guru Nanak replied "I am sending water to my farm which is dry". They asked, "How will water reach your crops so far away?" Guru Nanak replied, "If your water can reach your ancestors in the region of the sun, why can't mine reach my fields a short distance away?" The pilgrims realized their folly and fell at the Gurus feet.

On an eastern journey Guru Nanak visited Gorakhmata here he discussed the true meaning of asceticism with some yogis;

"Asceticism doesn't lie in ascetic robes, or in walking staff, nor in the ashes. Asceticism doesn't lie in the earring, nor in the shaven head, nor blowing a conch. Asceticism lies in remaining pure amidst impurities. Asceticism doesn't lie in mere words; He is an ascetic who treats everyone alike. Asceticism doesn't lie in visiting burial places. It lies not in wandering about, nor in bathing at places of pilgrimage. Asceticism is to remain pure amidst impurities (Suhi).

After his first long journey, Guru Nanak returned home after twelve years of propagating his message. He then set out on a second journey travelling as far south as Sri Lanka. On his return north he founded a settlement known as Kartharpur (the Abode of God) on the western banks of the Ravi river, Guru Nanak would one day settle down here in his old age. It was also here that he met a young devotee who would later go on to serve five of the following Gurus, Baba Buddha (the revered old one). On his third great journey Guru Nanak travelled as far north as Tibet. Wherever Guru Nanak travelled he always wore a combination of styles worn by Hindu and Muslim holy men and was always asked whether he was a Hindu or Muslim. Guru Nanak visited Sheikh Ibrahim the Muslim successor of Baba Farid the great Sufi dervish of the twelfth century at Ajodhan. When asked by Ibrahim which of the two religions was the true way to attain God, Guru Nanak replied; "If there is one God, then there is only His way to attain Him, not another. One must follow that way and reject the other. Worship not him who is born only to die, but Him who is eternal and is contained in the whole universe".

On his fourth great journeyin life Guru Nanak dressed in the blue garb of a Muslim pilgrim travelled to the west and visited Mecca, Medina and Baghdad. Arriving at Mecca, Guru Nanak fell asleep with his feet pointing towards the holy Kabba. When the watchman on his night rounds noticed this he kicked the Guru, saying, "How dare you turn your feet towards the house of God". At this Guru Nanak woke up and said, "Good man, I am weary after a long journey. Kindly turn my feet in the direction where God is not". When pilgrims and the holy men of the shrine gathered to hear Guru Nanak and questioned him, he sang in Persian;

"I beseech you, O Lord! pray grant me a hearing. You are the truth, the great, the merciful, and the faultless Creator. I know for certain, this world must perish, and death must come, I know this and nothing else. Neither wife, nor son, nor father, nor brothers shall be able to help. I must go in the end, none can undo what is my fate. I have spend days and nights in vanity, contemplating evil. Never have I thought of good; this is what I am ill-starred, miserly, careless, short-sighted, and rude. But says Nanak, I am yours, the dust of the feet of your servants". (Tilang)

While in Baghdad contradicting the Muslim priests views that there were only seven upper and as many lower regions Guru Nanak shouted out his own prayer saying.

"There are worlds and more worlds below them and there are a hundred thousand skies over them. No one has been able to find the limits and boundaries of God. If there be any account of God, then alone the mortal can write the same; but Gods account does not finish and the mortal himself dies while still writing. Nanak says that one should call Him great, and God himself knows His ownself". (Japji)

In 1916 a tablet with the following inscription was uncovered in Baghdad, "In memory of the Guru, the only Baba Nanak, King of holy men, this monument has been raised anew with the help of the seven saints". The date on the tablet 927 Hijri corresponds to A.D. 1520-1521.

On his return journey home he stopped at Saidpur in western Punjab during the invasion of the first Mughal Emperor Babar. On seeing the extent of the massacre by the invaders, Mardana asked Guru Nanak why so many innocent people were put to death along with those few who were guilty. Guru Nanak told Mardana to wait under a banyan tree and after a while he would return to answer his question. While sitting under the tree Mardana was suddenly bitten by an ant. In anger Mardana killed as many ants as he could with his feet. Guru Nanak said to him, "you know now Mardana, why do the innocents suffer along with the guilty?"

Guru Nanak and Mardana were both taken prisoner by the Mughal's. While in jail Guru Nanak sang a divine hymn about the senseless slaughter of the innocents by the Mughal invaders, Upon hearing it the jailer reported it to his king. Babar sent for the Guru and upon hearing him realized that Guru Nanak was a great religious figure. He asked for the Gurus forgiveness and set him free offering him a pouch of hashish. Guru Nanak refused saying that he was already intoxicated with the love and name of God.

After having spent a lifetime of travelling abroad and setting up missions, an aged Guru Nanak returned home to Punjab. He settled down at Kartharpur with his wife and sons. Pilgrims came from far and near to hear the hymns and preaching of the master. Here his followers would gather in the mornings and afternoons for religious services. He believed in a casteless society without and distinctions based on birthright, religion or sex. He institutionalized the common kitchen called langer in Sikhism. Here all can sit together and share a common meal, whether they were kings or beggars.

While working the fields one day in 1532 Guru Nanak was approached by a new devotee who said, "I am Lehna," Guru Nanak looked at him and replied, "So you have arrived Lehna—the creditor. I have been waiting for you all these days. I must pay your debt". ("Lehna" in Punjabi means debt or creditor). Lehna was a great devotee of the Hindu God Durga. One day having hearing about Guru Nanak and his teachings, he decided to visit and see the Guru for himself. Once Lehna met Guru Nanak he left his previous beliefs and became an ardent disciple of the Guru. Lehna's devotion to Guru Nanak was absolute, when he was not working on the farm, he would devote his spare time to the contemplation of God. Over time he became Guru Nanak's most ardent disciple. Guru Nanak put his followers to many tests to see who was the most faithful. Once while accompanied by Lehna and his two sons Guru Nanak came across what looked like a corpse covered with a sheet. "Who would eat it?" asked Guru Nanak unexpectedly.

His sons refused, thinking that their father was not in his senses. Lehna though agreed and as he removed the cover he found that it was a tray of sacred food. Lehna first offered it to Guru Nanak and his sons and then partook of the leftovers himself, Guru Nanak on seeing this replied.

"Lehna, you were blessed with the sacred food because you could share it with others. If the people use the wealth bestowed on them by God for themselves alone or for treasuring it, it is like a corpse. But if they decide to share it with others, it becomes sacred food. You have known the secret. You are my image". (Janamsakhi).

Guru Nanak then blessed Lehna with his ang (hand) and gave him a new name, Angad, saying "you are a part of my body". Guru Nanak placed five coins and a coconut in front of Guru Angad and then bowed before him. He then had Bhai Budhha anoint Angad with a Saffron mark on his forehead. When Guru Nanak gathered his followers together for prayers he invited Angad to occupy the seat of the Guru. Thus Guru Angad was ordained as the successor to Guru Nanak. Feeling his end was near, the Hindus said we will cremate you, the Muslims said we will bury you. Guru Nanak said; "You place flowers on either side, Hindus on my right, Muslims on my left. Those whose flowers remain fresh tomorrow will have their way." He then asked them to prey and lay down covering himself with a sheet. Thus on September 22, 1539 in the early hours of the morning Guru Nanak merged with the eternal light of the Creator. When the followers lifted the sheet they found nothing except the flowers which were all fresh. The Hindus took theirs and cremated them, while the Muslims took their flowers and buried them.

Thus having spread the words of reform, throughout his lifetime, Guru Nanak successfully challenged and questioned the existing religious tenants and laid the foundations of Sikhism.

The Second Master Guru Angad Dev (1504-1552)

The son of a prosperous Hindu trader, Bhai Pheru, Guru Angad was an ardent devotee of the Hindu goddess Durga. Lehna, as he was known before becoming Guru was born on March 31, 1504 in the village of Matte-di-Sari but eventually his family moved to Khadur. He was married to Khivi and had two sons. Datu and Dasu, and one daughter Amro. Lehna would annually lead groups of pilgrims to visit the temple of Durga at Jwalamukhi for preying and dancing. Here the flames emitted by the volcano are worshipped by devout Hindus. One day Lehna heard a Sikh named Bhai Jodha reciting the Japji, the early morning prayer composed by Guru Nanak. Finding out about Guru Nanak from Bhai Joda, Lehna decided to visit the Guru and pay his respects. Upon meeting Guru Nanak at the age of 27, Lehna became a devout disciple of Guru Nanak and renounced his former practices.

Guru Nanak instructed Lehna to return to Khadur to instruct people in the ways of Sikhism. Here Lehna spent his time in prayer and serving the people. He distributed food to the poor daily. Longing to be with Guru Nanak he eventually returned to Karthapur where he became totally devoted to the service of Guru Nanak. After undergoing countless tests. Guru Nanak eventually appointed Guru Angad as his successor on July 14, 1539 as described previously. Upon the death of Guru Nanak, Guru Angad returned to Khadur where he went into seclusion and meditation for six months. Eventually a delegation of Sikhs led by Baba Buddha convinced the Guru that they needed him. Guru Angad longed for Guru Nanak, when he said to Baba Buddha;

"He whom you love, die for him. Accursed is the life without the beloved. The head should be sliced that does not bow before the Master. O Nanak! the body should be burnt that suffers not the agony of separation". (Sri Rag) "He who has been blessed by Guru Nanak is lost in the praises of the Lord. What could one teach those, who have Divine Nanak as their Guru?" (Majh)

Guru Angad was the embodiment of humility as Guru Nanak had been before him. The renowned yogi Daya Nath visited Guru Angad to try to convert him. Daya Nath believed that mental purity could only be obtained through renunciation of the world, observance of rituals, introspection, and yoga. Guru Angad engaged him in discussion saying that only through living a simple truthful life as Guru Nanak had lived can God be realised, by remaining pure amidst impurity. The yogi was eventually won over by the purity and innocence of Guru Angad and asked the Guru if there was anything that he could do for him. The humble Guru Angad replied that he only seeked the learned yogis blessings.

Guru Angad followed the daily routine that Guru Nanak had. He would wake up early at dawn to recite Guru Nanak's Japji (morning prayer) as well as sing Asa di var with his congregation work during the daytime and then have evening prayers. Guru Angad also maintained langar where people of all religions and castes could gather for a free meal. Guru Angad also took a keen interest in physical fitness, and encouraged his devotees to be involved in sports after their morning prayers.

After the Mughal emperor Babur's death he was succeeded by his son Humayun. He was soon defeated by Sher Shah and on his retreat out of India he stopped at Khadur to seek the Guru's blessings. When Humayun arrived, Guru Angad and the congregation were absorbed in singing religious hymns. After a while Humayun became impatient and angry at being ignored and put his hand on the hilt of his sword to attack the Guru. Guru Angad was unmoved by this and said "when you should have used the sword you did not, rather you ran away from the battlefield like a coward. Here you show off, threatening to attack unarmed devotees engaged in prayer". Humayun was humbled by this and asked the Guru's forgiveness and blessings. Guru Angad blessed him, and as history was to have it he eventually regained his throne.

Guru Angad was very fond of children and took a great interest in their education. He advocated that they should be taught to read and write in their mother tongue, Punjabi. Although the origins of the Gurmukhi script are unclear, it is clear that Guru Angad popularized the use of this simplified script among the Sikhs starting around 1541. Being the successor of Guru Nanak he also got the first authorized biography of Guru Nanak written in 1544, as well as having a number of copies of Guru Nanak's hymns written out in the new Gurmukhi script. Guru Angad further expanded the number of Sikh religious centres.

There lived a very devout Vaishanavite Hindu named Amar Das. He had regularly, made pilgrimages to the Ganges river for ritual baths for over 20 years. While returning from his twelfth such pilgrimage he was asked by a monk "Who is your Guru?" Amar Das felt frustrated as he could not answer this question having searched his whole life, but still not achieving the peace of mind that he longed for. One day he heard Bibi Amro the daughter of Guru Angad, who was recently married to his nephew singing the hymns of Guru Nanak. Amar Das started to listen to them every day until he was enchanted by them. Bibi Amro told Amar Das about the mission of Guru Nanak and promised to introduce him to her father Guru Angad.

When the time finally came and they met. Guru Angad got up from his seat on his arrival to embrace Amar Das as he was his relative and also much older than the Guru. Amar Das instead fell to the Guru's feet out of respect and humility, forgetting his age and family status. On this day of their meeting, Guru Angad was eating meat and being a Vaishnav Hindu. Amar Das felt uncomfortable. Guru Angad told Amar Das that the meats one should avoid are envy, greed, ego, slander and usurpation of others rights. He told Amar Das that there is life in everything, whatever is eaten while remembering God is like nectar itself. Amar Das thus became a devoted disciple of Guru Angad.

One of the Guru Angad's wealthy disciple named Gobind decided to build a new township on the river Beas to honour the Guru. Guru Angad sent Amar Das to supervise the construction of this new township which came to be known as Goindwal. When it was completed Guru Angad instructed Amar Das and his family to move there. Amar Das compiled. Every morning he would get up early in the morning and carry water from the river to the Guru and remain in his company the entire day before returning to Goindwal in the evenings. Each year Guru Angad would present a turban as a symbol of honour to his devoted followers. Such was the devotion of Amar Das that he would wear one on top of the other, refusing to discard the Guru's gift. People ridiculed Amar Das for his blind faith, but he was never concerned.

As Guru Angad's popularity continued to spread among the people, this caused much jealousy among the Hindu high castes because Guru Angad was gaining popularity with his preaching about a casteless society. They conspired to turn the people away from the Guru. During a drought year a Hindu recluse told the villagers "You go to Guru Angad day and night for spiritual guidance, why can't he get rain for your dying crops?" The recluse forecasted that there would only be rain when Guru Angad left the village. When confronted by the desperate farmers Guru Angad replied, "nature cannot bend to your will merely by human sacrifice to the gods, or by injuring someone's heart. But if your rain god is satisfied by my leaving this village, I shall do so without a moment's hesitation". "Leaving the village Guru Angad was refused shelter in neighbouring villages and finally settled in a forest south of Khadur. When the rains did not come as promised the villagers grew angry at the Hindu recluse and wanted to kill him. Amar Das was disappointed with the way that the villagers had treated Guru Angad. He suggested that instead of killing the recluse the farmers tie the recluse to a plow and drag him through their fields. The rains finally came. The villagers now emplored to Guru to return to the village. When Guru Angad heard to the punishment the Hindu recluse had received he told Amar Das; "you should have shown endurance, in the face of adversity, like the earth, steadfastness like a mountain and compassion like a river. For the wise and the holy, it is unforgivable if they practice not humility and remain not even-minded in weal or woe". Amar Das asked for and received forgiveness.

Guru Angad did not believe in performing miracles unnecessarily. When Amar Das blessed a devotee of the Guru's with a son, Guru Angad warned him, "do not go about disbursing your blessings and curses without due deliberation. God is merciful to all men of prayer and good intentions, and one need not exhibit one's spiritual prowess by such showmanship".

A village women once ridiculed Amar Das for his faithful devotion as being that "homeless old man who carries water every day for his Guru daily". When Guru Angad heard this he embraced Amar Das and told his congregation; "Amar Das is not homeless, he is the shelter of the unsheltered. He is the strength of the weak and the emancipation of the slave!" Finding that Amar Das was his most worthy disciple and feeling that his end was near Guru Angad announced that Amar Das would be his successor. Guru Angad's two sons were unhappy with their fathers decision but the Guru told them that the honour would go to Amar Das because he was the most worthy and humble. Guru, Angad bowed before Guru Amar Das placing five copper coins and a coconut before him signifying as Guru Nanak had done before him. Guru Angad then had Baba Buddha anoint the forehead of Guru Amar Das with a saffron mark. Shortly thereafter, Guru Angad left this world on March 28, 1552.

The Third Master Guru Amar Das (1479-1574)

Guru Amar Das born in the village of Basarke on May 5, 1479. He was the eldest son of Tej Bhan a farmer and trader. Guru Amar Das grew up and married Mansa Devi and had two sons Mohri and Mohan and two daughters Dani and Bhani. He was a very religious Vaishanavite Hindu who spent most of his life performing all of the ritual pilgrimages and fasts of a devout Hindu.

It was not until his old age that Amar Das met Guru Angad and converted to the path of Sikhism. He eventually became Guru at the age of 73 succeeding Guru Angad as described previously.

Soon large numbers of Sikhs started flocking to Goindwal to see the new Guru. Datu one of Guru Angad's sons proclaimed himself as Guru at Khadur following his fathers death. He was so jealous of Guru Amar Das that he proceeded to Goindwal to confront the Guru. Upon seeing Guru Amar Das seated on a throne surrounded by his followers he said. "You were a mere menial servant of the house until yesterday and how dare you style yourself as the master?" "He then proceeded to kick the revered old Guru, throwing him off his throne. Guru Amar Das in his utter humility started caressing Datu's foot saying; "I'm old. My bones are hard. You may have been hurt". As demanded by Datu, Guru Amar Das left Goindwal the same evening are returned to his native village of Basarke.

Here Guru Amar Das shut himself in a small house for solitary meditation. There he attached a notice on the front door saying, "He who opens this door is no Sikh of mine, nor am I his Guru". A delegation of faithful Sikhs led by Baba Buddha found the house and seeing the notice on the front door, cut through the walls to reach, the Guru. Baba Buddha said, "the Guru being a supreme yogi, cares for nothing in the world—neither fame, nor riches nor a following. But we cannot live without his guidance. Guru Angad has tied us to your apron, where should we go now if your are not to show us the way?" At the tearful employment of the Sikhs, Guru Amar Das was overwhelmed by their devotion and returned to Goindwal. Datu having been unable to gather any followers of his own had returned to Khadur.

Guru Amar Das further institutionalized the free communal kitchen called langer among the Sikhs. The langer kitchen was open to serve all day and night. Although rich food was served there. Guru Amar Das was very simple and lived on coarse bread. The Guru spent his time personally attending to the cure and nursing of the sick and the aged. Guru Amar Das made it obligatory that those seeking his audience must first eat in the langer. When the Raja of Haripur came to see the Guru. Guru Amar Das insisted that he first partake a common meal in the langer, irrespective of his caste. The Raja obliged and had an audience with the Guru. But one of his queens refused to lift the veil from her face, so Guru Amar Das refused to meet her. Guru Amar Das not only preached the equality of people irrespective of their caste but he also tried to foster the idea of women's equality. He tried to liberate women from the practices of purdah (wearing a veil) as well as preaching strongly against the practice of sati (Hindu wife burning on her husbands funeral pyre). Guru Amar Das also disapproved of a widow remaining unmarried for the rest of her life.

Goindwal continued to experience growth as many Sikhs thronged there for spiritual guidance. Pilgrims moved there in large numbers to be closed to the Guru. Muslims and Hindus also moved to the thriving town. When there was racial fighting between the three groups and calls for revenge. Guru Angad instructed his Sikhs; "in God's house, justice is sure. It is only a matter of time. The arrow of humility and patience on the part of the innocent and the peaceful never fail in their aim".

Once during several days of rain while Guru Amar Das was riding by a wall which he saw was on the verge of falling he galloped his horse past the wall. The Sikhs questioned him saying; "O Master, you have instructed us, 'fear not death, for it comes to all" and 'the Guru and the God-man are beyond the pale of birth and death", why did you then gallop past the collapsing wall?" Guru Amar Das replied; "Our body is the embodiment of God's light. It is through the human body that one can explore one's limitless spiritual possibilities. Demi-god's envy the human frame. One should not, therefore, play with it recklessly. One must submit to the Will of God, when one's time is over, but not crave death, nor invite it without a sufficient and noble cause. It is self surrender for the good of man that one should seek, not physical annihilation".

With a view of providing the Sikhs with a place where they could have a holy dip while visiting Goindwal the Guru had a type of deep open water reservoir called a baoli dug. As the Hindus believed in reincarnation in 84 hundred thousand species. Guru Amar Das had the well dug with exactly 84 steps. To symbolize that God could be reached through his remembrance rather than just a cycle of reincarnations he declared that who ever would descend the 84 steps for a bath while reciting the Japji of Guru Nanak at each step would be freed from the cycles of births and deaths.

When it came time for the Guru to marry his younger daughter Bibi Bani, he selected a pious and diligent young follower of his called Jetha from Lahore. Jetha had come to visit the Guru with a party of pilgrims from Lahore and had become so enchanted by the Guru's teachings that he had decided to settle in Goindwal. Here he earned a living selling wheat and would regularly attend the services of Guru Amar Das in his spare time.

In 1567 while on his way to Lahore the Emperor Akbar decided to visit and see for himself Guru Amar Das. He stopped at Goindwal to meet the Guru, whose teachings had heard about. The Guru agreed only to see Akbar if he would first eat in the langer. Akbar agreed and here the Emperor sat down and ate with the poorest of the poor in his company. Akbar was so impressed by Guru Amar Das that he wanted to give the Guru a parting gift of the revenue collected from several villages to help support the langer kitchen. Guru Amar Das refused saying that the langer must be self supporting and only depend upon the small offerings of the devout.

The jealousy of the teachings of the Gurus by the high caste Khatris and Brahmins continued. They pleaded with Akbar at the royal court that the teachings of Sikhism would lead to disorder as they went against the teachings of Hindus and Muslims. Akbar summoned the Guru to his court for an explanation. Guru Amar Das politely excused himself on account of his old age, but sent Jetha to answer the charges leveled against the Sikhs. In the royal court Jetha explained the teachings of Sikhism. Akbar was open minded and deeply impressed by the religious doctrine of the Sikhs and decided that no further actions were required.

Guru Amar Das continued a systematic planned expansion of the Sikh Institutions. He trained a band of 146 apostles (52 were women) called Masands and sent them to various parts of the country. He also set up 22 dioceses called manjis across the country. These twenty two dioceses helped to spread Sikhism among the population while collecting revenues to help support the young religion. Guru Amar Das also declared Baisakhi (April 13), Maghi (1st day of Magha, mid January) and Diwali (festival of light in October/November) as three special days where all the Sikhs should gather to hear the Guru's words. Although advanced in years, Guru Amar Das undertook a tour of a number of Hindu places of pilgrimage along the banks of the Yamuna and Ganga rivers as well as Kurukshetra. Here the Guru would hold religious services and large numbers of people would come to hear his preaching.

For their religious scriptures Guru Amar Das collected an anthology of writings including hymns of Guru Nanak and Guru Angad and added his own as well as those of other Hindu saints whose poems conformed to the teachings of Sikhism. All of these were in Punjabi and easily understood by the common people. When a learned Brahmin once questioned the Guru; "Why do you impart instruction to your disciples not in Sanskrit, the language of gods in which all the Hindu lore is written, but in their mother-tongue, like Punjabi, the language of the illiterate mass". To this Guru Amar Das replied; "Sanskrit is like a well, deep, inaccessible and confined to the elite, but the language of the people is like rain water—ever fresh, abundant and accessible to all". He said; "I want my doctrines to be propagated through every language which the people speak, for it is not language but the content that should be considered sacred or otherwise".

Seeing the rapid expansion of Sikhism, Guru Amar Das asked his son-in-law and trusted follower Jetha to oversee the founding of another city. He wanted him to dig a tank there and to build himself a house. Jetha first purchased the lands for the price of 700 Akbari rupees from the Zamindars of Tung. Here he started the digging on the tank. This new township called Ramdaspur would in due time become present day Amritsar, the holiest city of the Sikhs.

On September 1, 1574 sensing that his end was near, Guru Amar Das sent for Baba Buddha and other prominent Sikhs including his two sons Mohan and Mohri. He declared; "according to the tradition established by Guru Nanak, the leadership of the Sikhs must go to the most deserving. I, therefore, bestow this honour on my son-in-law Jetha". Guru Amar Das then renamed Jetha as Ram Das, meaning servant of God. As was the custom Baba Buddha was asked to anoint the forehead of Amar Das with the saffron mark. All those present bowed before Guru Ram Das except for Mohan. Guru Amar Das's eldest son. Shortly thereafter Guru Amar Das breathed his last on the full moon day of Bhadon in 1574 at the ripe old age of 95.

The Fourth Master Guru Ram Das (1534-1581)

Guru Ram Das was born on September 24, 1534 to simple God-fearing parents, Hari Das and Anup Devi of Lahore. Known as Jetha meaning the first born, he was a handsome young man. When he grew up he could always be found in the company of religious men. One day Jetha came across a party of Skihs who were on their way to Goindwal to pay homage to Guru Amar Das. Jegha decided to join them and also travel to Goindwal. Upon their arrival and meeting, Guru Amar Das at once noticed the young Jetha with his pleasant manner and sense of devotion. While his fellow travellers returned to Lahore, Jetha decided to stay and become a disciple of Guru Amar Das. His hard work, and devotion eventually won him the hand of Guru Amar Das's younger daughter, Bibi Bhani. They went on to have three sons, Prithi Chand, Mahadev and Arjan Dev.

Jetha became a trusted disciple of Guru Amar Das. As described previously he successfully represented Guru Ram Das before the Mughal royal court to defend the charges by jealous Hindus that Sikhism maligned both the Hindu and Muslim religions. "Birth and caste are of no avail before God. It is deeds which make or unmake a man. To exploit ignorant people with superstitions and to call it religion is a sacrilege against god and man. To worship the infinite, formless and absolute God in the form of a totem, an image or an insignificant or time-bound object of nature, or to wash one's sins not through compassion and self-surrender, but through ablutions; to insist upon special diets, languages and dresses, and fads about what to eat and what not, and to condemn the mass of human beings, including women, to the status of sub-humans and to deny them the reading of the scriptures and even work of every kind is to tear apart man from man. This is not religion, not is it religion to deny the world through which alone man can find his spiritual possibilities". The Emperor Akbar was greatly impressed by the tenants of Sikhism as explained by Jetha and dismissed all of charges.

Eventually Jetha was ordained as Guru Amar Das's successor and named Guru Ram Das (meaning servant of God). These events have previously been described.

When the aged ascetic son of Guru Nanak Baba Sri Chand came to visit Guru Ram Das he asked him why he kept such a long beard? Guru Ram Das replied; "to wipe the dust off the feet of holy men like yourself" and then proceeded to perform this supreme act of humility. Sri Chand held his hand and embraced Guru Ram Das saying; "it's enough. This is the kind of character by which you have deprived me of my ancestral heritage. Now, what more is left with me that I could offer you for your piety and goodness of heart?"

Guru Ram Das now eagerly continued the building of the city of Ramdaspur (the abode of Ram Das) by digging of the second sacred pool as he had been instructed by Guru Amar Das. Pilgrims came in large numbers to hear the Guru and to help in the excavation work of the tank. The holy tank would be called Amritsar meaning pool of nectar. Today the city which is the holiest centre of Sikhism has come to be known as Amritsar. Guru Ram Das urged his Sikhs that one could fulfil one's life not merely by quiet meditation but in actively participating in the joys and sorrows of others. This is how one could also rid oneself of the prime malady—Ego, and end their spiritual loneliness.

One of the new entries into the Sikh fold at this time was Bhai Gurudas Bhalla, the son of the younger brother of Guru Amar Das. Bhai Gurdas was a superb poet and scholar of comparative religion who would later go on become the scribe of the first edition of the Guru Granth Sahib. Guru Amar Das was impressed with Bhai Gurdas's existing knowledge of Hindi and Sanskrit and the Hindu scriptures. Following the tradition of sending out Masandas across the country Guru Amar Das deputed Bhai Gurudas to Agra to spread the gospel of Sikhism. Before leaving Guru Amar Das prescribed the following routine for Sikhs.

"He who calls himself a Sikh of the True Guru, He must get up in the morning and say his prayers. He must rise in the early hours and bathe in the holy tank. He must meditate on God as advised by the Guru. And rid himself of the afflictions of sins and evil. As the day dawns, he should recite scriptures, and repeat God's name in every activity. He to whom the Guru's takes kindly is shown the path. Nanak! I seek the dust of the feet of the Guru's Sikh who himself remembers God and makes others remember him". (Gauri).

The standard Sikh marriage ceremony known as the Anand Karaj is centred around the Lawan, a four stanza hymn composed by Guru Ram Das. The marriage couple circumscribe the Guru Granth Sahib as each stanza is read. The first round is the Divine consent for commencing the householders life through marriage. The second round states that the union of the couple has been brought about by God. In the third round the couple is described as the most fortunate as they have sung the praises of the Lord in the company of saints. In the fourth round the feeling of the couple that they have obtained their hearts desire and are being congratulated is described.

Guru Ram Das's first cousin Sahari Mal came to invite the Guru to visit Lahore in connection with the marriage of his son. The Guru being much too busy with his work promised to send one of his sons instead. Guru Ram Das asked his eldest son Prithi Chand to attend on his behalf, but he refused. Prithi Chand feared that his father was perhaps trying to eliminate him in order to install his youngest brother Arjan as the next Guru. Arjan was a great favourite of his father, Mahadev the Guru's middle son was a recluse and excused himself on the ground that he was not interested in the affairs of the world. The Guru therefore asked his youngest son Arjan Dev to attend, which he agreed to do with such grace and humility, that Guru Ram Das was very pleased.

Arjan Dev now proceeded to Lahore, where his father asked him to remain until called for and to take charge of the needs and education of the Sikhs in Lahore, his ancestral home. After two years of feeling intensely homesick. Arjan Dev composed a poem of love and devotion and sent it to Guru Ram Das. This poem along with another one a few month's later were intercepted by the Guru's jealous son Prithi Chand who made sure his father never received them. Finally Arjan wrote a third poem and numbered it with a 3 and gave strict instructions to the messenger to only hand it over to the Guru personally.

"A moment's separation and it was like an age. When do I see you now, my beloved Lord? My night does not pass, nor do I get sleep, without seeing the Guru's darbar. I am a sacrifice, I am a sacrifice again to the true darbar of the Guru. 3" (Majh)

Upon finally receiving this poem, Guru Ram Das sensed what must have happened to the earlier two messages so he confronted his eldest son Prithi chand. At first, Prithi Chand denied everything, but seeing the insistence of the Guru and the consequences of refusal to obey him, he finally confessed his treachery and produced the other two letters. When Guru Ram Das read them, he was moved to tears by the humility and sincerity of his son Arjan's compositions.

Guru Ram Das immediately sent for Baba Buddha to journey to Lahore and to bring back his son Arjan Dev with full honour. The Guru then had Bhai Buddha apply the saffron mark to the forehead of Arjan Dev and declared him his successor. Prithi Chand would not accept his fathers wishes and continued to misbehave and abuse Guru Arjan Dev. Guru Ram Das had to publicly condemn his son Prithi Chand for his actions. Shortly thereafter Guru Ram Das breathed his last of September 1, 1581.

The Fifth Master Guru Arjan Dev (1563-1606)

Guru Arjan Dev was the youngest son of Guru Ram Das and Mata Bhani. He was born at Goindwal on April 15, 1563. In 1579 Guru Arjan was eventually married to Ganga Devi daughter of Krishan Chand in 1579.

Eventually Arjan Dev was invested with the Guruship by his father Guru Ram Das in 1581 as narrated previously. Guru Arjan now left Goindwal for Ramdaspur (Amritsar) to complete the work started there by his father and to get away from his jealous older brother Prithi Chand. Guru Arjan Dev completed the two tanks of Santoksar and Amritsar and undertook the expansion of Ramdaspur.

The Guru laid the foundation of the Harmandir Sahib (Golden Temple) in the middle of the tank of Amritsar. All of the Sikhs desired that it should be the tallest building in the new town. Guru Arjan Dev however felt otherwise. He reminded his followers that humility should be a great virtue. The temple was therefore built on as low an elevation as possible. To counter the Muslim belief that God's house is in the west and the Hindu belief that it is in the east where the sun rises, the Harmandir Sahib had entrances on all four sides. Guru Arjan Dev exclaimed; "My faith is for the people of all castes and all creeds for whichever direction they come and to whichever direction they bow". To help raise money for these monumental public works projects, the Guru declared that all Sikhs should donate 1/10th of their earnings to charity.

Around the year 1590 Guru Arjan Dev decided to go on an extensive tour of Punjab accompanied by such trusted Sikhs as Bhai Gurdas and Bidhi Chand. He visited Khadur, Goindwal, Sarhali, Bhaini, Khanpur, Taran Taran, Lahore, Dera Bhaba Nanak, as well as Barath were he met the aged ascetic son of Guru Nanak, Baba Sri Chand. Guru Arjan Dev also purchased some land near Jullundur and laid the foundations of a new township called Kartarpur as well as digging a well called Ganga Sagar.

The Guru eventually returned to Amritsar to find his eldest brother Prithi Chand jealous as ever. With the Guru having no children as yet, Prithi Chand hoped that his own son Mehrban would be able to succeed Guru Arjan Dev as the next Guru. Guru Arjan in his humility asked his wife Ganga Devi; "If you need a boon, ask not me but a pious Sikh like Baba Buddha, the aged seer and devout disciple of Guru Nanak". She proceeded with a large entourage and much fanfare to Baba Buddha who lived in a jungle near Amritsar. There she presented him with many delicacies to eat. Baba Buddha resented this and refused to provide any blessings. Upon hearing what happened, Guru Arjan Dev told his wife to return this time on foot, with a simple meal prepared by herself. This time Baba Buddha was delighted and partook of the simple food. He prophesied; "A son will be born to thee who will crush the enemies of Nanak's house, just as I have crushed this piece of onion with my hand".

Soon thereafter Ganga Devi became pregnant. Prithi Chand meanwhile cultivated Sulhi Khan, a revenue officer of the Mughal court to raid Amritsar on the pretext of collecting a tribute. Guru Arjan Dev along with his family left Amritsar and settled at Wadali a few miles away. It was here that on June 14, 1595 that the Guru was blessed with a son, Hargobind. The love of a father for his son can be seen in the following lines:

"My true Guru is my savior and protector. Showering us with his mercy and grace, God extended His Hand, and saved Hargobind, who is now safe and secure. The fever is gone—God Himself eradicated it, and preserved the honour of his servant. I have obtained all blessings from the Saadh Sangat, the Company of the Holy; I am a sacrifice to the true Guru". (Guru Arjan Dev, Sorath, pg. 620).

Meanwhile Sulhi Khan upon hearing that both Guru Arjan Dev and his treasure were no longer in Amritsar put off his attack on the city. In Amritsar Prithi Chand tried to convince the Sikhs that he was the real Guru and not Arjan Dev. He only met with disappointment though, as the Sikhs continued to flock to see Guru Arjan Dev. Prithi Chand therefore concocted a plan to assassinate the Guru's only child Hargobind. He sent a wet-nurse with poison, got a snake charmer to release a snake near Hargobind, and on another attempt sent a servant with poison milk. All of these attempts failed with the perpetrators all publicly confessing that Prithi Chand had sent them.

"The poison had absolutely no harmful effect. But the wicked Brahmin died in pain ||1|| The Supreme Lord God himself has saved his humble servant. The sinner died through the Power of the Guru". (Guru Arjan Dev, Bhairon, pg, 1137).

Eventually a large delegation of Sikhs were able to convince the Guru to return to Amritsar. [Guru Arjan now started the training for his son Hargobind for the responsibilities which he would one day have to face. He had the young Hargobind not only trained in languages and religious philosophy, but also in riding, the use of weapons, astronomy, medicine, agriculture, public administration and the sciences. Baba Buddha was put in charge of the religious education of the young Hargobind, while a team of experts were employed for instruction in their areas of expertise. Guru Arjan Dev meanwhile kept quite busy attending to the spiritual needs of the large masses of Sikhs who came to see him daily. He would daily perform devotional music from the Harmandir Sahib, being a great instrumentalist and vocal singer.

A situation now arose which would require the Guru's complete attention. Reports came to the Guru that Prithi Chand was composing his own hymns and was passing them to the visiting Sikhs as the compositions of Guru Nanak as well as other Guru's. Others were also passing of their own compositions as the work of the Sikh Guru's. Guru Arjan Dev realized that if this situation was allowed to continue, it would be the undermining of the Sikh religion. Having given the Sikhs a central place of worship, they now needed an authentic compilation of the hymns of their Guru's. Thus Guru Amar Das started collection the original verses of all the Guru's. He sent trusted Sikhs such as Bhai Piara, Bhai Gurdas and Baba Buddha across the country in search of original manuscripts. Guru Arjan Dev made trips to Goindwal, Khadur and Kartarpur to visit the families of the previous Guru's. Guru Arjan Dev collected original manuscripts of the Guru's from Mohan (son of Guru Amar Das), Datu (son of Guru Angad) as well as Sri Chand (son of Guru Nanak). Putting Baba Buddha in charge of the spiritual needs of the large number of pilgrims visiting Harmandir Sahib. Guru Arjan now pitched a tent by the side of Ramsar tank and started the arduous task of compiling the first edition of the Holy Guru Granth Sahib. Bhai Gurdas was entrusted as the Guru's scribe for the master copy. Unlike any other religious book in history. Guru Arjan Dev decided to also include the compositions of Hindu and Muslim saints which he considered consistent with the teachings of Sikhism and the Guru's. Guru Arjan Dev included the works of such Hindu Bhaktas as Kabir, Jaidev, Namdev, Dahna, Ravidas, Pipa and Ramanand. The Guru also included the works of such Muslim divines as Farid, Mardana, Satta and Balwand, the Guru's minstrels, as well as several bards (Bhatts). Bhai Gurdas was invited by the Guru to include his own verses, but declined out of modesty.

The monumental task was finally completed. The first edition of the Guru Granth Sahib known at that time as Pothi Sahib was installed on a high pedestal within the Harmandir Sahib in August 1604. Guru Arjan Dev seated himself at a lower level and instructed all Sikhs to bow before it, not as an idol, but as the book of divine inspiration which instructed living men in the ways of God and dedicated secular life. The revered Baba Buddha was appointed the first Granthi (custodian) of the book. Guru Arjan Dev dictated that unlike the Hindu scriptures, the Pothi Sabhi could be open to reading by anyone of any caste, creed or sex. This original copy is still in existence today.

A rich arrogant Hindu banker of Delhi called Chandu Shah tried to marry his daughter to Hargobind. But due to his arrogance Guru Arjan Dev refused the match. Prithi Chand knew that Chandu Shah welded some influence with the imperial court. He used Chaneu Shah's anger at being rejected to cause further trouble. Prithi Chand had Chandu Shah complain to the Emperor Akbar that the Guru had prepared a book which was derogatory in nature to Muslim's and Hindu's. Upon hearing this Akbar ordered the Guru to be brought before him along with the Granth. Guru Arjan Dev sent the revered Baba Buddha and Bhai Gurdas to the Mughal court along with a copy of the Holy Granth. Akbar opened the holy book and the first hymn read out was;

"My God has breathed His Light into the dust. And so brought the world into being. He it is who created the sky, the earth, the waters and all vegetation. O man, whatever one sees, passes away. But the world usurps another due and is forgetful of God. It is the world of the animal, nay, of ghosts and goblins. It eats the forbidden fruit, usurping what belongs to another. Hold thy mind, O man, or God will burn thee in the fire of Hell. Thy benefactors, thy brothers, thy courts and kingdoms and thy homes. Are of no avil to thee, when seized thee the Angel of Death. My Lord, purest of the pure, knows all that is within thee. Nanak: pray thou to His Saints that they lead thee on the truth Path". (Tilang)

Upon hearing this Akbar was satisfied as he had always looked upon the Sikh Gurus as social reformers and believed in the unity of God and the brotherhood of man. However Chandu Shah accused Bhai Gurdas of not really read the text but recited a hymn from memory. Akbar therefore got one Sahib Dyal who could read Gurmukhi to appear before the court and opened a page at random for him to read, he read the following;

"You don't see God who dwells in your heart. And you carry about an idol around your neck. A non-believer, you wander about churning water. And you die harassed in delusion. The idol you call God will drown with you. The ungrateful sinner. The boat will not ferry you across. Says Nanak, I met the Guru who led me to God. He who lives in water, earth, nether region, and firmament." (Sulhi).

The Emperor now exclaimed; "excepting love and devotion to God, I so far find neither praise nor blame to anyone in this Granth. It is a volume worthy of reverence". Not only this but Akbar wanted to offer Guru Arjan a suitable gift. Guru Arjan asked the emperor to instead exempt the people of Punjab from the annual land revenue that year since their was a severe drought. Akbar graciously compiled with the Guru's wishes, this greatly increased the Guru's popularity with the ..nts.

On October 17, 1605 Akbar died and was succeeded by Jahangir as emperor. Jahangir was a person of lax morals, pleasure loving and fond of drinking. He left much of the administration duties of running his kingdom to others. Because of his lax morals Jahangir set out to please the orthodox Muslim clergy which he knew did not approve of his actions, or the tolerant attitude that his father Akbar had previously displayed to other religions, Jahangir wrote the following in his memories called Tuzak-i-Jahangiri; "at Goindwal on the banks of the river Beas, lived a Hindu, Arjan by name, in the garb of a Pir or Sheikh. Thus, many innocent Hindus and even foolish and ignorant Muslims he brought into his fold who beat the drum noisily of his self-appointed prophethood. He was called Guru. From all sides, worshippers came to offer their homage to him and put full trust in his word. For three or four generations, they had warmed up this shop. For a long time I had harboured the wish that I should set aside this shop of falsehood or I should bring him into the fold of Islam". Jahangir further writes; "in these days, Khusro (Jahangir's rebel son) passed through this way. The foolish person resolved to call on him. Khusro (Jahangir's rebel son) passed through this way. The foolish person resolved to call on him. Khusro halted for a time at this place and this man came to see him and discoursed with him on many matters and also applied with saffron on is forehead what the Hindus call kashkeh (tilak) and consider a good omen. When I heard this account personally, I knew about his false pretenses. So I ordered that he be brought into my presence, that his property be confiscated and his sons and other possessions be made over to Murtaza Khan and he be dealt with in accordance with the political and common law of the land".

When Guru Arjan received the summons to appear before Jahangir, he knew that it was not a good sign. The Guru declared that his son Hargobind should be installed as the next Guru. Prominent Sikhs gathered are revered Baba Buddha applied the saffron mark on Hargobind's forehead anointing him as Guru Hargobind.

Upon reaching Lahore, Jahangir demanded that Guru Arjan Dev revise the Holy Granth, removing all references to Islam and Hinduism. This of course the Guru refused to do. Since Jahangir was on his way to Kashmir, he asked Murtaza Khan to deal with the Guru.

Murtaza Khan immediately jailed the Guru, and ordered the Guru Arjan Dev to be tortured to death if he did not agree to remove the alleged derogatory references in the Holy Granth. The Guru was cruelly tortured. He was made to sit on a red hot iron sheet. They poured burning hot sand on his body. The Guru was dipped in boiling water. The bore all of these brutalities with calm serenity, for five long days he was tortured. When the torturers found the Guru unresponsive to their torture they did not know what to do. On May 30, 1606 the Guru asked for a bath in the river Ravi by the side of the Mughal fort. Thousands of followers watched the Guru who could barely walk make his way to the river with tears in their eyes. His bare body was covered with blisters, Guru Arjan Dev repeated over and over; "Sweet is your will, O God; the gift of your Name alone I seek". The Guru then calmly walked into the river bank, bidding his farewell to his followers and was gone forever, his body carried away by the currents. This act of brutality in ending such a saintly life with such cruelty was to forever change the course of Sikhism.

The Sixth Master Guru Hargobind (1595-1644)

Guru Hargobind was born at Wadali village in June 1595 and was the only child of Guru Arjan Dev. He was invested with the Guruship on May 25, 1606 just days before his fathers martyrdom. From a young age he was educated in the sciences, sports and religion as his father had insisted. Baba Buddha was responsible for overseeing the Guru's religious teachings.

During the Guruship ceremony Guru Hargobind respectfully declined to wear the Seli (woollen cord worn on the head) which had been passed down on each successive Guru since Guru Nanak. Instead the Guru asked for a sword. Baba Buddha, never having handled a sword before, placed it on the wrong side of the Guru. Guru Hargobind noticing this, asked for another sword saying "I'll wear two swords, a sword of shakti (power) and a sword of bhakti (meditation)". Henceforth the Guru would always carry two swords to symbolize his dual role of holding secular power (Miri) and spiritual authority (Piri).

Soon after his ascension to Guruship in 1606, Guru Hargobind laid to foundation of a new temple at Amritsar; the Akal Takht. The Akal Takht was built facing Harmandir Sahib (the Golden Temple). Guru Hargobind had a throne built, and would administer sikh affairs from here. The temporal nature of the Akal Takht balanced the spiritual nature of the Golden Temple, emphasizing the dual concepts of Miri and Piri introduced by the Guru. Guru Hargobind donned the royal regalia of a King and was known by the Sikhs as Sacha Padshah (The True King).

Guru Hargobind knew that the Sikh's would no longer take their freedom for granted, he undertook to steel his Sikhs against tyranny and oppression. The Guru now gave instructions to the Masands and to all the other Sikhs that they should make offerings in the future of horses and weapons rather than just money. The Hindus had become so weak that they could not contemplate any kind of resistance to the rulers of the date. The Sikhs did not believe in self-denial alone; they grew increasingly aware of the need for assertion also. They wielded arms and lived an active life, reared horses, rode on them, and racing and hunting became their pastimes. Guru Hargobind encouraged Sikhs in physical activity and weapons training as well as prayers. Soon an army of one thousand horses was raised. The spiritual side was not neglected. Guru Hargobind would rise long before the day dawned and after his bath in the holy tank, would go into meditation. The Guru would then join his Sikhs for prayers both in the mornings and evenings. Guru Hargobind did not want his emphasis on the temporal caused by the necessity for a war like posture to detract his followers from the spiritual ideals of Sikhism.

The Gurus military activities were soon reported to Emperor Jahangir by the ever jealous Chandu Shah, who still had an unmarried daughter on his hands as a constant reminder of the indignity hurled at him. Guru Hargobind was summoned by Jahangir and decided to go see the Emperor. Many Sikhs were apprehensive about the Guru going as they feared for his life. Before setting out for Delhi Guru Hargobind assigned the secular duties of running the Golden Temple to the honoured Baba Buddha and the spiritual instructions to the great scholar and scribe of the Guru Granth Sahib, Bhai Gurdas. Guru Hargobind then set out for Delhi accompanied by three hundred horses.

When Jahangir met Guru Hargobind, he was quickly won over by the young Gurus charm and holiness. The Guru had a number of religious discourses with the emperor who wanted to be sure that no harm was intended to Islam by the propagation of Sikhism. When asked which religion was better Hinduism or Islam, Guru Hargobind replied quoting Kabir:

"God first created light, All men are born out of it. The whole world came out of a single spark; who is good and who is bad? The Creator is in the creation, and the creation in the Creator. He is everywhere. The clay is the same, the potter fashions various models. There is nothing wrong with the clay or the potter. God the true resides in all. Whatever happens is His doing. He who surrenders to Him gets to know Him. He is His slave. God is invisible. He cannot be seen. The Guru has granted me this sweet gift, says Kabir, my doubts are dispelled. I have seen the pure with my own eyes". (Prabhati)

When Jahangir found out that Guru Hargobind was a great lover of sports, he invited the Guru to accompany him on a tiger hunt. During the chase the emperor was attacked by a ferocious tiger. The attendants accompanying the royal party lost their nerve and their horses and elephants panicked. Guru Hargobind rushed his horse and pulling out his sword, he engaged and killed the dangerous tiger single handed. Jahangir was full of gratitude towards the Guru for risking his life. Jahangir became so fond of the Guru that he asked him to accompany him on a number of visits. Once while visiting Agra a poor grass-cutter follower of the Guru came to seem him. The grass-cutter, crying that he wanted to see the vision of the True King, was led by the royal attendants into the camp of the Emperor. The grass-cutter put a coin before him and stood with folded hands, praying, his eyes filled with tears and his throat choked with emotion. The Emperor was overwhelmed with the devotion of a loyal subject and offered him a large gift. The Sikh replied, "O True King, if you are so pleased, bless me with the glory of God's name that I be emancipated". When the devotee was told that he had come to the wrong camp, and that the one who granted redemption was housed in the opposite camp, the devotee unhesitatingly left the presence of the emperor picking up his coin saying "then this too is meant for him, not your majesty".

While at Agra Jahangir suddenly fell ill. The ever scheming Chandu Shah conspired with astrologers to tell the Emperor that he would only be cured if a holy man was sent to Gwalior Fort and undertook penance on the emperors behalf. Guru Hargobind was now requested to go to Gwalior Fort. Fully aware of Chandu's scheming, the Guru agreed, and accompanied by an escort of five Sikhs left for the fort. Guru Hargobind spent a number of months within the fort sometime between 1617 and 1619 as a virtual prisoner. Here were also imprisoned a number of princes who lived in deplorable conditions. Guru Hargobind uplifted their spirits with daily prayers and distributed much of his rations to them. Chandu Shah even tried unsuccessfully to have the Guru poisoned. Eventually many months after Jahangir's recovery he was finally convinced by Wazir Khan an admirer of the Guru in the Mughal court to release the Guru and invite him back to Delhi. Guru Hargobind refused to leave the fort unless all of the princes who were political prisoners were also not released. Jahangir agreed after he was reminded by Wazir Khan that the emperor owed his life to the Guru.

Upon his return to Delhi, Guru Hargobind told the emperor about the intrigue and scheming of Chandu Shah. Jahangir handed over Chandu to Guru Hargobind to avenge the death of his father Guru Arjan. Guru Hargobind handed over Chandu Shah to his Sikhs who eventually took Chandu to Lahore where he was killed by an indignant Sikh who had seen Guru Arjan tortured with his own eyes. Upon hearing this news Guru Hargobind asked God to pardon Chandu Shah's sins.

Guru Hargobind now proceeded to visit Lahore. A devout Sikh from Kabul called Sujan brought a magnificent horse to present to the Guru as a gift. The horse was seized by a Muslim Qazi who refused to return it unless he received a large ransom. Guru Hargobind remarked that "the horse must come to him to whom he was intended". Soon the horse stopped eating and its health deteriorated. The Qazi sold the horse to the Guru for a minimal rate, thinking that the horse would die anyway. Instead the horse regained its health and Guru Hargobind would ride it regularly. The Qazi became angry and felt that he had been cheated and launched a complaint with the authorities. The authorities did not take any action against the Guru. Meanwhile the Qazi's daughter ran away from her fathers tyranny and sought refuge with the Guru at Amritsar. There she lived her whole life as a devout Sikh, and Guru Hargobind got a tank known as Kaulsar dug up in her memory.

Guru Hargobind now undertook extensive travels. The Guru founded the town of Kiratpur in 1626 where the land had been gifted to the guru by one of the princes who had been freed from Gwalior by the Guru. While visiting Srinagar the Guru had a discourse with Swami Ramdas Samrath a great spiritual teacher who would later go on to instruct Shivaji, the founder of the Maratha empire. Swami Ramdas asked the Guru "you are on the spiritual throne of Guru Nanak, a great saint. You are wearing arms and maintain troops and horses. You allow yourself to be addressed as Sachcha Padsah, the True King. What sort of saint are you?" Guru Hargobind replied, "I display royalty only from the outside; inwardly, I'm detached like a hermit. Guru Nanak had not renounced the world. He had only renounced maya (illusion and ego)". The Swami answered that this idea appealed to him and thus he thereafter changed his teachings of Hindu renunciation.

While visiting the shrine of Guru Nanak, Guru Hargobind met and received the blessing of Baba Sri Chand, Guru Nanak's son. Soon thereafter in 1613 a son was born called Gurditta. In 1617 another son was born, Suraj Mal. In 1618 a third son, Ani Rai was born and in 1620 Atul Rai was born. Finally in 1622 the last and fifth son, Tegh Bahadur was born. During the life of Guru Hargobind some of the most influential Sikhs of the time passed away. Baba Buddha passed away in 1631 at Ramdas, Bhai Gurdas in 1636 at Goindwal and Baba Sri Chand at Kiratpur in 1629. In October 1627 emperor Jahangir died and Shah Jahan ascended the throne in Delhi.

The Mughal emperor Jahangir was out hunting one day in the vicinity of Amritsar. A favourite hunting hawk of the emperors flew into the camp of Guru Hargobind who was also hunting. When the emperors soldiers came to reclaim the hawk, a brief skirmish ensued and the hawk was not returned. Jahangir was so enraged that he sent an army of 7000 cavalry under the command of his general Mukhlis Khan to recover both the hawk and capture the Guru for his insolence. In the ensuing battle the Gurus forces emerged victorious after the Guru killed Mukhlis Khan in single combat with his sword. This battle took place in 1634. This battle marked a turning point as the Sikhs, now turned militant under mughal persecution.

After the battle Guru Hargobind left Amritsar never to return. The Guru shifted to Kartarpur and went on to build the city of Hargobindpur on the banks of the river Beas. The local villagers who were members of the Gherar tribe were very excited, but the headman of the tribe Bhagwan Das did not want the Guru to settle there. Bhagwan Das who was friendly with the Mughal authorities made derogatory remarks against the Guru, the Sikhs lost their temper and in the ensuing scuffle, Bhagwan Das was killed. His son Ratan Chand went to Abdullah Khan the Subedar of Jullundur and convinced him to attack the Guru at Hargobindpur with a force of 10,000 troops. The Guru felt that he was being forced into a fight when all he wanted was to be left alone to pursue his religious pursuits. He said, "we are fighting for a righteous cause—our right to live with honour and in peace—and not for the sake of self glory or rule over others".

A fierce battle ensued in which the Guru's forces were only half of the invading Mughals. Karam Chand the son of Chandu Shah joined Rattan Chand the son of Bhagwan Das for revenge. In the ensuing battle both the Subedar Abdullah Khan as well as his two sons were killed. Rattan Chand was also killed while Karam Chand was captured by the Sikh Bidhi Chand. Guru Hargobind ordered Karam Chand released but he soon returned to battle again. At this Guru Hargobind engaged Karam Chand in single hand to hand combat without any weapons and killed him with his bare bands. The Mughal forces were completely defeated and forced to retreat. After the battle the construction of a Gurdwara at Hargobindpur resumed and the Guru ordered that a mosque also be built for Muslims.

Friction with the Mughal authorities were to continue. A group of devoted Sikhs from Afghanistan were on their way to present the Guru with two extraordinary horses. The horses were seized by the Muslim authorities at Lahore and presented to Shah Jahan who was visiting there. When the Sikhs heard about this, Bidhi Chand decided to rescue the horses for the Guru. He gained the confidence of the keeper of the royal stable at Lahore first disguised as a grass cutter and then as a magician. Both times he was able to safely spirit away both horses to the Gurus household. The fact that the Mughals would retaliate was a foregone conclusion, therefore Guru Hargobind shifted his base deep into the forest in the district of Nabha. Here a large contingent of Mughal troops sent by the emperor under the control of Lala Beg found there way. A bloody battle lasting 18 hours took place in which the Sikhs suffered over 1,200 casualties but were able to inflict even heavier losses to the mughals and send them retreating in defeat. This battle took place in 1631.

Before the death of Guru Nanaks son Baba Sri Chand, he asked Guru Hargobind if he could adopt one of the Gurus sons since he had no children. Out of respect for Sri Chand, Guru Hargobind offered him the choice of his eldest son Baba Gurditta. Baba Sri Chand then chose Baba Gurditta as his successor. Baba Gurditta who was married to Natti gave birth to a son called Dhir Mal who was to later cause much trouble to the Guru and his family. In 1630 Baba Gurditta had another son called Har Rai who was to prove to be a blessing. The son of guru Hargobind, Atal Rai started displaying his supernatural powers by performing miracles and revived a dead playmate of his. When Guru Hargobind heard about this he reprimanded his son saying. "My son has started dissipating his spiritual powers without discrimination. Shall our occupation now be to revive everyone's dead son and interfere ever in God's will, we who are enjoined to accept whatever good or bad comes to us is His pleasure".

Atal Rai took the Guru's reprimand so seriously that he soon passed away after that. His death caused Guru Hargobind much grief and he constructed a nine storey structure called the Bunga of Baba Atal at Amritsar to commemorate the nine short years of his sons life.

Trouble soon evolved among some of the Gurus troops. One of the Gurus favourite soldiers Painda Khan let the honour and gifts presented to him by Guru Hargobind go to his head. He gave the choice gifts which he had personally received to his son in law Asman Khan who also captured one of the Gurus favourite hunting hawks and refused to return it. When Guru Hargobind asked Painda Khan for an explanation he replied in a rude and insulting manner. Therefore the Guru regrettably terminated the services of Painda Khan. The disgruntled Painda Khan along with 500 troops loyal to him approached the emperor in Lahore and offered to join the imperial forces against the Guru. The emperor was pleased to have the help of such a close confident of the Gurus. Painda Khan told the emperor that the Gurus army was only composed of poor peasants. In the year 1634 fifty thousand troops under the command of Kale Khan and supported by Painda Khan were dispatched to attack the sikhs at Kartarpur. When the Guru's forces heard about the impending attack, Dhir Mal the Guru's grandson sent a secret letter to Painda Khan pledging him his full support. The battle was fierce with Guru Hargobinds two sons Gurditta and Tegh Bahadur also fighting along with their father. Many great soldiers fell on the battlefield including Kale Khan. The Mughal forces were decimated until among the remaining Painda Khan engaged Guru Hargobind in battle. Guru Hargobind had raised Painda Khan from a young age and loved him like a son, therefore he refused to strike the first blow. Painda Khan struck two times unsuccessfully missing the Guru both times. Painda Khan continued to taunt and insult the Guru until finally Guru Hargobind killed him with his sword. Seeing his body in the dust, Guru Hargobind clasped his old comrade in his arms and put his shield over Painda Khan's face to shade it from the scorching sun. Guru Hargobind then wept over the death of one so dear to him and prayed that God grant Painda Khan forgiveness and a place in heaven. In another part of the battlefield Baba Gurditta also wept at killing another mughal general Asman Khan who had been his childhood friend. The Mughal forces were successfully routed and retreated with heavy losses although the Sikhs suffered over 700 dead.

Immediately following the battle Guru Hargobind and his family left Kartarpur to retire to the out of the way town of Kiratpur in order to avoid further bloodshed. Here the Guru had also promised to visit a Muslim devotee of his Budhan Shan who was near death and had previously met Guru Nanak. The Guru's grandson Dhir Mal refused to move, instead he remained in Kartarpur and with possession of the original copy of the Granth Sahib which he refused to hand over. Dhir Mal had aspirations of succeeding Guru Hargobind as the next Guru because he had the Holy Granth.

Here are Kiratpur Guru Hargobind remained the rest of his life peacefully. He kept a small army of men and 900 soldiers as his protection. The Guru continued to receive countless devotees who flocked to Kiratpur to hear and see the Guru and Sikhism continued to spread throughout the Indian subcontinent. The most accurate eye witness account of Guru Hargobind's life appears in the Dabistan-i-Mazahib written by the Muslim Mohsin Fani. In this he writes about the Sikhs, "the Guru believes in one God. His followers put not faith in idol worship. They never pray or practice austerities like the Hindus. They believe not in their incarnations, or places of pilgrimage nor the Sanskrit language which the Hindus deem to be the language of the Gods. They believe that all the Gurus are the same as Nanak. The Sikhs are not restricted in the matter of eating and drinking".

Soon the Guru received the shocking news of the death of his eldest son Baba Gurditta who passed away at age 24. He passed in much the same manner as Atal Rai, having taken to heart the reprimand of the Guru for reanimating a dead cow of an angry farmer which he had accidentally killed while out hunting. Guru Hargobind was much saddened by the death of his son and requested his grandson Dhir Mal to appear for his fathers last rites and receive his fathers turban. Dhir Mal refused to come even on such a solemn occasion, only caring about styling himself as the next Guru, especially now with his fathers untimately demise.

Guru Hargobind now started training his grandson Har Rai the other son of Baba Gurditta as his natural successor. The Guru's own sons; Gurditta had passed away, Suraj Mal and Ani Rai were too worldly while Tegh Bahadur preferred solitude and meditation. Har Rai was a pious young man and Guru Hargobind proceeded to train him in the use of arms as well as spiritual matters. At the age of fourteen Har Rai was ordained by Guru Hargobind as the seventh Sikh Guru. Guru Hargobind bowed before Guru Har Rai as his successor. Soon thereafter Guru Hargobind passed away in 1644 having in his lifetime transforming the Sikhs into soldier-saints.

The Seventh Master Guru Har Rai (1630-1661)

Guru Har Rai was born on January 16, 1630 in Kiratpur to Baba Gurditta the eldest son of Guru Hargobind. From a very young age he exhibited a sensitivity to all living things and endeared himself to his grandfather Guru Hargobind. One day while young Har Rai was returning home he got off his horse upon seeing Guru Hargobind and in his hurry his robe got caught in a bush and some flowers were broken from their steams. It is said that it pained Har Rai's heart so much that he started crying. At the age of 14 after having received suitable training Har Rai was invested with the Guruship by his grandfather Guru Hargobind shortly before his death in March 1644. Like Guru Hargobind, Guru Har Rai kept a contingent of 2,200 cavalry as his personal guard. After the many battles of Guru Hargobind, the times of Guru Har Rai were a time of consolidation for the Sikh community without any major battles in the Guru's lifetime.

The Guru was fond of hunting but due to his sensitive nature he would not kill the animals but keep them as pets in his zoo. Once while in the forest the Guru came upon a large snake basking in the sunlight. Pointing to it, Guru Har Rai exclaimed, "this serpent might as well have been a pundit in his previous life; beautiful to behold in his dress, but the knowledge he has is to bite. Men also bite others through jealousy; even when they teach about God it is not through love or self-surrender, but through the sharp wits and poisonous fangs of controversy and argument". Guru Har Rai spent his life at his birthplace of Kiratpur. Guru Har Rai would spend the mornings and evenings listening to devotional music and giving lectures on the writings of the Gurus. The Guru would also eat simple food which was earned by the labour of his own hands. Followers from far would come to Kiratpur to seek the blessings of Guru Har Rai. The Guru continued to spread the message of Sikhism. He sent Bhagwan Gir to eastern India to preach Sikhism. Another disciple Bhai Pheru was sent to Rajasthan and Suthre Shah was appointed to Delhi.

When Mughal Emperor Shah Jahan's eldest son Dara Shikoh was seriously ill, Guru Har Rai sent a herbal medicine which cured him. Thus relations with the mughals remained on a good footing for a short time. There was eventual unstability in the Delhi royal court when Shah Jahan fell ill and his second son Aurangzeb aligned himself with his youngest brother Murad against their eldest brother Dara Shikoh, Shah Jahan's approved successor. Aurangzeb imprisoned his father in Agra and his soldiers as well as those of his youngest brother Murad forces

Dara Shikoh to flee towards Punjab. Guru Har Rai was visiting Goindwal in June 1558 and here he met Dara Shikoh who had come to receive his blessings. Dara Shikoh remembered that the Guru had been responsible for saving his life when he was sick. Dara Shikoh was both an intellectual and liberally tolerant towards other religions. He was a great admirer of the Muslim Sufi Saint Mian Mir who was in turn a great admirer of the Gurus. Guru Har Rai granted Dara Shikoh an audience and received the prince with due courtesy. After some time Dara Shikoh was eventually captured by the forces of Aurangzeb. Aurangzeb had Dara Shikoh executed, then killed his own youngest brother Murad and appointed himself as the emperor.

With such a ruthless person on the throne in Delhi, relations with the Sikhs would never be the same during Aurangzeb's long reign. Once settled into the throne, Aurangzeb turned his attention to the new faith, Sikhism. It was reported to the emperor that Guru Har Rai has had blessed Dara Shikoh and assisted his escape. Aurangzeb ordered the Guru to appear in the royal court of Delhi. Guru Har Rai did not go himself but instead sent his son Ram Rai to meet the emperor. Before leaving Ram Rai was instructed by his father to not engage in any miracles and to not allow the teaching of the Sikhs to be compromised in any way. When Ram Rai presented himself allow the teaching of the Sikhs to be compromised in any way Aurangzeb with his intellect and charm that Sikhism did not present any threat to the mughals. Aurangzeb took exception to a verse in the Guru Granth Sahib;

"*God alone knows who burns in hell (the Hindu or the Muslim), for (like the Hindus whom fire consumes here), the earth of the Muslims graves also suffers being fired by the potter who fashions bricks and vessels out of its clay". (Guru Nanak, Asa Var)*

Ram Rai explained to Aurangzeb that the words of Guru Nanak had been incorrectly written by the scribe, and that the word was not "Muslim" but "Baiman" (meaning faithless). By intentionally changing the words of Guru Nanak. Ram Rai was able to gain the emperors friendship. When it was reported back to Guru Har Rai what his son had done, he was deeply hurt. The Guru exclaimed, "Ram Rai was a genuine claimant for my throne. But the Guruship is like the milk of a tigress which can only be contained in a cup of gold. Now Ram Rai shall never see my face again". Ram Rai never saw his father again but maintained his friendship with Aurangzeb.

Since Ram Rai had proved a disappointment to his father, Guru Har Rai appointed his younger son Harkrishan as the next Guru and passed away soon thereafter on October 6, 1661.

The Eighth Master Guru Harkrishan (1656-1664)

Guru Harkrishan was born on July 7, 1656 to Guru Har Rai and Krishan Kaur. Before his death in October 1661 Guru Har Rai had appointed his younger son Harkrishan as the next Guru as opposed to his elder son Ram Rai who was in collusion with the mughals. Guru Harkrishan was only five years old when he received the Guruship.

The Guru's older brother Ram Rai complained to emperor Aurangzeb in Delhi that he had been discriminated against because of his loyalty to the emperor and had not received his due share of the property of his father Guru Har Rai. Ram Rai knew that before his death Guru Har Rai had instructed Guru Harkrishan to never meet Aurengzeb. Ram Rai hoped if Guru Harkrishan met the emperor he would be going against his fathers wishes and the Sikhs would be displeased with their Guru. On the other hand if Guru Harkrishan refused to come to Delhi, then he would be attacked by the emperors forces. Since Aurangzeb was very friendly with Ram Rai he summoned Guru Harkrishan to appear before him in Delhi. The Sikhs were very apprehensive about allowing young Guru Harkrishan to go to Delhi. Aurangzeb sent Raja Jai Singh a high court official known for his devotion to the Guru to escort the Guru to Delhi.

Raja Jai Singh assured the Guru that he would not have to meet the emperor personally while in Delhi, and that there were a large number of devotees in Delhi who were anxious to see and hear their Guru. Guru Harkrishan convinced the Sikhs at Kiratpur that he should go to Delhi. As a result Guru Harkrishan along with his mother and a group of devotees set out for the long journey to Delhi. On their journey the Guru was met by large crowds of devotees. At Panjolhara a jealous Brahmin taunted the Guru, "Your Guru is called Hari Krishna, a mere child of eight years! Krishna, the incarnation of Vishnu, uttered the Gita which is the repository of all the eternal truths, if your Guru also calls himself Krishna, let him expound the truths of Gita to us". Hearing this a poor water carrier called Chhajju stood up and proclaimed that anyone could expound on the Gita if he were so blessed by the Guru. Guru Harkrishan touched Chhajju with his walking stick and Chhajju immediately began explaining the philosophy of the Gita. The Brahmin was so humbled by the spectacle that he fell to the Gurus feet and asked forgiveness for his arrogance.

Upon reaching Delhi the Guru and his party were the guests of Raja Jai Singh who had promised to uphold the safety of the Guru. Every day large numbers of devotees started flocking to see the Guru. At this time a small pox epidemic was raging in Delhi. The Guru helped to heal many sick people, naturally coming in contact with so many people every day, the Guru was also infected and taken seriously ill. On March 30, 1664 Guru Harkrishan decided to announce his successor, the Guru called for five coins and a coconut. He took them and being too weak to move, weaved his hand three times in the air and said "Baba Bakala". Guru Harkrishan then suddenly passed away at the tender age of eight years old.

The Ninth Master Guru Tegh Bahadur (1621-1675)

Guru Tegh Bahadur was the youngest son of Guru Hargobind and Bibi Nanki and was born at Amritsar on April 1, 1621. From a young age Tegh Bahadur was trained in the martial arts of swordsmanship and horse riding as well as religious training by the wise Baba Buddha and Bhai Gurdas. In February 1633 Tegh Bahadur was married to Gujari daughter of Lal Chand and Bishan Kaur. During his young years Tegh Bahadur fought along his father's side but after Guru Hargobind's fierce and bloody battle in 1634 at Kartarpur he turned to the path of renunciation and meditation. When Guru Hargobind settled down at Kiratpur to live the rest of his life in peace, Tegh Bahadur spent nine years with his father before settling down at the isolated village of Bakala in 1656 and retired to a life of contemplation. He became known as "Tyag Mal" meaning "the Master of Renunciation". Here Tegh Bahadur would spend many long years in meditation and prayer.

Guru Hargobind did not choose Tegh Bahadur as his successor because the Sikhs needed a lead[illegible] of men, something still lacking in his young son, who had now ch[illegible]n a path of renunciation. Instead Guru Hargobind chose Guru Har Rai his grandson as his natural successor. Guru Har Rai in turn chose his youngest son Guru Harkrishan as his successor. When Guru Harkrishan had suddenly fallen ill at Delhi in 1664, before his death, being too weak to move or speak the Guru had said his successor was "Baba Baka[illegible]

Following the untimely death of Guru Harkrishan large numbers of Sikhs flocked to the village of Bakala looking for the new Guru. When the Sikh went in large numbers to Bakala to find the Guru, they were instead confronted by twenty two members of the Sodhi family, each claiming that they were the Guru and successor as named by Guru Harkrishan. The Sikh were in a quandary as to who was really the true Guru?

Meanwhile a wealthy merchant Makhan Shah had his ships carrying valuable cargo caught in a fierce storm at sea. He vowed to offer five hundred gold coins to the Guru if his goods safely reached home. His wish was fulfilled and his merchandise safely arrived at their port. Makhan Shan immediately set our for Delhi where he received the tragic news that Guru Harkrishan had passed away and that his successor was at Bakala. Makhan Shah set out for Bakala to pay his homage to the Guru. When he finally got there he was confronted with all the same quandary as the rest of the Sikhs, who was the real Guru? Being a businessman Makhan Shah decided that he would pay homage to all of the twenty two claimants and placed two gold coins before each of them as tribute. When he had visited all of the claimants, a child pointed out to him that a holy man lived across the street. Makhan Shah decided that he may as well pay him tribute also. When Makhan Shah entered the house he found that Guru Tegh Bahadur was in meditation. He was told that Tegh Bahadur did not like to receive visitors but spent his time in meditation. Makhan Shah waited until he met the Guru and placed two gold coins before him. At this Guru Tegh Bahadur smiled and said to Makhan Shah, "I thought that you had pledged five hundred coins". Makhan Shah became so elated that he kissed the Gurus feet and started shouting from the rooftop "I've found the Guru, found the Guru!" All the Sikhs rushed to the house of the quiet saint and when they heard the story there was much rejoicing for many days. Thus the pious, humble saint Tegh Bahadur was acclaimed as being the true Guru for the Sikhs and natural successor of Guru Harkrishan.

Sikhs flocked to see the Guru and presented him with many gifts and offerings. One who was not so happy about the whole affair was the troublesome Dhir Mal, grandson of Guru Hargobind who had wanted people to acclaim him as the Guru since he was in possession of the Guru Granth Sahib written by Guru Arjan Dev. Dhil Mal became so angry that he planned as assassination attempt. He sent Shihan a masand (priest) loyal to him and some men to attack the Guru while he slept. Dhir Mal's men attacked the house of Guru Tegh Bahadur, shot the Guru and ransacked his belongings. Luckily Guru Tegh Bahadur was not seriously wounded. In retaliation loyal Sikhs raided Dhir Mal's house, looting in including the original copy of the Guru Granth Sahib and presented all of the bounty to the Guru as revenge. Guru Tegh Bahadur believed in forgiveness and ordered all of his property returned, including the original copy of the Guru Granth Sahib.

Guru Tegh Bahadur now accepted the role of leading the Sikhs and set out on a number of missionary journeys. He visited Kiratpur and then made his way to the other great centres of Sikhism, Tarn Taran, Khadur Sahib, Goindwal and Amritsar. At Amritsar Guru Tegh Bahadur bathed in the sacred pool but he was refused entry into the Golden Temple which was under the control of Harji, grandson of that other famous troublemaker to the Gurus, Prithi Chand. Guru Tegh Bahadur then journeyed back to Kiratpur. Here he encountered some Sodhi family jealousy and decided to found a new township. The Guru acquired a tract of land from the raja of Kahlur and founded the town of Chak Nanaki in 1665, named in honour of his mother (later to be known as Anandpur Sahib). The Guru now continued his journeys to spread the messages and teachings of Sikhism among the masses across the land.

Accompanied by his wife and mother Guru Tegh Bahadur travelled across the country. The Guru travelled throughout Punjab, wherever he would stop the Guru would get wells dug for the people and community kitchens set upon. Guru Tegh Bahadur continued his tour through Haryana and arrived at Delhi. Here the Guru met the congregations of Delhi who came out in large numbers to see the Guru. The emperor Aurangzeb was away from Delhi at this time. Guru Tegh Bahadur then continued his mission of preaching to the masses, visiting Kurekshetra, Agra, Ittawa and Allahabad. Wherever the Guru stopped he would preach about honest work and charity. The Guru would also give away all the offerings that he would receive from devotees. At Priyag, the Gurus wife Gujri conceived a child. The Guru then traveled onto the holy Hindu city of Banaras and then onto Gaya and Patna. Guru Tegh Bahadur was requested by custodians of the various temples that he visited to perform rituals and ceremonies for himself and his ancestors, but the Guru refused saying, "He who trusts in God and makes an honest living to share with others and injures no one, nor harbours ill-will against another need perform on other rituals. His soul ever stays in health. And, as for the ancestors, they gather the reward of what they themselves have sown and no one can bless or curse them after they are gone".

Guru Tegh Bahadur now arrived at Patna where he stayed for some time. The Guru left his family here, as his wife Mata Gujri was expecting their child and moved onwards with his tour to Dacca and the eastern most parts of India not visited since the time of Guru Nanak. Sikh congregations were very jubilant to see their Guru. In December of 1666 while on his eastern tour Guru Tegh Bahadur received the news that he had been blessed with a child, a son named Gobind Rai. This eastern tour would last three years as Guru Tegh Bahadur visited as many people as he could. While in Assam in 1668 Guru Tegh Bahadur was able to achieve a peace treaty between the ruler of Ahom and a large force sent by Aurengzeb under the command of Raja Ram Singh of Amber. In 1669-1670 Guru Tegh Bahadur started the journey homeward and travelled to Patna to see his young son Gobind Rai for the first time. Here Guru Tegh Bahadur spent over a year with his family training his son in the Sikh Scriptures, horse riding and swordsmanship. Guru Tegh Bahadur then sent his family onto Punjab while he continued his missionary work. The Guru finally returned home to Anandpur Sahib in 1672-1673. Here thousands of devotees flock to see and hear the Guru.

While the Guru attended to his devotees to Anandpur, things in the country were rapidly deteriorating under the tyrannous rule of emperor Aurangzeb. Since coming to power by imprisoning his father and killing his two brothers. Aurangzeb had been consolidating his power base. After ten years he now began to apply his power throughout the country. Aurangzeb was an orthodox Muslim who dreamed of purging India of all 'infidels' and converting it into a land of Islam. Aurangzeb had no tolerance for other religions and proceeded on a brutal campaign of repression. Famous Hindu temples throughout the country were demolished and mosques built in their place. Hindu idols were placed in the steps of mosques to be trodden on by the feet of Muslims pilgrims. Aurangzeb issued a number of harsh decrees. In 1665 he forbade Hindus to display illuminations at Diwali festivals. In 1668 he forbade. Hindu Jatras, in 1671 he issued and order that only Muslims could be landlords of crown lands, and called upon provincial Viceroys to dismiss all Hindu clerks. In 1669 he issued a general order calling upon all governors of all provinces to destroy with a willing hand the schools and temples of the infidels; and they were told to put a stop to the teachings and practising of idolatrous forms of worship. In 1674 lands held by Hindus in Gujarat, in religious grants were all confiscated.

In this climate of intolerance the viceroy of Kashmir Iftikhar Khan took to the task of forcibly converting the Hindu population to Islam by the sword. The Hindu Brahmin Pandits of Kashmir were among the most highly learned and orthodox of the Hindu leadership. Aurangzeb felt if they could be converted, the rest of the country would easily follow. He did not want to see the tilak (holy mark on the forehead) or janaeu (sacred thread) on any of his subjects. Given this ultimatum, a large delegation of 500 Kashmiri Pandits decided to journey to Anandpur Sahib to seek the help of Guru Tegh Bahadur. The delegation was led by Pandit Kirpa Ram Datt (who would later on become the Sanskrit teacher of Guru Gobind Singh and eventually become a Khalsa and died fighting in the battle of Chamkaur). The pandits met the Guru and explained their dire predicament to the Guru and requested the Guru to intercede on their behalf. As the Guru was pondering over the issue his nine year old son Gobind Rai walked into the room, noticing the serious and gloomy mood in the room the young Gobind asked his father what was happening. Guru Tegh Bahadur replied, "unless a holy man lays down his head for the sake of the poor Brahmins, there is no hope for their escape from imperial tyranny". Young Gobind replied, "Revered father, who would be better equipped for this than yourself?" Guru Tegh Bahadur hugged his son and wept for joy. "I was only worried about the future, for you are far too young". "Leave me to God", Gobind replied, "and accept the challenge of the Mughals".

Even though Guru Nanak had refused to wear the sacred thread when he was young, the Gurus still believed in the freedom of religion and the right of the Hindus, Muslims and Sikhs to live in peace and practice their own religions. With this Guru Tegh Bahadur laid down the gauntlet in the fight for freedom of religion and told the Pandits to inform Aurangzeb that the Brahmins would gladly accept and embrace Islam if Guru Tegh Bahadur can be convinced to do so. Guru Tegh Bahadur made preparations to leave for Delhi, he bid farewell to his family and followers and dictated that his son Gobind Rai should be installed as the next Guru. Accompanying the Guru on his journey and also prepared to accept the consequences of whatever happened were Bhai Mati Das, Bhai Dyala and Bhai Sati Das. As soon as Aurangzeb heard the news he ordered the immediate arrest of the Guru. Guru Tegh Bahadur and his party were arrested soon after they left Anandpur Sahib and taken in chains to Delhi.

When brought before Aurangzeb, he was asked why he was hailed as the Guru or prophet and called 'Sacha Padsah' (the True King) and if he really believed in his being one he should perform a miracle to justify his claim. Guru Tegh Bahadur reprimanded the emperor for his blind orthodoxy and his persecution of other faiths, "Hinduism may not be my faith, and I may believe not in the supremacy of Veda or the Brahmins, nor in idol worship or caste or pilgrimages and other rituals, but I would fight for the right of all Hindus to live with honour and practice their faith according to their own rites". The Guru answered further, "Every ruler of the world must pass away, but not the Word of God or His Saint. This is how people not only call me a True King but have done so through the two centuries before me in respect of my House and also in respect of others who preceded them and identified themselves not with the temporal and the contingent, but with the eternal and the ever dying". The Guru refused to perform any miracles saying, "this is the work of charlatans and mountebanks to hoodwink the people. Man of God submit ever to the Will of God". Guru Tegh Bahadur refused to embrace Islam, saying "For me there is only one religion—God—and whosoever belongs to it, be he a Hindu or a Muslim, him I own and he owns me. I neither convert others by force, nor submit to force to change my faith". Aurengzeb was enraged and ordered Guru Tegh Bahadur to be forced to convert to Islam through torture or be killed.

Guru Tegh Bahadur was subjected to many cruelties, he was kept in an iron cage and starved for many days. The Guru was made to watch as Bhai Mati Das the devoted Sikh was tied between two pillars and his body split in two by being sawn alive. Bhai Dyala was boiled alive in a cauldron of boiling water and Bhai Sati Das was wrapped in cotton wool and set on fire. The Guru bore these cruelties without flinching or showing any anger or distress. Finally on November 11, 1675 Guru Tegh Bahadur was publicly beheaded with the sword of the executioner as he prayed. The Gurus body was left in the dust as no one dared to pick up the body for fear of the emperors reprisal. A severe storm swept through the city and under the cover of darkness a Sikh named Bhai Jaita managed to collect the Guru's sacred head and carried it off to Anandpur Sahib to the Guru's son. Another Sikh Bhai Lakhi Shah who had a cart, was able to smuggle the Gurus headless body to his house. Since a public funeral would be too dangerous, Bhai Lakhi Shah cremated the body by setting his house on fire. Meanwhile the head was taken to the grief stricken young Guru Gobind Singh and the widow Mata Gujari. On November 16, 1675 at Anandpur Sahib, a pyre of sandlewood was constructed, sprinkled with roses and the head of Guru Tegh Bahadur was cremated by young Guru Gobind Singh.

Thus ended the earthly reign of the ninth Nanak, Guru Tegh Bahadur. Never in the annals of history has the religious leader of one religion sacrificed his life to save the freedom of another religion.

The Tenth Master Guru Gobind Singh (1666-1708)

'I establish thee as my son, that you spread My Path. Go and instruct men in Righteousness and the Moral Law, and make people desist from evil".

I stood up, with joined palms, and bowing my head to Lord God, I said: Thy Path I shall spread only if Thou be at my back.

For this was I born into the world, I utter only how and what God uttered to me, for I am the enemy of no one. He who calls me God will surely burn in the fire of hell. For I am only the servant of God: doubt not the veracity of this statement. I am but the slave of the Supreme Being come to witness His Play. I tell the world only what my God said to me, for I will not be silenced through fear of the mere mortals. I utter as is the instruction of my God, for I consider no one greater than Him. I am pleased not with any religious garb, so I shall sow the seeds of the Unaccountable One. Nay, I worship not stones, nor I am attracted by denominational coats. I utter only the name of the Infinite and so attain unto the supreme Being. I wear not matted hair, nor ear-rings, nor have regard for any such ritual, and do only what God bids me do. I repeat only the name of one God who fulfils us, at all places. No, I utter not another's name, nor establish another God. I dwell upon the Name of the Infinite One and so realise the essence of the Supreme Light. I give thought to none else, nor utter another's name. O God, with Thy one Name I am imbued. I have no other pride. Yea, I utter only Thy Name and eradicate my endless sins. (Guru Gobind Singh, Vachitra Natak).

The Religion and Social Organisation of the Sikhs

Sikhism is the religion of some six and a quarter million Indians. The homeland of the Sikhs is the Sutlej valley, the region around Amritsar, Jullundur, and Ludhiana in the Punjab. Smaller numbers of Sikhs, in service or commerce, are to be found in many other parts of India, especially since the exodus from West Pakistan at the time of partition. The Sikhs are not racially distinct from other Punjabis, from whose main stocks they are drawn.

Sikhism began as one of the many religious movement is called forth in northern India by the confrontation of Hinduism and Islam. What has survived of the teaching of its founder, Nānak, is not so vigorous as that of this predecessor Kābir, nor so original as that of the later Dādu, both of whom founded small sects which survive to this day. But Sikhism revealed a power of growth, religious and political, nor possessed by the Kābir-or Dādū-panthīs, so that whereas they are today minor sects, the Sikh community is still politically important. Sikhism has a double interest then, as an example, first, of syncretist religious thought in Nānak's teaching, and second, of the clothing of a spiritual idea in corporate institutions.

The Punjab, when Nānak was born (A.D. 1469), had been for four centuries under Muslim rule and influence. More particularly, from the thirteenth century onward the Sufi-orders had been active, first the Chishti and Suhrawadi, and the Qadiri and Naqshbandi orders. The teaching and shrines of the Sufi saints alike were venerated—by Hindus as well as by Muslims. The Punjab was also influenced profoundly by the Bhakti movement, the outburst of devotional religion which swept across India, a vigorous Hindu reaction to the shock of persecution and the monotheistic teaching of the Muslim invaders.

Between the two movements, Sufi and Bhakti, for both of which doctrine was unimportant and the personal, emotional relation of the individual to God vital, there was much in common. The three successive exponents in northern India of this new religious approach were a Muslim Kabīr (1440-1518), a Hindu, Nānak (1469-1538), and a Muslim, Dādu (1544-1603). All three used a common Bhakti vocabulary to preach a message which, under different emphasis, remained at root the same. Indeed the Sikh and Dādūpanthī scriptures incorporate much of Kabīr's teaching and verse. Both Hindus and Muslims were attracted by their preaching, and the popular accounts of Kabīr and Nānak picture Muslims and Hindus claiming the bodies of the dead teachers as theirs to bury and to cherish.

So far did the *rapprochement* go that the orthodox on either side took alarm. At the very moment when, under Aurangzeb, orthodox Muslims were acting to restrain the Sufis, orthodox Hindus were denouncing the Sikh gurus for betraying Hinduism. As Dādu cried; "Fierce and terrible have they become, when they saw I was of neither faction"[1].

NĀNAK AND HIS TEACHING

The founder of Sikhism, Nānak, was a Hindu and a kshatriya. His native village, largely Hindu, had a Muslim zamīndār (landholder), however, and it is said that a Muslim neighbour provided for Nānak's further education after he had finished the schooling given by the village pandit[2]. Nānak married a Hindu girl, who bore him two sons, and possibly a daughter also. Through his brother-in-law's influence he secured a job as storekeeper in the service of Daulat Khān Lodi, the greater Afghan governor of the province.

Nānak's early life thus illustrates the interdependence of Muslims and Hindus in the Punjab. The accounts of his life also speak of his early interest in the teachings of wandering ascetics; Muslims-Fānī[3] suggests that Nānak, a Hindu, finally decided to adopt the wandering religious life at the prompting of a Muslim darwish. Leaving the service of Daulat Khān Lodi in early middle age, he abandoned his wife and family, and, accompanied by a Muslim musician, Mardāna, began a period of wandering which traditionally took him all over India, to Ceylon, and even to Mecca and Medina. At intervals he revisited the Punjab where he spent the last ten or fifteen years of his life at Kartarpur, a newly founded "Sikh" village. There he lived with his family as a householder,[4] preaching in the villages and teaching the disciples gathered round him, until his death in 1538.

Nānak was not a systematic theologian, and his thought, drawn from many sources, is not always coherent. But his personal working faith proclaims insistently the majesty and unity of God, the comparative insignificance of prophets or avatārs, the fleeting vanity of worldly life, and the need to approach God in fear and love. God creates, God disposes, but God is gracious. All can approach Him, therefore, in a spirit of service and devotion, without which all formal ritual is worthless.

God, and the worship of God, rather than man's salvation, is at the centre of Nānak's preaching. His Being is beyond men's capacity to know, relate, or understand shrouded in mystery, "The Unseen, Infinite, Inaccessible, Inapprehensible God"[5]. But if there is something here of the Hindu attitude (or the Mu 'tazilite), defining God by negatives until God becomes a mere philosophical abstraction, normally Nānak stresses the reality of God, whose power and glory are displayed in His creation. "There is but one God whose name is true, the Creator"[6]. Here the influence of Islam is evident and strong. And it is seen again in the vision of God sustaining and disposing by His will. The transcendence and omnipotence are carried indeed to the logical conclusion of orthodox Islam, to predestination and a fatalistic acceptance of God's decree.

But the background of Nānak's thought is Hindu—the metaphors and basic concepts of Hinduism come naturally to him. So, though in his writings as a whole, the vision of God the creator is dominant, there are also passages about the immences of God—"He Himself is the Relisher; He Himself is the Relish; He Himself is the Enjoyer[7] —which strike a quite different note. In the same way he accepts the Hindu doctrines of māyā and rebirth, though forcing them into a form which is scarcely reconcilable with Hindu philosophy. Thus the almost autonomous system of karma to which that philosophy consigns men is in Nānak made subject to the Will of God. The round of transmigration becomes a punishment, a hell, to which God may condemn men, but from which, whatever, his burden of evil action, God in His grace may save man. "Even if he be drowning in sin, God will still take care of him"[8].

What then is the relationship of men and God? It has already been suggested that for the Muslim "the reason for man's existence on earth, the purpose of his daily life, was submission to and worship of the One God, the Omnipotent". Nānak, when he is thinking of God as Omnipotent, likewise urges absolute and joyful submission. He stresses man's weakness, his own consciousness of failure or sin, and his consequent wholesome fear of the Lord.

But he also thinks of God as a loving God—a bestower of unmerited grace:

As a herdsman guardeth and keepeth watch over his cattle,

so God day and night cherisheth and guardeth man and keepeth him in happiness.

O thou compassionate to the poor, I seek Thy protection; look on me with favour[9].

In this mood Nānak throws himself upon God's mercy, calling upon Him also to pity all suffering humans.

But Nānak does not conceive of man as merely passive. Man may be misled by māyā—but here māyā is not that pure illusion of Vedantic monism which keeps man from the realization that God alone exists, but something much nearer the Puritans' view of a snare and a delusion. If man chooses the world, the flesh, and the devil, he is to some degree responsible; Nānak contritely recognises that he has sinned, if only by omission, "I have done no good act"[10]. He outlines how responsible men should act in this world so as to "abide pure amid the impurities of the world"[11].

There is no constant belief, however, in human free will, and even where man chooses the good life, he is still utterly dependent upon God's grace. He cannot earn, still less compel the gift of salvation. "God cannot be overcome by other ceremonial acts"[12]. Nevertheless, worship and devotion are given as the means of approaching God. He is in fact bounteous, the great giver, but even if He were not, wholehearted devotion would be man's only way.

Man may avoid entanglement in māyā by surrender and devotion to God.

By obeying him wisdom and understanding enter the mind.

By hearing the name [God revealed] sorrow and sin are no more[13].

But God does not reveal Himself directly, nor can man learn to love the Creator unaided. A mediator is needed between the transcendent lord and man. That mediator is the guru.

With Nānak, who had no human guru of his own, the word is used less of human guides than for God himself, for the holy spirit. But his teaching accorded well with the ancient Hindu doctrine of the teacher being all in all for the pupil, with the emphasis on the relationship of pīr and murīd among Sufis, even perhaps with the Shīa doctrine of the Imām. The doctrine of the guru was one destined to grow in importance in Sikhism.

Finally, what of the negative, the puritan, aspect of Nānak's teaching? There is an attack upon whatever sunders man from the One True Name—pride in book learning, pride in fasts and penances, pride in ritual purity or the five prayers daily made. There is an attack upon whatever is set up as a substitute for God, whether it be prophet or avatār. There is an attack upon whatever distracts—wealth, leisure, even family ties. And there is the most relentless attack upon idol worship.

Kabīr had been a trenchant iconoclast: "The beads are of wood, the gods of stone, the Jumnā of water. Rāma and Krishna are dead. The four Vedas are fictitious stories"[14]. Nānak's monotheism is not quite so unqualified. Sometimes he echoes Kabīr, pointing out the inconsistencies in the four Vedas,[15] the false lesson taught in the *Rāmāyana* and *Mahābhārata*[16]. He several times makes the point continued in the lines.

At God's gate there dwelt thousands of Muhammads, thousands of Brahmas, of Vishnus, and of Sivas.

There is one Lord over all spiritual lords, the Creator, whose name is true[17].

But the Prophet, or the Hindu Gods, though creator, have a reality, and honest worship of them has some value. It is hard to be a good Muslim or Hindu, hard to give alms, fast, or say one's prayers meaningfully, but to be or do so is good. Caste, which he treats as irrelevant is seen as a source of spiritual pride. In all of these what Nānak deplores is the confusion of outward form for inner purpose. "Thou shalt not go to heaven by lip service, it is by the practice of truth thou shalt be delivered"[18].

NĀNAK

The teachings of Nānak, which have come down in the *Ādi Granth* are in the form of hymns and of sayings, often short and pithy, which are made more memorable by being in vigorous verse. His verses, like those of all the gurus, are often repetitious, for they represent his preaching to many different audiences, and to unlettered villagers at that.

Sikhs hold that the essence of Nānak's teaching is found in the Japji, or morning prayer. From it, the opening invocation, three of the thirty-eight verses, and the conclusion are given below. Here we find Nānak's conception of God, the transcendent Creator, the Disposer of all things; and also his view of man, predestined sinful, brought to judgement.

[From M.A. Macauliffe, *The Sikh Religion*, I, 195-98, 204, 217]

There is but one God, whose name is true, the Creator, devoid of fear and enmity, immortal, unborn, self-existent; God the great and bountiful. Repeat His Name.

The True One was in the beginning, the True One was in the primal age, the True One is now also, O Nānak; the True One also shall be.

By His order bodies are produced; his order cannot be described.

By His order souls are infused into them; by His order greatness is obtained.

By His order men are high or low; by His order they obtain preordained pain or pleasure.

By his order some obtain their reward; by His order others must ever wander in transmigration.

All are subject to His order; non is exempt from it.

He who understandeth God's order, O Nānak's is never guilty of egoism. [pp. 195-96]

. . .

True is the Lord, true is His name, it is uttered with endless love.

People pray, and beg, "give us give us"; the Giver His gifts;

Then what can we offer Him whereby His court may be seen?

What words shall we utter with our lips on hearing which he may love us?

At the ambrosial hour of morning meditate on the true Name and God's greatness.

The Kind One will give us a robe of honour, and by His favour we shall reach the gate of salvation.

Nānak, we shall thus know that God is altogether true. [pp. 197-98]

. . . .

Numberless are the fool appallingly blind;

Numberless are the thrives and devourers of others' property;

Numberless are those who establish their sovereignty by force;

Numberless the cut-throats and murderers;

Numberless the liars who roam about lying;

Numberless the filthy who enjoy filthy gain;

Numberless the slandered who carry loads of calumny on their heads;
Nānak thus describeth the degraded.

So lowly am I, I cannot even once be a sacrifice unto Thee.

Whatever pleaseth Thee is good.

O Formless One, Thou art ever secure. [p. 204]

. . . .

Merits and demerits shall be read out in the presence of the judge.

According to men's acts, some shall be near, and others distant from God.

They who have pondered on the Name and departed after the completion of their toil,

Shall have their countenances made bright, O Nānak; how many shall be emancipated in company with them! [p. 217]

The Guru and the Ungodly

[From Macauliffe, *The Sikh Religion*, I, 228, 272-83, 326-31]

As a fish out of water, so is the infidel—dying the thirst.

If thy breath be drawn in vain, O Man, thou shalt die without God.

O Man, repeat God's name and praises;

But how shalt thou obtain this pleasure without the guru? It is the guru when uniteth man with God.

Meeting the society of holy men is as a pilgrimage for the holy. [pp. 330-31]

. . . .

Man is led astray by the reading of words; ritualists are very proud.

What availeth it to bathe at a place of pilgrimage, if the fifth of pride be in the heart?

Who but the guru can explain that the King and Eemperor dwelleth in the heart?

All men err; it is only the great Creator who erreth not.

He who admonisheth his heart under the guru's instruction shall love the Lord.

Nānak, he whom the incomparable Word hath caused to meet God, shall not forget the True One. [pp. 272-73]

. . . .

The Hindus have forgotten God, and are going the wrong way.

They worship according to the instruction of Nārad.

They are blind and dumb, the blindest of the blind.

The ignorant fools take stones and worship them.

O Hindus, how shall the stone which itself sinketh carry you across?

[p. 326]]

. . . .

What power hath caste? It is the reality that is tested.

Poison may be held in the hand, but man dieth if he eat it.

The sovereignty of the True One is known in every age.

He who obeyeth God's order shall become a noble in His court.

[p. 383]

They who have meditated on God as the truest of the true, have done real worship and are contended;

They have refrained from evil, done good deeds, and practiced honesty;

They have lived on a little corn and water, and burst the entanglements of the world.

Thou art the great Bestower; ever thou givest gifts which increase a quarter fold.

They who have magnified the great God have found him. [p. 228]

REFERENCES

1. W.G. Orr, *A Sixteenth-century Indian Mystic*, p. 63.
2. Ghulām Husayn Khān Tabātabā'i, *Siyar-ul-Mutaak-khirin*, I, 110.
3. Mushin-i-Fānī, *Dabistān-i-Mazāhib*, II, 247-48.
4. Bhāi Gurdās, *War*, I, 38.
5. M.A. Macauliffe, *The Sikh Religion*, I, 330.
6. *Ibid.*, I, 195.
7. *Ibid.*, I, 265.
8. Macauliffe, *The Sikh Religion*, I, p. 107.
9. *Ibid.*, p. 301.
10. *Ibid.*, p. 178.
11. *Ibid.*, p. 60.
12. *Ibid.*, I, 308.
13. *Ibid.*, I. 201.
14. G.H. Westcott, *Kabir and the Kabir Panth*, p. 58.
15. Macauliffe, *The Sikh Religion*, I, 236.
16. *Ibid.*, I, 269.
17. *Ibid.*, I, 40-41.
18. Macauliffe, *The Sikh Religion*, I. 39.

Women in Sikhism

At the time of the Gurus women were considered very low in society. Both Hindus and Muslims regarded women as inferior and a man's property. Women were treated as mere property whose only value was as a servant or for entertainment. They were considered seducers and distractions from man's spiritual path. Men were allowed polygamy but widows were not allowed to remarry but encouraged to burn themselves on their husbands funeral pyre (sati). Child marriage and female infanticide were prevalent and purdah (veils) were popular for women. Women were also not allowed to inherit and property. Many Hindu women were captured and sold as slaves in foreign Islamic countries.

In such a climate Guru Nanak Dev, the founder of Sikhism shocked the entire society by preaching that women were worthy of praise and equal to men. Five hundred years later, the rest of mankind is only now waking up to this fundamental truth. The Gurus actively encouraged the participation of women as equals in worship, in society, and on the battle field. They encouraged freedom of speech and women were allowed to participate in any and all religious activities including reading of the Guru Granth Sahib.

VIEWS OF THE GURUS

Guru Nanak Dev

Guru Nanak Dev broke the shackles of women by admitting them into the sangat (congregation) without any restrictions or reservations.

Guru Nanak felt that his message was meant as much for women as for men.

Guru Angad Dev

Guru Angad encouraged the education of all Sikhs, men and women.

Guru Amar Das

Guru Amar Das condemned the cruel custom of sati, female infanticide and advocated widow remarriage. Guru Amar Das also believed that women wearing veils (purdah) was demeaning. The Guru refused to meet the queen of Haripur or the allow any women into the congregation wearing a veil.

Guru Hargobind

Guru Hargobind respected women and declared, "women is the conscience of man".

Guru Gobind Singh

Guru Gobind Singh made the Khalsa initiation ceremony open to men and women alike, a women being just as worthy. At the time of Amrit a man is given the name Singh meaning lion, the women is given the name Kaur, meaning princess. A Sikh women is an individual in her own right, she does not have to take her husband's name a and is Kaur till her death. Guru Gobind Singh did not see any distinction between the Khalsa, men or women could keep the 5 K's. Guru Gobind Singh issued orders forbidding the Khalsa having any association with those that practiced female infanticide. Guru Gobind Singh also forbade Sikhs to exercise any proprietary rights over women captured in battle, they could not be kept as slaves or wives but were to be treated with the utmost respect.

In Praise of Women

"We are born of women, we are conceived in the womb of women, we are engaged and married to women. We make friendship with women and the lineage continued because of women. When one women dies, we take another one, we are bound with the world through woman. Why should we talk ill of her, who gives birth to kings? The woman is born from woman; there is none without her. Only the One True Lord is without woman" (Guru Nanak Dev, Var Asa, pg. 473).

Marriage is an equal partnership of love and sharing between husband and wife. "They are not said to be husband and wife, who merely sit together. Rather they alone are called husband and wife, who have one soul in two bodies". (Guru Amar Des, Pauri, pg. 788).

Women have an equal right to participate in the congregation.

"Come my sisters and dear comrades! Clasp me in thine embrace. Meeting together, let us tell the tales of our Omnipotent Spouse (God). In the True Lord are all merits, in us all demerits". (Guru Nanak Dev, Sri Rag, pg. 17).

God is the husband and we are all his brides.

"The spouse is but One and all others are His brides. The false bride assumes many religious garbs. When the Lord stops her going into another's home, then is she summoned into her lord's mansion without any let and hindrance. She is adorned with the Name and is dear to her True Lord. She alone is the true bride and the Lord lends her His support". (Guru Nanak Dev, Ramkali, pg. 933).

God is our Mother as well as our Father.

"Thou O lord, art my Father and Thou my Mother, Thou art the Giver of peace to my soul and very life". (Guru Arjan Dev, Bhairo, pg. 1144).

Faithfulness to ones spouse is stressed.

"The blind-man abandons the wife of his home, and has an affair with another's woman. He is like the parrot, who is pleased to see the simbal tree, but at last dies clinging to it". (Bhagat Nam Dev, Bhairo, pg. 1165).

The rape and brutalities committed against women by the Mughal invader Babar condemned.

"Modesty and righteousness both have vanished and falsehood moves about as the leader, O Lalo. The function of the Qazis and the Brahmins is over and the Satan now reads the marriage rites (rape). The Muslim women read the Quran and in suffering call upon God, O Lalo. The Hindu women of high caste and others of low caste, may also be put in the same account, O Lalo". (Guru Nanak Dev, Tilang, pg. 722).

The practice of women burning themselves on their husband's funeral pyre (sati) condemned.

"They cannot be called satis, who burn themselves with their dead husbands. They can only be called satis, if they bear the shock of separation. They may also be known as satis, who live with character and contentment and always show veneration to their husbands by remembering them". (Guru Amar Das, Var Suhi, pg. 787)

The ritual of dowry so prevalent in Indian society condemned.

"Any other dowry, which the perverse place for show, that is false pride and worthless gliding. O' my Father! Give me the Name of Lord God as a gift and dowry". (Guru Ram Das, Sri Rag, pg. 79).

FAMOUS WOMEN

Bibi Nanaki

Bibi Nanaki was the first person to recognize Guru Nanak as a prophet and missionary early in his life. Bibi Nanaki (Guru Nanak's sister) and Mata Tripta (Guru Nanak's mother) played very important roles in encouraging young Nanak to pursue his lifelong mission.

Mata Khivi

Mata Khivi was the wife of Guru Angad Dev and was in charge of the langar (community kitchen). She was an unlimited source of bounty and helped create a new social consciousness for women.

Sikh Missionaries

Guru Amar Das trained missionaries to spread Sikhism throughout the country. Of the 146 missionaries Guru Amar Das trained and sent out, 52 were women. At one time the country of Afghanistan and Kashmir were under the jurisdiction of women masands (priests). These women had complete jurisdiction in decision making, collection of revenues as well as preaching to congregations.

Bibi Bhani

Bibi Bhani has a unique position in Sikh history as the daughter of a Guru (Guru Amar Das), wife of a Guru (Guru Ram Das) and mother of a Guru (Guru Arjan Dev). Bibi Bhani was an inspiration during the formative period of Sikh history and symbolizes responsibility, dedication, humility and fortitude.

Mata Gujri

Mata Gurji was an illuminating force behind her husband Guru Tegh Bahadur and her son Guru Gobind Singh. After the martyrdom of Guru Tegh Bahadur, Mata Gujri guided and inspired her son Guru Gobind Singh. She was responsible for the training of the Sahibzadas (the four sons of Guru Gobind Singh) who gave up their lives for Sikhism at a young age. Mata Gujri was an inspiring force during one of the most difficult times in Sikh history.

Mai Bhago

Mai Bhago was the brave women who shamed the 40 deserters to return to the battle of Muktsar. She led them into battle where they achieved martyrdom and were blessed by Guru Gobind Singh.

Mata Jitoji

During the baptism ceremony of the Khalsa in 1699, Guru Gobind Singh asked Mata Jitoji to participate in the first baptism by adding sugar cakes (patashas) to water which was stirred with the knanda (double edged sword) and administrated to the Khalsa as amrit (sweet water).

Mata Sahib Kaur

Because of her purity, Guru Gobind Singh declared that Sikhs should consider Mata Sahib Kaur as the spiritual mother of the Khalsa.

Mata Sundri

The widow of Guru Gobind Singh, Mata Sundri helped provide leadership for the Sikhs in a very difficulty and tumultuous time following the death of Guru Gobind Singh. She helped maintain the sanctity of the Guru Granth Sahib as the only successor of Guru Gobind Singh and dealt strictly with pretenders and aspires of Guruship.

Gender and the Sikh Panth

This paper begins with an apology, not for its content, but rather for the fact that the content is being raised by a man. By treating this subject. I must surely be giving the impression that, in my opinion at least, the subject of women's rights is best treated by a man—the old, old story. I do not think I shall apologise though, as my intention is not to provide any answers to the question. It is merely to raise it as a question and to see what answers are forthcoming from those who are entitled to give them.

There were actually three reasons which accounted for the decision to set down my thinking on this subject, the hope being that it will prompt others to carry both discussion and (if necessary) action much further. The first was that 1993 was the centennial year of the granting of women's suffrage in New Zealand. As a result, those of us who live in that country have been constantly reminded that it was the first country to introduce the reform, and our consciousness really has been raised during the course of the year by the incessant bombardment of material relating to women's suffrage. The second reason was the questions which my students have voiced during the last five years in classes on Sikh religion in the university of Toronto. These questions have come particularly from female students and particularly during the last two years. And the third reason was my reading of that excellent booklet by Jagtar Singh Grewal entitled *Guru Nanak and Patriarchy*. This showed that the subject was certainly alive and provides a very useful analysis of the first Guru's teachings on the subject[1].

We begin our discussion not with the situation in the Sikh Panth (in the Sikh community), but with a note on the situation in the West. Western society is the context within which the Sikh diaspora has largely taken place and Western society poses for the Panth questions both new and insistent. It is, after all, the context in which those students of mine were being raised and which supplied them with questions which they felt (rightly or wrongly) that their traditional faith was answering inadequately. There can be no doubt that in some areas of Western society gender issues are certainly well and truly alive, and that this awareness is forcing some substantial changes in our conventional ways.

But let us not exaggerate the extent of the progress. The dramatic changes are both recent and few, and within Western society there are still powerful forces opposing true equality. There may indeed be voiced sentiments favouring the movement, but subtle influences can be very effective in slowing the process or even in stopping it altogether. My own university in New Zealand adheres most explicitly to the doctrine of equal opportunity, but that does not alter the fact that only one-twentieth of its full professors are women.

And note too that in Western society many of the areas where progress is positively opposed are areas occupied by religion. This is not saying of course that the Roman Catholic Church (for example) is necessarily wrong in its adamant opposition to the admission of female priests. This paper is not concerned with what is right or wrong, but merely with things as they are. The sphere of religion in general is actually an area where the Sikh religion, with regard to the place of women, is favourably situated in comparison with practically all examples drawn from the Western experience. This is the case in theory and it is also largely the case in practice.

So what is the place of women in the Sikh religion? In explaining the position that women occupy Sikhs invariably turn to the *Guru Granth Sahib* and there they almost always turn to a famous shalok by Guru Nanak from *Asa di Var*:

Each [man] took birth from a woman, the woman in whom he was conceived; each is engaged to a woman and with that woman is wed. With [that] woman affection develops; through [that] woman new offspring are born.

If one woman dies he seeks another; with a woman he orders his life.

Why cast aspersions on her, she who gives birth to rajas.

[And] a woman herself is born of the woman; none [takes birth] except from a woman.

Only the True One, Nanak, needs not the assistance of a woman…[2]

This shalok is held to summarise completely the attitude of all Sikhs to the place that women occupy and it would seem to maintain complete equality for women with men, not just for the Sikh but for everyone. Certainly Guru Nanak's words carry us well beyond the conventional view of his time or, for that matter, the present time as well. Without a woman man is as nothing, so should she ever be called weak or polluting?

The other Gurus support the stand taken by Guru Nanak, opposing such practices as dowries, seclusion and female infanticide as reflecting unmistakably the view held by Indian society in general of the place in that society occupied by women. The views of the Sikh Gurus were vastly ahead of those of their contemporary society—or at least (assuming we are not in the business of apportioning praise and blame) they were vastly different from them. The standard Sikh view, as spelt out by *Sikh Rahit Maryada*, fully supports the Gurus. The very first sentence begins with the words *jo istari jan purus,* 'That woman or man"[3]. Women are not to be veiled in a sangat; a woman is entitled to sit in attendance on the *Guru Granth Sahib*; a woman can receive initiation into the Khalsa; and she can also be one of the Panj Piares who gives it[4]. One cannot, it seems, go much further than that.

But here we encounter the first signs of difficulty and very quickly they grow into a substantial quantity. In the first place we must note that all the Gurus were men—not just some of the Gurus, or most of the Gurus, but all of them. When we observe the testimony of Sikh history we find that it consists almost wholly of 500 years of the doings of men. We proceed on to the situation today and here we find that contemporary Sikh institutions are strongly male-dominated—very strongly indeed.

Clearly (but scarcely surprisingly) the difficulties that accumulate are very substantial. And they do not end here. If we travel right back to the beginning we find that the interpretation which we placed upon Guru Nanak's *Var Asa* shalok may have been a little naive. If we think about it more carefully we may come to the conclusion that the position adopted by Nanak comes very close to the situation commonly argued as ideal today. In other words, we may conclude that although women deserve every respect it is nevertheless the duty of men to protect them and that in so doing men must assume the role of leaders in the affairs of the family, locality and nation.

It amounts, that is, to what is normally assumed to be the ideal order, the order symbolically enshrined in Anand Karaj (the wedding ceremony of the Sikhs). The bridegroom is addressed first by the officient and enjoined to be "the protector of [the bride's] person and her honour". Then comes the address to the bride, wherein she is counselled to accept her future husband as "a master of all love and respect". The hem of one of the groom's garments is then placed in the bride's hand and *she* follow *him* round the sacred scripture four times[5]. The ceremony is a beautiful one and it indicates symbolically what the nature of the union is intended to be. It very definitely is what the modern Panth regards as ideal.

Let us return to Sikh history and look again at the general scarcity of women on the historical scene. With this we shall group the absence of female Gurus. This latter issue is reasonably easy to answer and can be dealt with summarily. Consider the circumstances of the time. It would have been altogether impossible for a woman to occupy the position of Guru and even if she had, it is unlikely that anyone would have listened to her. The point is taken, but there is a hint of reluctance from those who know the Christian scene. The twelve disciples of Jesus were all men and this fact is a prime argument used by the Roman Catholic Church to refuse the admission of women to the priesthood.

Consider next the entire span of Sikh history and, as we have already indicated, it is immediately evident that Sikh history is almost completely the history of the doings of men. Almost all the Gurus had wives, but inevitably they performed their roles in the shadow of their husbands. How much attention, for example, is Sulakhani given? Like all wives of the Gurus she comes across as an ideal wife, but inevitably the attention she receives is the tiniest fraction of that given to Nanak[6]. Mata Jito certainly made an important contribution to the first Khalsa initiation but there was no doubt that it was her husband who stood at the centre of that event[7]. The case was similar with the Gurus' daughters. Bibi Bhani occupies an important position, but it is exceptional and she receive much less attention than her father, her husband, or her son[8]. The wives and daughters of the Gurus are certainly noticed, but the notice is a brief one.

And so to for the remainder of Sikh history. Mai Bhago wins renown, but there are very few like her whose names are known[9]. Sada Kaur is very definitely an exception[10] and Rani Jindan is one about whom the Khalsa is distinctly ambivalent[11]. Very quickly we run out of names, leaving a mere handful. Yet who is surprised by this? After all, the history of the West shows exactly the same phenomenon and it is the same with all histories. The question is not whether there is any scarcity of female figures, nor whether they have been omitted because they occupied strictly subordinate positions. The question is rather one of whether, in these modern times, the situation has been significantly improved.

When we turn to contemporary times the answer is both yes and no. Within the Panth the situation of women definitely has been improved, largely as a result of the Singh Sabha reformers. *Sikh Rahit Maryaada* is the product of their activities (that is of the Tat Khalsa group within the Singh Sabha) and there can be no doubt that in this area, as in many others, there is the clear mark of their reforming hands[12]. The position of women within the Panth has been advanced during the early decades of the present century.

Yet one has difficulty in picking out areas of benthic leadership where women are conspicuous. There are of course numerous doctors in the Punjab and overseas, and there are likewise women engaged in teaching or in the bureaucracy. These positions do not involve leadership within the Panth, but rather in society at large. Within the Panth activities in which women predominate, or at least are strongly represented, are very few and command little influence in changes affecting the Panth. Practically all offices are held by men, from the President of the SGPC down to the humblest granthi or sevadar. This is not to say that women are debarred from occupying such positions. They assuredly are not. The fact is, though, that they do not hold them.

It is this situation of what is construed as female subordination which causes some Sikh women to raise insistent questions—my Toronto students for example. These women may not number many at present, but they are articulate members of the Panth and they may be held to represent many more. Partly their puzzlement or their incipient sense of injustice can be explained by the fact that most of them live in Western society as well as retaining their original Punjabi domicile, picking up ideas which do not seem to harmonise well with the traditional values with which they were raised. Those who attend the gurdwara regularly may find themselves asking why the institution is largely controlled by men, while the women must content themselves by singing gurbani and serving in the langer. The question is: are these women right? Are women really being given their legitimate place in the life of the Panth?

The intention of this paper is merely to raise the question and to point out that there are two possible answers to it. Actually there are three answers, but no one is likely to own up to an acceptance of the third one, even though it may accord best with a man's current way of life. This third answer is that the Panth rightly imposes subordination on women. It is an answer which may meet with widespread covert approval (particularly in some areas of rural society where it is likely to be overt), but it is hardly likely to win the same approval in a discussion such as this.

We are left therefore with a decision between two options. Should the Panth recognise differences of role distinguishing men from women, and retain men in positions of authority in order that they may discharge their designated role? Men have traditionally been the protectors of women and this particular option assumes that they still are. Women deserve love and respect, but when it comes to making important panthic decisions the role should remain firmly that of the men.

This is one option. The other is that the Panth should subscribe to the theory of complete equality, total and absolute, between men and women. The supporters of this view will maintain that, in common with all modern societies, the Panth still has some considerable distance to go before the ideal is achieved. This, however, should be the objective and all enlightened Sikhs should press on towards it. Needless to say this particular option will meet with strong if subtle opposition and the way ahead will be paved with all manner of compromise and imperfection, but the ideal must be won. Women can do anything, including the presidency of the SGPC.

These are the two options and Sikhs, in seeking an answer, will turn to the *Guru Granth Sahib*. Even here they will find themselves confronted by what is essentially the same problem. Remember that we have been dealing largely with Sikhs of the diaspora and for many of these Sikhs English is the language in which they think. English uses pronouns which are either female or male and traditionally God has been male. He (or she) may well be called *Waheguru*, but that certainly does not overcome the problem. Even in SLS[13] on Punjabi the problem is present in adjectival agreement and verb endings. It may be answered that *Waheguru* has female characteristics and that the use of male terminology is merely because the dilemma is otherwise insoluble. To this the reply is that there is indeed another way and that is to refer to *Wagegure* as female. At this the traditional mind must balk and the only possible solution lies in finding some acceptable dual usage.

I have gone far enough for an outsider and must at this point withdraw from the discussion, leaving its continuation to members of the Panth. In concluding I would repeat a plea already made. Let not the discussion and deciding be done by men, predominantly or exclusively. This is the danger for sikhs as it is for any other group of people.

—W.H. McLeod

REFERENCES

1. The thought provoking work by Nikky-Guninder Kaur Singh. *The Feminine Principle in the Sikh Vision of the Transcendent* (Cambridge: Cambridge University, Press, 1994), will be examined in a series of lectures which are being prepared for the Indian Institute of Advanced Study, Shimla.
2. *Var Asa* 19:2, Adi Granth, p. 473.
3. *Sikh Rahit Maryada* (Amritsar: Shromani Gurduara Prabandhak Kameti, 16th ed., 1983), p. 8.
4. *Ibid.*, pp. 12, 13, 24.
5. *Ibid.*, pp. 19-20.
6. W.H. McLeod, *Guru Nanak and the Sikh Religion* (Oxford Clarendon Press, 1968), p. 104.
7. Harbans Singh. *The Heritage of the Sikhs* (New Delhi: Manohar, 1983), p. 95.
8. Bibi Bhani was the daughter of Guru Amar Das, the wife of Guru Ram Das, and the mother of Guru Arjan. Harnam Singh, *The Encyclopaedia of Sikhism*, ed. Harbans Singh, Vol. 1 (Patiala: Punjabi University, 1992), p. 346.
9. Piara Singh Padam, *The Encyclopaedia of Sikhism*, ed. Harbans Singh, Vol. 1, pp. 323-24.
10. J.S. Grewal, *The Sikh of the Punjab*, Vol. II. 3 of *The New Cambridge History of India* (Cambridge: Cambridge University Press, 1990), pp. 101-103.
11. *Ibid.*, pp. 122-25.
12. W.H. McLeod, *Who is a Sikh?* (Oxford: Clarendon Press, 1989), pp. 94-95.
13. The Sacred Language of the Sikhs, the language of the Adi Granth. We owe this name of Professor Christopher Shackle.

Sikh Code of Conduct

What is the Rehat Maryada?

This document is the official *Sikh Code of Conduct*. There were a number of unsuccessful attempts in the eighteenth century following the death of Guru Gobind Singh to produce an accurate portrayal of sikh conduct and customs. These attempts were contradictory and inconsistent with many of the principles of the Gurus and were not accepted by the majority of Sikhs. In 1931, an attempt was made by the Shromani Gurudwara Prabandhak Committee (S.G.P.C.) to produce a modern standard Rehat. These efforts involved the greatest Sikh scholars and theologians of this century who worked to produce the current version. The document produced has been accepted as the official version which provides guide lines against which all Sikh individuals and communities around the world can measure themselves. The Rehat Maryada is the only version authorized by the Akal Takht, the seat of supreme temporal authority for Sikhs. It's implementation has successfully achieved a high level of uniformity in the religious and social practices of Sikhism.

Rehat Maryada

The Code of Sikh Conduct and Conventions

Dharam Prachar Committee

Shiromani Gurdwara Prabandhak Committee, Amritsar

SIKH REHAT MARYADA (CODE OF CONDUCT)

1. The Definition of Sikh

Article I

Any human being who faithfully believes in

(i) One immortal being.

(ii) Ten Gurus, from Guru Nanak Dev to Guru Gobind Singh,

(iii) The Guru Granth Sahib,

(iv) The utterances and teachings of the ten Gurus and

(v) The baptism bequeathed by the tenth Guru, and who does not owe allegiance to any other religion, is a Sikh.

2. Sikh Living

Article II

A Sikh's life has two aspects: individual or personal and corporate or panthic.

3. Sikh's Personal Life

Article III

A Sikh's personal life should comprehend:

(i) meditation on Nam (Diving substance) and the scriptures,

(ii) leading life according to the Gurus teachings and

(iii) altruistic voluntary service.

4. Meditation on Nam (Divine substance) and Scriptures

Article IV

1. A sikh should wake up in the ambrosial hours (three hours before the dawn), take bath and, concentrating his/her thoughts on one immortal being, repeat the name Waheguru (Wondrous destroyer of darkness).
2. He/she should recite the following scriptural compositions every day:

   (a) the Japji, the Jappu and the ten Sawayyas (Quartets)—beginning "Sarawag sudh"—in the morning;

(b) Sodar Rehras compromising the following compositions:

(i) nine hymns of the Guru Granth Sahib, occurring in the holy book after the Japuji Sahib, the first of which begins with "Sodar" and the last of which ends with "saran pare ki rakh sarma".

(ii) The Benti Chaupai of the tenth Guru (beginning "hamri karo hath dai rachha" and ending with "dusht dokh te leho bachai"

(iii) the Sawayya beginning with the words "pae geho jab te tumre"

(iv) the Dohira beginning with the words "sagal duar kau chhad kai"

(v) the first five and the last pauris (stanzas) of Anand Sahib

(vi) and Mundawani and the slok Mahla 5 beginning "tere kita jato nahi" in the evening after sunset.

(c) the Sohila—to be recited at night before going to bed.

The morning and evening recitations should be concluded with Ardas (formal supplication litany).

3. (a) The text of the Adras:

One Absolute Manifest; victory belongeth to the Wondrous Destroyer of darkness. May the might of the All-Powerful help!

Odc to the might by the tenth lord.

Having first thought of the Almighty's prowess, let us think of Guru Nanak. Then of Guru Angad, Amardas and Ramdas—may they be our rescuers! Remember then Arjan, Hargobind and Harirai. Meditate then on revered Hari Krishan on seeing whom all suffering vanishes. Think then of Tegh Bahadur, remembrance of whom brings all nine treasures. He comes to rescue everywhere. Then of the tenth lord, revered Guru Gobind Singh, who comes to rescue everywhere. The embodiment of the light of all ten sovereign lordships, the Guru Granth Sahib—think of the view and reading of it and say, "Waheguru (Wondrous Destroyer of darkness)". Meditating on the achievement of the dear and truthful ones, including the five beloved ones, the four sons of the tenth Guru, forty liberated ones, steadfast ones, constant repeaters of the Divine Name, those given to assiduous devotion, those who repeated the Nam, shared their fare with others, ran free kitchen, wielded the sword and overlooked faults and shortcomings, say "Waheguru", O Khalsa.

Meditating on the achievement of the male and female members of the Khalsa who laid down their lives in the cause of dharma (religion and righteousness), got their bodies dismembered bit by bit, got their skulls sawn off, got mounted on spiked wheels, got their bodies sawn, made sacrifices in the service of the shrines (gurdwaras), did not betray their faith, sustained their adherence to the Sikh faith with sacred unshorn hair uptil their last breath say, "Wondrous Destroyer of darkness", O Khalsa.

Thinking of the five thrones (seats of religious authority) and all gurdwaras, say, "Wondrous Destroyer of darkness", O Khalsa.

Now it is the prayer of the whole Khalsa. May the conscience of the whole Khalsa be informed by Waheguru, Waheguru, Waheguru and, in consequence of such remembrance, may total well-being obtain. Wherever there are communities of the Khalsa, may there be divine protection and grace, and ascedance of the supply of needs and of the holy sword, protection of the tradition of grace, victory to the Panth, the succour of the holy sword, ascedance of the Khalsa. Say, O Khalsa, "Wondrous Destroyer of darnkess".

Unto the Sikhs the gift of the Sikh faith, the gift of the untrimmed hair, the gift of the disciple of their faith, the gift of sense of discrimination, the gift of truest, the gift of confidence, above all, the gift of meditation on the Divine and bath in the Amritsar (holy tank at Amritsar). May hymns-singing missionary parties, the flags, the hostels, abide from age to age. May righteousness reign supreme. Say, "Wondrous Destroyer of darkness". May the Khalsa be imbued with humility and high wisdom! May Waheguru guard its understanding!

O immortal being, eternal helper of Thy Panth, benevolent Lord, bestow on the Khalsa the beneficence of unobstructed visit to the free management of the Nankana Sahib and other shrines and places of the Guru from which the panth have been separated.

O Thou, the honour of the humble, the strength of the weak, aid unto those who have none to rely on, True Father, Wondrous Destroyer of darkness, we humbly render to you (mention here the name of the scriptural composition that has been recited or, in appropriate terms, the object for which the congregation has been held.)

Pardon any impermissible acceretions, omissions, errors mistakes.. Fulfil the purposes of all.

Grant us the association of those dear ones, on meeting whom one is reminded of Your Name. O Nanak, may the Nam (Holy) be ever in ascendance! In Thy will may the good of all prevail!

(a) On the conclusion of the Ardas, the entire congregation participating in the Ardas should respectfully genuflect before the revered Guru Granth, then stand up and call out, "The Khalsa is of the Wondrous Destroyer of darkness; victory also is His". The congregation should, thereafter, raise the loud spirited chant of Sat Sri Akal (True is the Timeless Being).

(b) While the Ardas is being performed, all men and women in the congregation should stand with hands folded. The person in attendance of the Guru Granth should keep waving the whisk standing.

(c) The person who performs the Ardas should stand facing the Guru Granth with hands folded. If the Guru Granth is not there, the performing of theArdas facing any direction is acceptable.

(d) When any special Ardas for and on behalf of one or more persons is offered, it is not necessary for persons in the congregation other than that person or those persons to stand up.

Rehat Maryada: Section Three

The congregation for understanding of and reflecting on Gurbani

Article V

(a) One is more easily and deeply affected by gurbani (the holy bani bequathed by the Gurus) participating in congregational gatherings. For this reason, it is necessary for a Sikh that he visits the places where the sikhs congregate for worship and prayer (the gurudwaras), and joining the congregation, partake of the benefits that the study of the holy scriptures bestows.

(b) The Guru Granth should be ceremonially opened in the gurdwara every day without fail. Except for special exigencies, when there is need to keep the Guru Granth open during the night, the Holy Book should not be kept open during the night.

It should, generally, be closed ceremonially after the conclusion of the Rehras (evening scriptural recitation). The Holy Book should remain open so long as a granthi or attendant can remain in attendance, persons seeking darshan (seeking a view of or making obeisance to it) keep coming, or there is no risk of commission of irreverence towards it. Thereafter, it is advisable to close it ceremonially to avoid any disrespect to it.

(c) The Guru Granth should be opened, read and closed ceremonially with reverence. The place where it is installed should be absolutely clean. An awing should be erected above. The Guru Granth Sahib should be placed on a cot measuring up to its size and overlaid with absolutely clean mattress and sheets. For proper installation and opening of the Guru Granth, there should be cushions/pillows of appropriate kind etc. and, for covering it, romalas (sheet covers of appropriate size). When the Guru Granth is not being read, it should remain covered with a romal. A whisk, too, should be there.

(d) Anything except the afore-mentioned reverential ceremonies, for instance, such practices as the arti with burning incense and lamps, offering of eatables to Guru Granth Sahib, burning of lights, beating of gongs, etc., is contrary to gurmat (the Guru's way). However, for the perfuming of the place, the use of flowers, incense and scent is not barred. For light inside the room, oil or butter-oil or butter-oil lamps, candles, electric lamps, kerosene oil lamps, etc. may be lighted.

(e) No book should be installed like and at par with the Guru Granth. Worship of any idol or any ritual or activity should not be allowed to be conducted inside the gurdwara. Nor should the festival of any other faith be allowed to be celebrated inside the guruwara. However, it will not be improper to use any occasion or gathering for the propagation of the gurmat (The Guru's way).

(*f*) Pressing the legs of the cot on which the Guru Granth Sahib is installed, rubbing nose against walls and on platforms, held sacred, or massaging these, placing water below the Guru Granth Sahib's seat, making or installing statues, or idols inside the gurduwaras, bowing before the picture of the Sikh Gurus or elders—all these are irreligious self-willed egotism, contrary to gurmat (the Guru's way).

(*g*) When the Guru Granth has to be taken from one place to another, the Ardas should be performed. He/she who carries the Guru Granth on his/her head, should walk barefoot; but when the wearing of shoes is a necessity, no superstitions need be entertained.

(*h*) The Guru Granth Sahib should be ceremonially opened after performing the Ardas. After the ceremonial opening, a hymn should be read from the Guru Granth Sahib.

(*i*) Whenever the Guru Granth is brought, irrespective of whether or not another copy of the Guru Granth has already been installed at the concerned place, every Sikh should stand up to show respect.

(*j*) While going into the gurduwara, one should take off the shoes and clean oneself up. If the feet are dirty or soiled, they should be washed with water.

(*k*) No person, no matter which country, religion or caste he/she belongs to, is debarred from entering the gurduwara for darshan (seeing the holy shrine). However, he/she should not have on his/her person anything, such as tobacco or other intoxicants, which are tabooed by the Sikh religion.

(*l*) The first thing a Sikh should do on entering the gurduwara is to do obeisance before the Guru Granth Sahib. He/she should, thereafter, having a glimpse of the congregation and bid in a low, quite voice, "Waheguru ji ka Khalsa, Waheguru ji ki Fateh".

(*m*) In the congregation, there should be no differentiation or discrimination between sikh and non-Sikh, persons traditionally regarded as touchable and untouchable, the so called high and low caste persons, the high and the low.

(n) Sitting on a cushion, a distinctive seat, a chair, a stool, a cot, etc. or in any distinctive position in the presence of the Guru Granth or within the congregation is contrary to gurmat (Guru's way).

(o) No Sikh should sit bare-headed in the presence of the Guru Granth Sahib or in the congregation. For the Sikh women, joining the congregation with their persons uncomfortable draped and with veils drawn over their faces is contrary to gurmat (Guru's way).

(p) There are five takhts (lit, thrones, fig., seats of high authority) namely:

(i) The holy Akal Takht Amritsar

(ii) The holy Takht, Patna Sahib

(iii) The holy Takht, Kesgarh Sahib, Anandpur

(iv) The holy Takht Hazur Sahib, Nanded

(v) The holy Takht Damdama Sahib, Talwandi Sabo.

(q) Only an Amritdhari (baptized) Sikh man or woman, who faithfully observes the discipline ordained for the baptized Sikhs, can enter the hallowed enclosures of the takhts. (Adras for and on behalf of any Sikh or non-Sikh, except a fallen or punished (tankhahia) Sikh, can be offered at the takhts.

(r) At a high-level site in every gurdwara should be installed the nishan sahib (Sikh flag). The cloth of the flag should be either of xanthic or of greyish blue colour and on top of the flag post, there should either be a spearhead or a Khanda (a straight dagger with convex side edges leading to slanting top edges ending in a vertex).

(s) There should be a drum (nagara) in the gurduwara for beating on appropriate occasions.

5. Kirtan (Devotional Hymn Singing by a Group or an Individual)

Article VI

(a) Only a Sikh may perform kitran in a congregation.

(b) Kirtan means singing and scriptural compositions in traditional musical measures.

(c) In the congregation, kirtan only of Gurbani (Guru Granth' or Guru Gobind Singh's hymns) and, for its elaboration, of the compositions of Bhai Gurdas and Bhai Nand Lal, may be performed.

(d) It is improper, while singing hymns to rhythmic folk tunes or to traditional musical measures, or in team singing, to induct into them improvised and extraneous refrains. Only a line from the hymn should be a refrain.

6. Taking Hukam (Command)

Article VII

(a) Doing obeisance to the Guru Granth Sahib, respectfully, taking a glimpse of the congregation, an embodiment of the Guru's person, and taking the command: these together constitute the view of the Satguru (Immortal destroyer of darkness, the true guru). Raising the drapery covering the Guru Granth Sahib and merely taking a look or making others take a look at the exposed page, without taking the command (reading the prescribed hymn) is contrary to gurmat (Guru's way).

(b) In the course of the congregational sessions, only one thing should be done at a time; performing of kirtan, delivering of discourse, interpretative elaboration of the scriptures, or reading of the scriptures.

(c) Only a Sikh, man or woman, is entitled to be in attendance of the Guru Granth during the congregational session

(d) Only a Sikh may read out from the Guru Granth for others. However, even a non-Sikh may read from it for himself/herself.

(e) For taking the command (Hukam), the hymn that is continuing on the top of the left page must be read from the beginning. If the hymn begins on the previous page, turn over the page and read the whole hymn from the beginning to the end. If the scriptural composition that is continuing on the top of the left hand page is a var (ode), then start from the first of the slokas preceding the pauri and read upto the end of the pauri. Conclude the reading at the end of the hymn with the line in which the name 'Nanak' occurs.

(f) Hukam must also be taken at the conclusion of the congregational session or after the Ardas.

7. Sadharan Path (Completion of Normal Intermittent Reading of the Guru Granth Sahib)

Article VIII

(a) Every Sikh should as far as possible, maintain a separate and exclusive place for the installation of Guru Granth Sahib, in his home.

(b) Every Sikh man, woman, boy or girl, should learn Gurmukhi to be able to read the Guru Granth Sahib.

(c) Every Sikh should take the Hukam (Command) of the Guru Granth in the ambrosial (early), hours of the morning before taking meal. If he/she fails to do that, he/she should read or listen to reading from the Guru Granth some time during the day. If he/she cannot do that either, during travel etc., or owing to any other impediment, he/she should not give into a feeling of guilt.

(d) It is desirable that every Sikh should carry on a continuous reading of the Guru Granth and complete a full reading in one or two months or over a longer period.

(e) While undertaking a full reading of the Guru Granth, one should recite the Anand Sahib (the first five and the last stanzas) and perform the Ardas. One should, thereafter, read the Japuji.

Akhand Path (uninterrupted Non-stop completion of the reading of the Guru Granth Sahib)

Article IX

(a) The non-stop reading of the Guru Granth is carried on at hard times or on occasions of elation or joy. It takes forty-eight hours. The non-stop reading implies continuous uninterrupted reading. The reading must be clear and correct. Reading too fast, so that the person listening in to it cannot follow the contents, amounts to irreverence to the scriptures. The reading should be correct and clear, due care being bestowed on consonant and vowel, even though that takes a little longer to complete.

(b) Whichever family or congregation undertakes the non-stop reading should carry it out itself through its members, relatives, friends, etc., all together. The number of reciters is not prescribed.

If a person himself, cannot read, he should listen into the reading by some competent reader. However, it should never be allowed to happen that the reader carries on the reading all by himself/herself and no member of the congregation or the family is listening into the reading. The reader should be served with food and clothing to the best of the host's means.

(c) Placing a pitcher, ceremonial clarified butter fed lamp, coconut, etc. around, during the course of the uninterrupted or any other reading of Guru Granth Sahib, or reading of other Scriptural texts side by side with or in the course of such reading is contrary to the gurmat (Guru's way).

Commencing the Non-stop Reading

Article X

While undertaking the intermittent reading of the whole Guru Granth Sahib, the sacred pudding (Karhah Prashad) for offering should be brought and after reciting the Anand Sahib (six stanzas) and offering Ardas, Hukam should be taken.

While beginning the unbroken reading, the sacred pudding should first be laid. Thereafter, after reciting, the Anand Sahib (six stanzas), offering the Ardas and taking the Hukam, the reading should be commenced.

Concluding the Reading

Article XI

(a) The reading of the whole Guru Granth Sahib (intermittent or non-stop) may be concluded with the reading of the Mundawani or the Rag Mala according to the convention traditionally observed at the concerned place. (Since there is a difference of opinion within the panth on this issue, nobody should dare to write or print a copy of the Guru Granth Sahib excluding the Rag Mala). Thereafter, after reciting the Anand Sahib, the Ardas of the conclusion of the reading should be offered and the sacred pudding (Karhah Prashad) distributed.

(b) On the conclusion of the reading, offering of draperies, fly whisk and awning, having regard to the requirements of the Guru Granth Sahib, and of other things, for panthic causes should be made to the best of means.

8. Karhah Prashad (Sacred Pudding)

Article XII

(a) Only the sacred pudding which has been prepared or got prepared according to the prescribed method shall be acceptable in the congregation.

(b) The method of preparing the Karhah Prashad is this: In a clean vessel, the three contents (wheat flour, pure sugar and clarified butter, in equal quantities) should be put and it should be made reciting the scriptures. Then covered with a clean piece of cloth, it should be placed on a clean stool in front of the Guru Granth Sahib, the first five and the last stanza of the Anand Sahib should be recited aloud (so that the congregation can hear) [If another vessel of the sacred pudding is brought in after the recitation of the Anand, it is not necessary to repeat the recitation of the Anand Sahib. Offering of the pudding brought later to the sacred Kirpan is enough.], the Ardas, offered and the pudding tucked with the sacred Kirpan for acceptance.

(c) After this, before the distribution to the congregation of the Karhah Prashad, the share of the five beloved ones should be set apart and given away. Thereafter, while commencing the general distribution, the share of the person in attendance of the Guru Granth Sahib should be put in a small bowl or vessel and handed over [giving double share to the person in attendance constitutes improper discrimination.] The person who doles out the Karhah Prashad among the congregation should do so without any discrimination on the basis of personal regard or spite. He should dole out the Karhah Prashad equally to the Sikhs, the non-Sikhs or a person of high or low caste. While doling out the Karhah Prashad, no discrimination should be made on considerations of caste or ancestry or being regarded, by some, as untouchable, of persons within the congregation.

(*d*) The offering of Karhah Prashad should be accompanied by at least two pice in cash.

9. Exposition of Gurbani (Sikh Holy Scriptures)

Article XIII

(*a*) The exposition of the Gurbani in a congregational gathering should be carried out only by a Sikh.

(*b*) The object of the exposition should only be promoting the understanding of the Guru's tenets.

(*c*) The exposition can only be of the ten Gurus writings or utterances, Bhai Gurdas's writings, Bhai Nand Lal's writings or of any generally accepted Panthic book or of books of history (which are in agreement with the Guru's tenents) and not of a book of any other faith. However, for illustration, references to a holy person's teachings or those contained in a book may be made.

Expository Discourse

Article XIV

No discourse contrary to the Guru's tenets should be delivered inside a gurduwara.

Gurduwara Service

Article XV

In the gurdwara the schedule of the congregational service is generally; Ceremonial opening of the Guru Granth Sahib, Kirtan, exposition of scriptures, expository discourses, recitation of Anand Sahib, the Ardas (see Article IV (3) (a), the raising of Fateh slogan and then the slogan Sat Sri Akal and taking the Hukam.

Rehat Maryada: Section Four

10. Living in Consonance with Guru's Tenets

Article XVI

A Sikh's living, earning livelihood, thinking and conduct should accord with the Guru's tenets. The Guru's tenets are:

(a) Worship should be rendered only to the one timeless being and to no god or goddess.

(b) Regarding the ten Gurus, the Guru Granth and the ten Gurus word alone as saviors and holy objects of veneration.

(c) Regarding ten Gurus as the effulgence of one light and one single entity.

(d) Not believing in caste or descent, untouchability, magic, spells, incantation, omens, auspicious times, days and occasions, influence of start, horoscopic dispositions, shradh (ritual serving of food to priests for the salvation of ancestors on appointed days as per the lunar calendar), ancestor worship, khiah (ritual serving of food to priests—Brahmins—on the lunar anniversaries of the death of an ancestor), pind (offering of funeral barley cakes to the deceased's relatives), patal (ritual donation of food in the belief that that would satisfy the hunger of the departed soul), diva (the ceremony of keeping an oil lamp lit for 360 days after the death, in the belief that that lights the path of the deceased), ritual funeral acts, hom (lighting of ritual fire and pouring intermittently clarified butter, food grains etc. into it for propitiating gods for the fulfillment of a purpose) jag (religious ceremony involving presentation of oblations), tarpan (libation), sikha-sut (keeping a tuft of hair on the head and wearing thread), bhadan (shaving of head on the death of parent), fasting on new or full moon or other days, wearing of frontal marks on the forehead, wearing thread, wearing of a necklace of the pieces of tulsi stalk [A plant with medicinal properties], veneration of any graves, of monuments erected to honour the memory of a deceased person or of cremation sites, idolatry and such like superstitions observances. [Most, though not all rituals and ritual or religious observances listed in this clause are Hindu rituals and observances. The reason is that the old rituals and practices, continued to be observed by large numbers of Sikhs even after their conversion from their old to the new faith and a large bulk of the Sikh novices were Hindu converts. Another reason for this phenomenon was the strangle-hold of the Brahmin priest on Hindus secular and religious life which the Brahmin priest managed to maintain even on those leaving the Hindu

religious fold, by his astute mental dexterity and rare capacity for compromise. That the Sikh novitiates include a sizable number of Muslims is shown by inclusion in this clause of the taboos as to the sanctity of graves, shirni, etc.]

Not owning up or regarding as hallowed any place other than the Guru's place—such, for instance, as sacred spots or places of pilgrimage of other faiths.

Not believing in or according any authority to Muslim seers, Brahmins holiness, soothsayers, clairvoyants, oracles, promise of an offering on the fulfillment of a wish, offering of sweet loaves or rice pudding at graves on fulfillment of wishes, the Vedas, the Shastras, the Gayatri (Hindu scriptural prayer unto the sun), the Gita, the Quran, the Bible, etc. However, the study of the books of other faiths for general self-education is admissible.

(e) The Khalsa should maintain its distinctiveness among the professors of different religions of the world, but should not hurt the sentiment of any person professing another religion.

(f) A Sikh should pray to God before launching off any task.

(g) Learning Gurmukhi (Punjabi in Gurmukhi script) is essential for a Sikh. He should pursue other studies also.

(h) It is a Sikh's duty to get his children educated in Sikhism.

(i) A Sikh should, in no way, harbour any antipathy to the hair of the head with which his child is born. He should not temper with the hair with which the child is born. He should add the suffix "Singh" to the name of his son. A Sikh should keep the hair of his sons and daughters intact.

(j) A Sikh must not take hemp (cannabis), opium, liquor, tobacco, in short any intoxicant. His only routine intake should be food.

(k) Piercing of the nose or ears for wearing ornaments is forbidden for Sikh men and women.

(l) A Sikh should not kill his daughter, nor should he maintain any relationship with a killer of daughter.

(m) The true Sikh of the Guru shall make an honest living by lawful work.

(n) A Sikh shall regard a poor person's mouth as the Guru's cash offerings box.

(o) A Sikh should not steal, form dubious associations or engage in gambling.

(p) He who regards another man's daughter as his own daughter, regards another man's wife as his mother, has coition with his own wife alone, he alone is a truly disciplined Sikh of the Guru.

(q) A Sikh shall observe the Sikh rules of conduct and conventions from his birth right upto the end of his life.

(r) A Sikh, when he meets another Sikh, should greet him with "Waheguru ji ka Khalsa, Waheguru ji ki Fateh" [The Khalsa is Waheguru's; victory too is His!]. This is ordained for Sikh men and women both.

(s) It is not proper for a Sikh woman to wear a veil or keep her face hidden by veil or cover.

(t) For a Sikh, there is no restriction or requirement as to dress except for he must wear Kachhehra [A drawer type garment fastened by a fitted string round the waist, very often worn as an underwear] and turban. A Sikh woman may or may not tie turban.

11. Ceremonies Pertaining to Birth and Naming of Child

Article XVII

(a) In a Sikh's household, as soon after the birth of a child as the mother becomes capable of moving about and taking bath (irrespective of the number of days which that takes), the family and relatives should go to a gurduwara with karhah prashad (sacred pudding) or get karhah prashad made in the gurduwara and recite in the holy presence of the Guru Granth Sahib such hymns as "parmeshar dita bana" (Sorath M. 5), "Satguru sache dia bhej" (Asa M. 5) that are expressive of joy and thankfulness. Thereafter if a reading of the holy Guru Granth Sahib had been taken up, that should be concluded. Then the holy Hukam (command) should be taken. A name starting with the first letter of the hymn of the Hukam

(command) should be proposed by the granthi (man in attendance of the holy book) and, after its acceptance by the congregation, the name should be announced by him. The boy's name must have the suffix "Singh" and the girl's the suffix "Kaur".

After that the Anand Sahib (short version comprising six stanzas) should be recited and the Ardas in appropriate terms expressing joy over the naming ceremony be offered and the karhah prashad distributed.

(b) The superstition as to the pollution of food and water in consequence of birth must not be subscribed to (There is a wide-spread belief among certain sections of Indian people that a birth in a household causes pollution (sutak) which is removed by the thorough bathing of the mother, the baby and persons attending on her as also by a thorough cleaning of the house, the utensils and the clothes, after prescribed periods of ten, twenty one and forty days], for the holy writ is: "The birth and death are by his ordinance; coming and going is by His will. All food and water are, in principle clean, for these life-sustaining substances are provided by him".

(c) Making shirts or frocks for children out of the Holy Book's draperies is a sacrilege.

Anand Sanskar (Lit. Joyful Ceremonial: Sikh Matrimonial Conventions and Ceremony)

Article XVIII

(a) A sikh man and woman should enter wedlock without giving thought to the prospective spouse's caste and descent.

(b) A Sikh's daughter must be married to a Sikh.

(c) A Sikh's marriage should be solemnized by Anand marriage rites.

(d) Child marriage is taboo for Sikhs.

(e) When a girl becomes marriageable, physically, emotionally and by virtue of maturity of character, a suitable Sikh match should be found and she be married to him by Anand marriage rites.

(f) Marriage may not be preceded by engagement ceremony. But if an engagement ceremony is sought to be held, a congregational gathering should be held and, after offering the ardas before the Guru Granth Sahib, a kirpan, a steel bangle and some sweets may be tendered to the boy.

(g) Consulting horoscopes for determining which day or date is auspicious or otherwise for fixing the day of the marriage is a sacrilege. Any day that the parties find suitable by mutual consultation should be fixed.

(h) Putting on floral or gilded face ornamentation, decorative headgear or red thread bands round the wrist, worshipping of ancestors, dripping feet in milk mixed with water, cutting a berry or jandi (Prosopis spicigera) bushes, filling pitcher, ceremony of retirement in feigned displeasure, reciting couplets, performing havens [sacrificial fire], installing vedi (a wooden canopy or pavilion under which Hindu marriages are performed), prostitutes dances, drinking liquor, are all sacrileges.

(i) The marriage party should b as small number of people as the girl's people desire. The two sides should greet each other singing sacred hymns and finally by the Sikh greeting of Waheguru ji ka Khalsa, Waheguru ji ki Fateh.

(j) For marriage, there should be a congregational gathering in the holy presence of Guru Granth Sahib. There should be hymn-singing by ragis or by the whole congregation. Then the girl and boy should be made to sit facing the Guru Granth Sahib. The girl should sit on the left side of the boy. After soliciting the congregation's permission, the master of the marriage ceremony (who may be a man or woman) should bid the boy and girl and their parents or guardians to stand and should offer the Ardas for the commencement of the Anand marriage ceremony.

The officiant should then appraise the boy and girl of the duties and obligations of conjugal life according to the Gurus tenets.

He should initially give to the two an exposition of their common mutual obligations. He should tell them how to model the husband-wife relationship on the love between the individual soul and the Supreme

Soul in the light of the contents of circumbulation (lavan) hymns in the Suhi measure (rag) section of the Guru Granth Sahib.

He should explain to them the notion of the state of "a single soul in two bodies" to be achieved through love and make them see how they may attain union with the Immortal Being discharging duties and obligations of the householders life. Both of them, they should be told, have to make their conjugal union a means to the fulfillment of the purpose of the journey of human existence; both have to lead clean and Guru-oriented lives through the instrumentality of their union. He should then explain to the boy and girl individually their respective conjugal duties as husband and wife. The bridegroom should be told that the girl's people having chosen him as the fittest match from among a whole lot, he should regard his wife as his better half, accord to her unflinching love and share with her all that he has. In all situations, he should protect her person and honour, he should be completely loyal to her.

Reht Maryada: Section Five

12. Voluntary Service

Article XXI

Voluntary service is a prominent part of Sikh religion. Illustrative models of voluntary service are organised, for imparting training, in the gurduwaras. Its simple forms are: sweeping and plastering the floors of the gurduwara [In olden times, buildings, particularly in rural areas had mud and not brick paved or cement floors. To give to these floors firmness and consistency, they were thinly plastered with a diluted compound of mud], serving water to or fanning the congregation, offering provisions to and rendering any kind of service in the common kitchen-cum-eating house, dusting the shoes of the people visiting the gurduwara, etc.

(a) Guru's kitchen-cum-Eating house. The philosophy behind the Guru's kitchen-cum-eating house is two fold: to provide training to the Sikhs in voluntary service and to help banish all distinction of high and low, touchable and untouchable from the Sikhs minds.

(b) All human beings, high or low, and or any caste or colour may sit and eat in the Guru's kitchen-cum-eating house. No discrimination on grounds of the country of origin, colour, caste or religion must be made while making people sit in rows for eating. However, only baptized Sikhs can eat off one plate.

Rehat Maryada: Section Six

13. Facets of Corporate Sikh Life

Article XXII

The essential facets of Panthic life are:

1. Guru Panth (the Panth's Guru status);
2. The ceremony of ambrosial initiation;
3. The statute of chastisement for aberrations;
4. The statute of collective resolution;
5. The appeal against local decisions.

Panth's Status of Guruhood

Article XXIII

The concept of service is not confined to fanning the congregation, service to and in the common kitchen-cum-eating house, etc. A Sikh's entire life is a life of benevolent exertion. The most fruitful service is the service that secures the optimum good by minimal endeavour. That can be achieved through organised collective action. A Sikh has, for this reason, to fulfil his Panthic obligations (obligations as a member of the corporate entity, the Panth), even as he/she performs his/her individual duties. This corporate entity is the Panth. Every Sikh has also to fulfil his obligations as a unit of the corporate body, the Panth.

(a) The Guru Panth (Panth's status of Guruhood) means the whole body of committed baptized Sikhs. This body was fostered by all the ten Gurus and the tenth Guru gave it its final shape and invested it with Guruhood.

Ceremony of Baptism or Initiation

Article XXIV

(a) Ambrosial baptism should be held at an exclusive place away from common human traffic.

(b) At the place where ambrosial baptism is to be administered, the holy Guru Granth Sahib should be installed and ceremonially opened. Also present should be six committed baptized Sikhs, one of whom should sit in attendance of the Guru Granth Sahib and the other five should be there to

administer the ambrosial baptism. These six may even include Sikh women. All of them must have taken bath and washed their hair.

(c) The five beloved ones who administer ambrosial baptism should not include a disabled person, such as a person who is blind or blind in one eye, lame, one with a broken or disabled limb, or one suffering from some chronic disease. The number should not include anyone who has committed a breach of the Sikh discipline and principles. All of them should be committed baptized Sikhs with appealing personalities.

(d) Any man or woman of any country, religion or caste who embraces Sikhism and solemnly undertakes to abide by its principles is entitled to ambrosial baptism. The person to be baptized should not be of very young age; he or she should have attained a plausible degree of discretion. The person to be baptized must have taken bath and washed the hair and must wear all five K's— Kesh (unshorn hair), strapped Kirpan (sword), Kachhehra (prescribed shorts), Kanga (comb tucked in the tied up hair), Karha (steel bracelet). He/she must not have on his/her person any token of any other faith. He/she must not have his/her head bare or be wearing a cap. He/she must not be wearing any ornaments piercing through any part of the body. The persons to be baptized must stand respectfully with hands folded facing the Guru Granth Sahib.

(e) Anyone seeking to be rebaptized, having committed an aberration, should be singled out and the five beloved ones should award chastisement to him/her in the presence of the congregation.

(f) One from amongst the five beloved ones administering ambrosial baptism to persons seeking to be baptized should explain the principles of the Sikh religion to them:

The Sikh religion advocated the renunciation of the worship of any created thing, and rendering of worship and loving devotion to, and meditating on, the one Supreme Creator. For the fulfillment of such devotion and meditation, reflection on the contents of Gurbani and practicing of its tenets, participation in the congregational services, rendering service to the Panth, benevolent exertion (to promote the good of others), love of God's name (loving reflection on the experience of the Divine), living within the Sikh discipline after getting baptized etc. are the principal means.

He should conclude his exposition of the principles of Sikh religion with the query: Do you accept these willingly?

(g) On an affirmative response from the seekers of baptism, one from amongst the five beloved ones should perform the Ardas for the preparation of baptism and take the holy Hukam (command). The five beloved ones should come close to the bowl for preparing the amrit (ambrosial nectar).

(h) The bowl should be of pure steel and it should be placed on a clean steel ring or other clean support.

(i) Clean water and sugar puffs should be put in the bowl and the five beloved ones should sit around it in bir posture [Sitting in bir posture comprises sitting resting the body on the right leg, the right calf and foot gathered inward and the left leg upto the shin kept in a vertical position] and recite the undermentioned scriptural compositions.

(j) The scriptural composition to be recited are: The Japuji, the Jaap, The Ten Sawayyas (commencing with sarawag sud), The Bainti Chaupai (from "hamri karo hath dai rachha" to "susht dokh te leho bachai"), the first five and the last one stenza of the Anand Sahib.

(k) Each of the five beloved ones who recites the scripture should hold the edge of the bowl with his left hand and keep stirring the water with a double-edged sword held in his right hand. He should do that with full concentration. The rest of the beloved ones should keep gripping the edge of the bowl with both hands concentrating their full attention on the ambrosial nectar.

(l) After the conclusion of the recitation, one from amongst the beloved ones should perform the Ardas.

(m) Only that person seeking to be baptized who has participated in the entire ceremony of ambrosial baptism can be baptized. One who has turned up while the ceremony was in progress cannot be baptized.

(*n*) After the Ardas as per clause (1) above, thinking of our Father, the tenth Master, the wearer of the aigrette, every person seeking to be baptized should sit in bir posture, putting his/her right hand cupped on the left cupped hand and be made to drink the ambrosial mix five times, as the beloved one who pours the mix into his cupped hand exclaims: say, Waheguru ji ka Khalsa, Waheguru ji ki Fateh! (The Khalsa is of the Wondrous Destroyer of darkness; victory too, is His!) The person being baptized should after imbibing the ambrosia, repeat: Waheguru ji ka Khalsa, Waheguru ji ki Fateh. Then five handfuls of the ambrosial mix should be sprinkled into the eyes of the person being baptized and another five into his hair. Each such sprinkling should be accompanied by the beloved one administering baptism saying, "Waheguru ji ka Khalsa, Waheguru ji ki Fateh," and the person being baptized repeating the chant. Whatever ambrosial mix is left over after the administration of the ambrosial baptism to all individual seekers, should be sipped by all (men and women) baptized, together.

(*o*) After this the five beloved ones, all together in chorus, communicating the name of Waheguru to all who have been administered the ambrosial baptism, recite to them the mul mantar (basic creed, seminal chant) and make them repeat it aloud; ik aunkar satnam karta purakh nirbhau nirwair akal murat ajuni saibhang gur prasad.

(*p*) After this, one from amongst the five beloved ones should explain to the initiates and discipline of the order: Today you are reborn in the true Guru's household, ending the cycle of migration, and joined the Khalsa Panth (order). Your spiritual father is now Guru Gobind Singh and, spiritual mother, Mata Sahib Kaur. Your place of birth is Kesgarh Sahib and your native place is Anandpur Sahib. You, being the sons of one father, are, inter-se yourselves and other baptized Sikhs, spiritual brothers. You have become the pure Khalsa, having renounced your previous lineage, professional background, calling (occupation) beliefs, that is, having given up all connections with your caste, descent, birth, country, religion, etc. You are to worship none except the one Timeless Being—

no god, goddess, incarnation or prophet. You are not to think of anyone except the ten Gurus and anything except their gospel as your savior. You are supposed to know Gurmukhi (Punjabi alphabet). (If you do not, you must learn it). And recite, or listen into the recitation of, the undermentioned scriptural compositions, the daily repetition of which is ordained, every day: (1) The Japuji Sahib, (2) The Jaap Sahib, (3) The Ten Sawayyas (Quartrains), beginning "sarawag sudh," (4) The Soddar Rahiras and the Sohila. Besides, you should read from or listen into the recitation from the Guru Granth. Have, on your person, all the time, the five K's: The Keshas (unshorn hair), the Kirpan (sheathed sword) [The length of the sword to be worn is not prescribed], the Kachhehra [The Kachhehra (drawers like garment) may be made from any cloth, but its legs should not reach down to below the shins], the Kanga (comb), the Karha (steel bracelet) [The kraha should be of pure steel].

The undermentioned four transgressions (tabooed practices) must be avoided:

1. Dishonouring the hair;
2. Eating the meat of an animal slaughtered the Muslim way;
3. Cohabiting with a person other than one's spouse;
4. Using tobacco.

In the event of the commission of any of these transgressions, the transgressor must get rebaptised. If a transgression is committed unintentionally and unknowingly, the transgressor shall not be liable to punishment. You must not associate with a sikh who had uncut hair earlier and has cut it or a Sikh who smokes. You must ever be ready for the service of the Panth and of the gurduwaras (Sikh places of worship). You must tender one tenth of your earnings to the Guru. In short, you must act the Guru's way in all spheres of activity.

You must remain fully aligned to the Khalsa brotherhood in accordance with the principles of the Khalsa faith. If you commit transgression of the Khalsa discipline, you must present yourself before the congregation and beg pardon, accepting whatever punishment is awarded. You must also resolve to remain watchful against defaults in the future.

(q) The following individuals shall be liable to chastisement involving automatic boycott:

1. Anyone maintaining relations or communion with elements antagonistic to the Panth including the minas (reprobates), the masands (agents once accredited to local Sikh communities as Guru's representatives, sine discredited for their faults and aberrations), followers of Dhirmal or Ram Rai, et. al., or users of tobacco or killers of female infants;
2. One who eats/drinks left-overs of the unbaptised or the fallen Sikhs;
3. One who dyes his beard;
4. One who gives off son or daughter in matrimony for a price or reward;
5. Users of intoxicant (hemp, opium, liquor, narcotics, cocaine, etc.);
6. One holding, or being a party to, ceremonies or practices contrary to the Guru's way;
7. One who defaults in the maintenance of Sikh discipline.

(r) After this sermon, one from among the five beloved ones should perform the Ardas.

(s) Thereafter, the Sikh sitting in attendance of the Guru Granth Sahib should take the Hukam. If anyone from amongst those who have received the ambrosial baptism had not earlier been named in accordance with the Sikh naming ceremony, he should renounce his previous name and be given a new name beginning with the first letter of the Hukam now taken.

(t) And finally, the karhah prashad should be distributed. All the newly launched Sikh men and women should eat the karhah prashad together off the same bowl.

Method of Imposing Chastisement

Article XXV

(a) Any Sikh who has committed any default in the observance of the Sikh discipline should approach the nearby Sikh

congregation and make a confession of his lapse standing before the congregation.

(b) The congregation should them, in the holy presence of Guru Granth Sahib, elect from among themselves five beloved ones who should ponder over the suppliant's fault and propose the chastisement (punishment) for it.

(c) The congregation should not take an obdurate stand in granting pardon. Nor should the defaulter argue about the chastisement. The punishment that is imposed should be some kind of service, especially some service that can be performed with hands.

(d) And finally an Ardas for correction should be performed.

Method of Adopting Gurmatta

Article XXVI

(a) The Gurmatta can only be on a subject that affects the fundamental principles of Sikh religion and for their upholding, such as the questions affecting the maintenance of the status of the Gurus or the Guru Granth Sahib or the inviolability of the Guru Granth Sahib, ambrosial baptism, Sikh discipline and way of life, the identity and structural framework of the Panth. Ordinary issues of religious, educational, social and political nature can be dealt with only in Matta [resolution].

(b) A Gurmatta [Holy resolution] can be adopted only by a select primary Panthic group or a representative gathering of the Panth.

Appeals Against Local Decisions

Article XXVII

An appeal can be made to the Akal Takht against a local congregation's decision.

The Concept of *Hukam* in Sikhism and Religious Experience

It has been observed by the scholars of world religions that a feeling of lowliness, rather nothingness is experienced by those who are confronted with the reality what Rudolf Otto Calls, the Holy or 'mysterium'. It is such an experience which, on the one hand, reduces its subject to naught, while on the other, exalts the object to the level of the 'supreme' or 'all in all'. Such a religious experience in monotheistic religions, is conceived as one amounting to a meeting with God. Numerous examples of this experience can be cited from the Old and New Testaments, from the Holy Qur'an and Bhagwad Gita. The concept of *Hukam* in Sikhism seems, to the present writer, somehow to stem out of such a realization of God. An attempt has been made in this article to show the relationship between the concept of *Hukam* in Sikhism and the religious experience as such.

The first stanza of *Jap-ji* ends with the following questions and its answer.

"How then shall the truth be known?

How the veil of false illusion torn?

O Nanak, thus runneth the writ divine,

Abide by His will and make it thine[1].

The theme is further elucidated in the second stanza as following:

"By Him are all forms created,
By Him infused with life and blessed,
By Him are some to excellence elated,
Others born lowly and depressed
By His writ some have pleasure, others pain,
By His grace some are saved,
Others doomed to die, re-live and die again,
His will encompasseth all, there be none beside".

The concept of Divine ordinance or '*Hukam*' as it is called in the original, running through these verses like a thread, is by no means restricted to this portion of *Jap-ji* only. In fact, it is one of the favourite and major ideas expounded by Guru Nanak and appears as a fundamental element in his religious experience. Numerous verses throughout *Guru Granth Sahib* by Guru Nanak as well as by other Gurus and saints embody the same idea.

At the end of 21st stanza in *Jap-ji Sahib* the experience of the Divine is summed up as follows:

"All I say is: Great is the Lord, great His name;
What He ordains comes to be,
O Nanak, he who sayeth more shall hereafter regret his stupidity".

Stanza 27 ends with these lines:

What He wills He ordains,
To Him no one can an order give,
for He, O Nanak, is the king of kings,
As he wills so we must live".

Many more verses can be added to this effect from *Granth Sahib*, which express the idea of the absolute supremacy of Divine will. These verses contain the elements of a doctrine which is called the doctrine of *Hukam* in Sikh theology.

Hukam, originally an Arabic word, has been used by Guru Nanak in a specialized sense giving this word much more extended and comprehensive connotation than it has in the original.

According to the verses quoted above, *Hukam* is the mystery underlying the phenomena giving rise to the multiplicity which is to be observed in the universe[2].

Sometimes, one is tempted to feel that a man is poor, because he is born of poor parents. Or he is able to receive good education because he was born in a prosperous family. But indeed, such an observation would be based on a facile perception of relationship between the 'cause' and 'effect'. Indeed, it is only a deep insight into the secret of *Hukam* which can provide an understanding of the Divine scheme controlling the universe. According to Guru Nanak, it is Divine will which is responsible for all the apparent contradictions. It is divine will which has put everything the way it is. It is divine ordinance or *Hukam* according to which all sentient or insentient beings have to traverse the course of their existence. Good and evil, happiness and misery, ignorance and enlightenment, ugliness and beauty are there because the Lord wants them to be like that. This concept of the divine rule working in every particle and every incident of the universe is precisely what is meant by the doctrine of *Hukam*.

In our ordinary consciousness we may have a feeling that there is some other power working through the events which supersedes our own desires and will, but it is only when the experience of *Hukam* becomes a fully realized fact of life that the true knowledge is achieved. It is only when such a person seeing the working of *Hukam* in every part of the universe completely surrenders himself to the will of God, that the 'veil of false illusion is torn'. It should be clear, however, that a complete and comprehensive understanding of the nature of *Hukam* is more than what any human consciousness can grasp. *Hukam* being part of the divine mystery, is an eternal abyss which no man can fathom[3].

Such an insight into the nature of the universe is by no means confined to the spiritual experience of Guru Nanak. In fact an overwhelming consciousness of a spiritual order of the universe is a necessary corollary of different types of religious experiences. While in Hinduism it may be expressed through the doctrine of rita (ऋत) and *Karama*, it is indistinguishable from the experience of the nameless *Tao* in Chinese mysticism.

Tao is all pervading,

And its use is inexhaustible!

Fathomless!
Like the fountainhead of all things.
I do not know whose son it is,
An image of what existed before God[4].

William James under the general title of mysticism in his epoch making book *Varieties of Religious Experience*, mentions 'passivity' as one of the fundamental characteristics of mystical experience. "When the characteristic sort of consciousness once has set", he says, "the mystic feels as if his own will were in abeyance, and indeed sometimes as if he were grasped and held by a superior power"[5]. Thus, he tends to believe it a constituent element of every mystical experience to realize the fact that there is some other, much stronger will or power existing in the universe. It is, however, particularly in the mysticism of devotional type that we find the concept of divine will most emphasized. Islam, one of the foremost monotheistic religions, has stressed this experience to such an extent that it can be said to be considerably obsessed by the idea of the supremacy of the divine will. Though plenty of verses containing this idea can be quoted from the Qur'an, yet I would like to cite an example from *sufi* literature which has an overtone of the devotional element in it. On the authority of Qushayri, R.C. Zaehner has cited a story about Abul Qasim Junaid of Baghdad, one of the patriarchs of sufism, in his book, *Hindu and Muslim Mysticism*, while still a young man, Junaid happened to be present in the company of the Shaykhs in Mecca. The Shaykhs who were discussing about love at that moment, asked Junaid about his opinion on the subject. "He cast down his head and tears began to flow. Then he said: (The lover is) a servant (of God) who departs from himself who cleaves to the recollection of his Lord, who undertakes to discharge his duty towards him, who contemplates him in his heart, whose heart has been set ablaze by the light of his essence (*huwiyya*)……And if he speaks, it is by god (that he speaks), and if he makes public discourse, it is of God (that he discourses) and if he is active, it is by God's command, and if he is silent, it is with god; and he (exists) through God, belongs to God, and (dwells) with God"[6]. Here again we find the same element which William James has described as being held and grasped by a superior power, which is God in this case, to the extent that the individual will is completely surrendered.

Among most of the mystics of devotional temperament we find that the ideals of poverty, chastity and obedience are emphasised[7]. These three concepts are but three aspects of the same consciousness, awakened as a result of mystical intuition, that the personal ego or individual self is only a tiny little part of a whole cosmic scheme. The realization by an individual of his being small in the grand divine plan, removes a fundamental ignorance of the ego, namely, the tendency of every ego to regard itself as the centre of the universe. Such a mystical intuition results in a feeling that it is only as a part of the whole organisation that an individual can be of any value. The mystic also realizes that as a small particle of the universe he belongs to the organiser who sustains and directs the whole show. He has to submit himself completely in order to be used wherever he is wanted, specially when he also perceives that revolt against the Divine will is of no avail. There is One and only One who is being obeyed, willingly or unwillingly, by everything in the universe. In such a situation relief can be achieved only through an unconditional surrender, a surrender of all personal desires and tendencies of the self to set up a small universe of its own. Evelyn Underhill has summed up the essence of spiritual life in subordinating all other interests to this single fact. "He made us in order to use us, and use us in the most profitable way for His purpose, not ours"[8].

It was this intuitive spark about the supra-rational structure of the universe, enflamed into a mystical vision, which made Guru Nanak see the nature of things as they really are, and thus his utterances which are the foundation of the doctrine of *Hukam* in Sikhism.

It is important to note here the difference between a scientific materialistic theory of pre-destination and spiritual experience of God's will ruling over the cosmos. It is not unusual to confuse both the concepts as one and the same. The concept of materialistic pre-destination is usually understood to imply that since everything in the phenomena has a cause behind it, whatever we are and whatever happens to us has many links of causal connections behind it. Therefore, whatever choices we make, thinking ourselves free in making our choices, are conditioned by our heredity, upbringing and other factors in which we did not have any choice. Such a view of pre-destination reduces all existence and activity, ultimately, to the natural laws which are inherent in all the manifestations of nature. This is a mechanical view of pre-destination which leaves no room for man's free will, everything being determined by natural laws.

A gross mistake is made when the spiritual experience of Divine ordinance or *Hukam* working through the universe, is understood in terms of the materialistic concept of cold blooded determinism. This is a view of pre-destination which is rooted in the philosophical thinking. It has been converted into a scientific religious theory from a materialistic one by substituting God or the supernatural as the 'head of the State' rather than the natural laws[9].

The genuine religious pre-destination, such as the concept of *Hukam* in Sikhism, originates from a spiritual experience rather than from an intellectual speculation. A spiritual experience is qualitatively different from intellectual reasoning; the former being based on a direct experience while the latter relying on an indirect knowledge from deduction or induction.

If we look for precisely that element in religious experience which is the source for the intuition of pre-destination we find that it is no other than what Rudolf Otto has described as 'The creature consciousness' "It is the emotion of a creature, submerged and overwhelmed by its own nothingness in contrast to that which is supreme above all creatures"[10]. It is the feeling which arises in man when he confronts the 'mysterium tremendum', which is described as aweful and extremely fascinating at the same time. The individual will is reduced to nothingness in the presence of the 'Numen'. The transcendent is experienced so overpoweringly that the subject is almost annihilated and submerged in it. Was this feeling intensified and truly experienced which made Guru Nanak exclaim, "Great is the Lord, Great His name; what He ordains comes to be"[11]. Abraham when attempting to plead to God for the people of Sodom could not but express himself in these words "Behold now, I have taken upon me to speak unto the Lord, which *am but* dust and ashes" (Gen. 18:27).

It would be a misunderstanding to regard the religious experience of divine ordinance as not allowing any free will to man. In fact, it is precisely in contrast to the free will of man that the supremacy of Divine will stands out so prominently. The verses like "He who hath the pride of power, let him try and see", in *Jap-ji* refer to the same fact that though man has an independent will and can exert it, yet it is naught and futile in comparison to the divine will. In the concept of *Hukam* in Sikhism, man is active but God is active too, the latter having infinite supremacy over man. It was in the background of such a concept of *Hukam* that Guru Nanak preached that man can be liberated only by merging his individual will into the will of God.

Thus, we understood that the doctrine of *Hukam* is fundamentally different from a materialistic view of pre-destination. The doctrine of *Hukam* is a necessary outcome of the religious experience of Guru Nanak in the same way as an insight into the spiritual order of the universe is present in other religious traditions particularly the monotheistic ones. The concept of *Hukam* necessarily entails free will of man.

REFERENCES

1. Vinobabhave, *Commentary on Jap-ji*, Panjabi University, Patiala, 1973. All quotations from Japji are from this book.
2. Gurubachan Singh Talib, *Guru Nanak His Personality and Vision*, Gurdas Kapur and Sons, Delhi, 1969, p. 147.
3. W.H. Meleod, *Guru Nanak and Sikh Religion*, Oxford University Press, London, 1968, p. 260.
4. Lin Yutang. *The Wisdom of China*, Michael Joseph Ltd. London, 1949, p. 29.
5. William James, *Varieties of Religious Experience,* New American Library, N.Y. 1958, p. 293.
6. R.C. Zaehner, *Hindu and Muslim Mysticism*, The Athlone Press, London, 1960, p. 138.
7. Evelyn Underhill, *Mysticism,* Methuen and Co., London, 1960, p. 205.
8. Evelyn Underhill, *Spiritual Life*. Hodder and Stoughton, London, 1961.
9. Rudolf Otto, *The Idea of the Holy,* Unwin Brothers, Old Working Surrey, 1959, p. 103.
10. *Ibid.,* p. 24.
11. Vinobabhave *op. cit.,* The last line of the 21st stanza.

Sikh Politics in India

India's internal and external affairs have been and still are strongly influenced by her emigrant communities (Tinker 1974 and 1976). Although such a situation is not unique to South Asia, and recent turmoil in India's Punjab and the influence and reactions by overseas Sikhs is indicative of how expatriates can exert leverage on and be influenced by the affairs in their land of origin. As international travel and communications become more efficient, and as the immigration stream to the West is dominated by the politically aware and highly educated, the migrant factor will become increasingly important in the domestic and international affairs of both sending and receiving countries.

The situation of India's Sikhs is a case in point: emigrant influence has contributed to and been affected by the turmoil in India's Punjab. An examination of overseas Sikh behaviour in connection with the recent political unrest provides clues to the linkages and influences expatriate communities have on the external and internal affairs of their land of origin. This factor has not been considered adequately in current political analysis.

The last several years have been times of tumult for India's Sikh. Violence has been continually reported, as waves of assassinations and counter murders between Sikhs and Hindus dominate Indian newspapers. On June 5, 1984, the Sikh's most sacred shrine, the Akal Takht, and other buildings around the Golden Temple of Amritsar were attacked by

India's armed forces on a day when pilgrims crowded the premises. On October 31, 1984, Indira Gandhi, Prime Minister of India, was assassinated by two of her trusted Sikh body guards. Recriminatory violence followed; vicious atrocities were committed on members of the Khalsa Sikh community, who were viciously beaten, tortured and burned by mobs in Delhi as police and army personnel passively looked on.

What was and is happening in India's Punjab and in Delhi is not confined to that region. In this context, statements such as Pran Chopra's reference to expatriate Sikhs as "fools, knaves and buffoons" (Chopra 1985: 337) and overseas influence being condemned by such notables as Khushwant Singh seem incongruous. In Vancouver, Canada one finds bumper stickers that state, "I love Bhindranwale". In fact, until his death, Sant Jarnail Singh Bhindranwale was considered a "potent source of terrorism on Canadian soil" (Baber 1986). After Airlines Flight 182 vanished from the skies on June 23, 1985, *Time Magazine* reported that the Royal Canadian Mounted Police would soon arrest those responsible from members of the Vancouver Sikh community.

When Mrs. Gandhi was assassinated, Sikhs in the U.S. were shown on national television drinking champagne. In Sydney, Australia, divisions developed among Sikhs over what was happening in India; while in England, debate took place as to whether the visiting religious figure Maharajah Darshan Das[1] was a plant by the Indian government to split the emigrant community, or a sincere preacher of love and reconciliation.

Many believe that India's emigrant Sikhs contribute to the unrest. There are, however, many endogenously based reasons for the political disruption taking place in India's Punjab. Increased concentration of wealth in the hands of a few; small farmers losing their land; the development of a young, educated but unemployed element; the rise of Hindu chauvinism; emigrant remittances; fear of being absorbed by Hindus; and Mrs. Gandhi's communal emphasis to maintain political power are all contributing factors (Jeffrey 1986; Leaf 1985; Nayar and Singh 1984; Singh, A. 1985; Singh and Malik 1985; Wallace 1986). The overseas Sikh community has influenced the situation faced by Sikhs in India, but analyses of the current crisis have neglected the role of the emigrant element (Leaf 1985; Nayar and Singh 1984; Singh, A. 1985; Singh and Malik 1985; Wallace 1986). As a result, this article focuses on the influence emigration and emigrants have on the current situation in India by setting forth three aspects; the effects of emigration on Punjab, the actual involvement of Sikh emigrants in Punjabi society, and the reasoning why emigrants remains involved in the situation of their home region.

Sikh Emigration and Punjab

Punjab has a tradition of emigration. The lead is fertile, but population density has made it necessary for people to emigrate; and the British rulers encouraged that behaviour pattern. Sikh soldiers were loyal to the British Raj during the Mutiny in 1857. As a result, Sikhs were favoured by their rulers and became a prominent part of Britain's armed forces. Sikh contingents developed in almost every corner of the empire. As they learned of opportunities across the seas, they took advantage of them by emigrating. Canada, the United Kingdom and the United States were dominant recipient countries, but Australia, Malaysia and other parts of the world had communities of Khalsa members also. Now, 8 to 10 per cent of the total world Sikh population of nearly 15 million live outside of India (Singh, I. 1986:3), and a third of those living in India reside outside Punjab.

What influence does this have on Punjab and on the Sikh situation there? One way to understand the situation is to look at Jandiali, a Sikh village in Punjab (discussed extensively in Helweg 1986). This village of 1703 individuals is located in the heart of the Jullundur Doab of Punjab, a high emigration area. In 1971, 515 of 1605 people lived abroad; a decade later, it was 923 of 1703. What effect did this have on Jandiali? Like the rest of Punjab, Jandiali received a great deal of capital from her expatriates. Money enabled the local residents to live better, invest in machinery, obtain and use new varieties of seeds and gain new ideas from abroad. With the outflow of people, pressure on the land decreased and there was more produced for few numbers.

Jandiali now reflects the prosperity of Punjab. The state has the second highest produce per acre of wheat and rice of any place in the world and five times the Indian average. It boasts the highest per capita rural income of India, provides 73 per cent of India's wheat for agricultural labour and has the highest number of banking offices per 100,000. Punjab is the bread basket of the country. Its high productivity is crucial for India's self-sufficiency in food grains. M.J. Akbar's description of Punjab also fits the village of Jandiali; he states:

> There were more advertisements for television sets and video-cassette-recorders in the Punjab in 1984 than in any other state of India. Hoarding and banners in profusion sold every consumer product on the Indian market; it was a startling visual confirmation of the fact that the state of Punjab no longer belonged to the Third World, where most of the rest of India still was. There were no mud huts in the villages; it was all brick and stone. The people worked hard; the fields were rich; water came streaming down from the nearby Himalayas; new strains of seed and fertilizers had turned this into the granary of India. If any one part of the country could be called a success story, this was it (Akbar 1985:103).

Although statistics are lacking, there is no doubt the remittances contributed to this prosperity. India's emigrants remitted 1.8 billion dollars (Rs. 2774.5 crores) in 1983-84[2] with an average of $200 million a year going to Punjab (Jeffrey 1986:35). Punjab's prosperity is linked fundamentally with this supply of external capital.

Money, however, does not necessarily bring social stability. One effect of remittances is inflation. In Jandiali the price of land rose as did the cost of services[3]. Those who had contacts abroad could compete in the village economy. Those who did not have overseas money had to accept a lower living standard or leave. Outflow was so extensive that by 1981 Jandiali was a ghost village. Relatives or hired managers commuted from Phagwara (three miles away) to manage land owned by emigrants. Emigrants provided money so that their family and representatives could buy or keep land, but for middle and lower income families without help from abroad, inflation made remaining in Jandiali impossible.

Next, social tensions developed in the village—the traditional leadership was challenged by the emigrant group. Those affiliated with emigrant money dictated how revenues were spent. For example, the emigrant faction wanted a new gurdwara with a tower so high that the city of Phagwara three miles away could be seen from its loft[4]. The traditional ruling family wanted their family gurdwara to be remodeled. After a bitter conflict, both goals were met. Morning prayers are now broadcast from two buildings to herald a new day.

Eventually prominent families had to have members emigrate to keep their position—their present income could not keep up with the inflation. Those who did not arrange for money to be remitted from abroad soon lost positions or prominence, as those with emigrant influence took over. Also, a disparity between the rich and the poor developed. The rich with emigrant connections could buy land, invest, and maintain a good standard of living, others could not. The middle class element began to decline—the rich became richer and the poor became poorer.

Immigrants from neighbouring states entered to work the land and were paid well, but their numbers were limited so that only those land owners with external support could pay current wages. Thus, a cadre in the village had to leave or remain unemployed; many left, emigrating to the Middle East or moving to the cities.

The school system in Jandiali was good, as emigrant money helped build the buildings and finance teachers. The poor as well as the rich were educated. As the poorer children became educated, their family land was in the process of being usurped by the rich; but in either case, they preferred jobs suitable to their education, most of which were in the city. Since Punjab is an agriculturally based economy, the number of jobs to the educated is limited and an unemployed but dissatisfied educated contingent developed.

In Jandiali the investment exceed production. Emigrants sent back much money which enabled farmers to mechanize and invest heavily in machinery and technology. Although more research is needed, I suspect that the money spent was not getting a sufficient return to warrant the investment. To illustrate, Jandiali had 22 tractors to till her 646 acres. Tractors in Jandiali did hire out, but the figure is indicative of an investment above that warranted by the output, possibly 20 times the amount. Part of the reason for excessive tractors is that they are a prestige item. When a surplus is obtained, people initially spend on food and immediate needs. Soon thereafter they focus on conspicuous consumption. Then they start investing in areas that will benefit the general economy.

Loss of talent was another problem. Many of the skilled trades people such as electricians, carpenters, and masons emigrated to the Middle East. Although the shortage was being felt, in Jandiali, the problem was more noticeable in cities like Phagwara and Chandigarh. Although more research needs to be done, it is likely that Jandiali reflects much of Punjab. Lessons from Jandiali's experience indicate that remittances and emigration can benefit an area but can also create problems (Helweg 1983, 1986).

Like Jandiali, Punjab as a state developed what I term an "external economy"—that is, the economic survival of the community is dependent on the influx of outside capital. One of the major questions not being asked is whether the productivity warranted the investment. Emigrants planned to return and assumed that in the long term their capital would provide for them in their twilight years. The prosperity was an illusion[5]. External money contributed to a plantation economy developing in Punjab. Landless agricultural labourers have risen from 17 per cent of the population in 1961 to 38.26 per cent in 1981. As land in production increased, jobs did not proportionately increase, wealth became concentrated in fewer hands. Ten per cent of the rural households now own 76 per cent of the agricultural wealth. Small farmers are being displaced, leaving a significant educated and dissatisfied element in the society. Immigrants from other states are being hired at cheaper wages than local workers, and since the Central Government will not grant permits to develop industry, a large urban unemployed cadre is developing. Also, without industry, the money in Punjab is being invested outside the state or being spent on conspicuous consumption (Gujral 1985; Singh, I, 1966:1, 135, 136).

Iqbal Singh sums up the situation well when he states:

> Despite Punjab's highest per capita income in India and a long list of enviable economic and social indicators, a sizable portion of its population lives under poverty level (between 30 and 45 per cent). Unemployment rose eight to ten times between 1966 and 1981. Area tilled per labourer dropped from 2.23 to 1.5 acres between 1961 and 1981. Forty five per cent of the land holders in Punjab own less than five acres of farm land and an average household consists of a little over five members. Of these sixty nine per cent were forced to liquidate their holdings between 1976 and 1981 for various reasons, economic non-viability being one of them. Overall, in the same period 31.78 per cent of all land holdings was absorbed into larger farms… In the light of Punjab's limited industrial base, its capacity to absorb these numbers is minimal (Singh, I. 1986:8).

Emigration helped Punjab become the most prosperous state in India. As one looks at the general situation and statistics like average income and gross productivity, one can understand why Mrs. Gandhi was reluctant to give more permits for industry and expand the water share for the state. Statistics, however, do not reveal the social situation. As a result, many wonder why this prosperous region is in social turmoil[6]. It is a lesson that most still have not learned—social affluence does not necessarily bring social stability. Emigration contributed greatly to Punjabi and Sikh prosperity but has its costs.

Although not part of Jandiali's story, there is another phenomenon developing in India which reflects on the situation—the emigrant is becoming the scape goat for India's ills. Some feel that when emigrants return to India, they are "square pegs in round holes" (Kabra 1976:12). A September, 1983 issue of *India Today* referred to emigrants as non-resident gods. In India, those Sikhs residing outside of Punjab are generally against the Khalistan movement because they are victims of Hindu reprisals. It is better to blame outsiders for social troubles than cause dissension in the community in India. Thus, one Sikh in Delhi summarized the view of many when he said, 'The Sikh abroad cause the trouble, give the money to terrorist and we pay the price". It is not surprising that blame goes to the expatriate community for the current problems.

Emigrant Involvement in Sikh Politics

Emigrant involvement in India's internal affairs is nothing new for Indian in general or Sikh in particular. For the Sikhs, it started at the turn of the century when Sardars (Sikhs) in Canada and the United States learned that Britain, the country they held in high esteem for fairness and loyalty, would not support them in their fight against racial discrimination on the West Coast of North America. Sikhs suffered discrimination and violence in the early 1900[7]. Also, Canada, with the consent of London and Calcutta, cancelled Indian rights of immigration even though Indians were British subjects. The United States soon followed suit. To combat their plight on the West Coast, the Vancouver Sikhs formed the Khalsa Diwan Society in 1907 which fought to safeguard economic interests and contest cases against immigration authorities. In California, the Sikh Diwan began publishing papers in Gurmukhi (the Sikh language), Urdu and English. Sikhs were prominent in the Indian emigrant drive to obtain rights in India as well as their country of residence. Lala Har Dayal, with the financial backing from a wealthy Sikh farmer Jwala Singh, organised the Sikh immigrants in Stockton, California under the banner of the Hindustani Workers of the Pacific Coast. They published a weekly paper called *Ghadar* (meaning revolutionary); they became known as the Ghadar Party. Copies of the paper were circulated to Indian settlers around the world, including, Canada, Japan, the Philippines, Hong Kong, China, Malaya, Singapore and India. When Sikhs abroad the *Komagata Maru* were barred from entering Canada in 1914, the *Ghadar* drew the attention of the world to their plight. The British monitored Indian emigrant activity and applied pressure and evidence which resulted in the "Hindoo Conspiracy Trial" and the conviction of some South Asians for violating U.S. Neutrality laws[8].

In spite of problems Sikhs faced abroad, those in India served the Crown and felt that their loyalty would be rewarded. They were mistaken. In the Fist World War, Sikhs fought on all fronts and received 14 of the 22 military crosses awarded to Indians. They sacrificed proportionately more in men and material to the war effort than did any other community. In spite of their contribution, local officials and police treated them as rustics. They also were not backed by Britain in their fight against discrimination in Canada or the United States (Singh, K. 1966:160, 161). This situation laid the foundations for revolutionary activity. The Ghadar movement in America unsuccessfully attempted to link up with revolutionary activities in India by supplying arms, money and men; but the atmosphere in India was not conducive for rebellion. The Ghadar movement was primarily an emigrant endeavour which failed, but it changed the Sikhs attitude towards the British and ended a lengthy period of unquestioned loyalty to the Raj (Singh, K. 1966:168-192; Kamath 1976: 103-130).

Since the Second World War there has been a great deal of Sikh emigration to Canada, England and the United States. Although emigrant involvement in Punjab has not been dramatic, it has been present as expatriates remitted money, influenced local policies, and contributed to national campaigns during elections; a few even return during elections to exert influence for their favourite party or candidate (Helweg, 1986:203-208).

The Khalistan Movement

Sikh agitation for Khalistan ("the country of the pure, the nation of the Khalsa") gained international attention in 1982 but had its foundations long before that time. Sikhs abroad, like their compatriots in India, felt it necessary to have a homeland if they were to survive[9]. The idea of

Khalistan started with Kapur Singh, an Oxford alumnus and member of the Indian Civil Service (ICS)[10]. He reminded Sikhs about the need for an independent nation. The claim was considered a joke and punned about: in Hindi *Khali* means "empty" and *stan* means "place," thus the proposed Sikh nation was joked about as being an empty place.

In 1971, Dr. Jagjit Singh Chauhan, a medical practitioner, former Akali Dal (Sikh political party) Secretary of the Master Tara Singh faction, and one time Finance Minister of Punjab, sought a British passport and announced plans to set up a "Rebel Sikh Government at Nankana Sahib," the birthplace of Guru Nanak which is in Pakistan. Initially Pakistan eagerly supported such a move because India was aiding the rebel government in East Pakistan (Akbar 1985:173, 174). In September 1971, Chauhan held a press conference in London and made allegations of the oppression of Sikhs in India. On October 13, 1971, he sponsored a half-page advertisement in *The New York Times* explaining why he wanted Khalistan and then went to Pakistan for the Birth Celebration of Guru Nanak at Nankana Sahib. At this time, however, he did not have the support of Sikhs. The Akali Dal U.K., and Akali Dal leaders in India, including Sant Fateh Singh, condemned his statements and expelled him from the party[11].

Little was heard concerning the movement until July 1977, when Chauhan returned to India. On November 12, 1979, a radio transmitter was installed in the Golden Temple and transmitted *Shabad Kirtan*[12]. One Sikh lady in California represented the views of many emigrants Sikhs when she justified her support for the project by stating, 'If the *gurbani*, prayers, are not broadcast, how will my children ever hear them?"

After he returned to Britain, the Indian government revoked Chauhan's passport but did not request extradition. It did, however, try to get the U.S., U.K., and Canadian government to restrict the activities of Chauhan and other Khalistan supporters. Since Khalistani sympathizers were not causing trouble in their country of residence, the host governments maintained that nothing could be done (Nayar 1981:1, 6).

On April 12, 1980, Shri Balbir Singh Sandhu, the Secretary General of the National Council of Khalistan announced an eleven member Council of Khalistan to strive for a sovereign Sikh state. It was Sandhu was made the first broadcast on the radio in the Golden Temple on June

8, 1980 and issued press notes proclaiming the Government of Khalistan. Jagjit Singh Chauhan circulated a U.K. press release of the International Council of Sikhs on June 16, 1980, stating that they would set up consulates in U.K., Germany and other West European countries. Khalistan was to be 850 miles long, stretching from Porbandar on the Arabian Sea, to Chamba in Himachal Pradesh. Its widest point scaled 200 miles, and the map bore the legend, "Approved by All Parties Sikhs Conference London". One other goal was to obtain counselor status in the United Nations. (Their bid was denied in 1987, but a group based in Kenya has passed through one stage of the approval process). They planned to set up an exile government in the U.S.A. and raise an army of 10,000 to reside and train in America. In fact Khalistan passports, money, and stamps were printed (Hudson 1981). Chauhan supporters and travel agents in India issued certificates to Sikhs to enter. Canada on a refugee status; and by October 1981, 1500 Sikhs entered Canada under this provision in their immigration laws[13]. Canada tried to pressure the Indian government to close travel agents in Punjab who Canadians claimed were running an organised racket by sending Sikhs to Canada under the guise of political refugees (Nayar 1981). It was due to the influx of Sikh refugees with "spurious claims" that India became the 12 country since 1977 and the third Commonwealth country to have its visa exempt status revoked by the Canadian government. Immigration Minister Lloyed Axworthy claimed his conclusions were based partly on information from the Sikh community in Canada and investigations in India (Jain 1981a). The action caused criticism from both the Indian High Commissioner in Ottawa and the Indian community in Canada (Jain 1981b).

Shri Ganga Singh Dhillon, a naturalized U.S. citizen and President of the Sri Nankan Sahib Foundation in Washington worked hard for the Khalistan cause in the United states. He visited India in March 1981 and on the way communicated with Pakistan's President concerning the administration of Sikh shrines in that country. He also became president of the Sikh Educational Conference organised at Chandigarh from March 13 to 15 by the Chief Khalsa Diwan, an organisation which had confined its operations to promoting cultural and educational activities. It was in March 1981 that the Chief Khalsa Diwan at Chandigarh called for associate United Nations membership for Sikhs. Ganga Singh Dhillon was instrumental in getting the resolution passed (Nayer 1981).

Both Dr. Jagjit Singh Chauhan and Shri Ganga Singh Dhillon were in contact with Pakistani officials through General Daniel Graham, Co-chairman of the American Security Council (a private organisation). He arranged a meeting between Chauhan and Agha Shahi, Pakistan's foreign minister. Dhillon claimed Senator Mark Hatfield and representative James C. Corman as patrons of his foundation,[14] and Chauhan maintained contact with Hatfield, Senator Jesse, Helms, Senator Sam Nunn, Charles Percy, and Alexander Haig.

In May and June of 1981, Gurucharan Singh Tohra, President of the Shiromani Gurdwara Prabandhak Committee (SGPC)[15] and Gurdial Singh Ajnoh of the Akal Takht toured the U.K., U.S.A., and Canada to acquaint themselves with the problems of Sikhs abroad and organise an Akali Dal of America. Dr. Jagjit Singh Chauhan organised conventions for these leaders; and, although there was no direct resolution demanding Khalistan, support was given to the concept of "Sikhs as a nation" and to establishing consular status for Sikhs in the United Nations. Despite Chauhan's support, Gurcharan Singh Tohra stated that he was not in favour of Khalistan. The visit abroad did result in the World Sikh Convention, organised by the Shiromani Akali Dal in Amritsar on July 26, 1981, raising the issue of the Indian Government's failure to protect Sikhs during the U.K. racial riots.

In 1982, the All India Sikh Student Federation (AISSF) called for a referendum on the "Sikh Nation" concept. Also in April 1982, the Indian government revoked Chauhan's passport. When he was denied a visa to enter (Keshavan 1982) the United States, Senator Jesse Helms helped circumvent the barrier by inviting Chauhan to testify before the U.S. Senate Agriculture Committee (Haniffa 1986). He travelled to the United States under a British certificate of identity. While in the U.S., he lead 200 Sikhs representing about 10 organisations Canada and the United States in a demonstration outside the United Nations asking, U.N. intervention for persecuted Sikhs in India. This was significant because it was the first time the supporters of Harchand Singh Longwal's Akali Dal faction openly joined forces with Chauhan. The change in Longwal's position was partly due to the fact that 20 to 38 Sikhs were killed in Punjab during a protest campaign he had called[16].

Anti-Indian government feelings were noticeable in Canada, by May of 1982 when the Indian High Commissioner, Dr. Gurdial Singh Dhillon, himself a Sikh, was pelted with eggs and rotten tomatoes during a visit to Vancouver, Canada. Press analysis of the event, however, argues that support for Khalistan was small (Jain 1982).

By July, 1983, relations between the Indian and Canadian governments improved and the Canadians denied Chauhan a visa for which the Indian government expressed gratitude (*India Abroad* 1983). On January 26, 1984, Chauhan in a letter to the Akali Dal president Harchand Singh Longowal, the SGPC president Gurcharan Singh Tohra and Sant Jarnail Singh Bhindranwale, asked for an assembly of Sikhs at the Akal Takht of the Golden Temple, the highest seat of Sikhs spiritual cum temporal authority, to declare a completely sovereign state for the Khalsa Panth. Chauhan's nephew,. Kanwar Singh, was residing near the Golden Temple at the time and was President of the Akal Foundation, an organisation of 2,000 committed to fighting for the establishment of a Sikh Raj. This organisation worked closely with Bhindranwale. However, there was divergence between Longowal and Chauhan as to the degree of autonomy that the Khalistan movement would take. Longowal never condoned the establishment of a separate Sikh state (*India Abroad* 1984).

As is evident from the above, the Khalistan movement was primarily an emigrant endeavour. It did not gain prominence in Punjab until receiving the support of Bhindranwale in 1982. Even then, its support abroad was small and centred in Canada until June 1984, when Indian army troops entered the Golden Temple premises. That one act united Sikhs around the world against the Central Government of India. Emigrant Sikh took to the streets. On June 8th, 250 Sikhs held a demonstration on Massachusetts Avenue in Washington, D.C., a few blocks from the Indian Embassy. On June 9th, 400 Sikhs protested outside the Indian Consulate in Chicago; while in Birmingham, England, 30,000 of England's 400,000 Sikhs demonstrated. On June 10th, 15,000 Sikhs marched in Vancouver wearing black arm bands and chanting "Death to Indira". On that same day in Toronto, 5,000 to 7,000 angry Sikhs marched up Queen's Park to the City Hall; and, in London 20,000 Sikh protesters expressed anger near India House. On June 11, 2,500 staged a protest outside the United Nations and marched to the Indian Consulate shouting slogans favouring Khalistan (Chhabra 1984).

When news of Mrs. Gandhi's assassination went on the air on October 31, 1984, Sikh jubilation was not broadcast in Delhi; but, in the United States, Sikhs were shown drinking champagne. Although the community was not unanimous in its reactions, the press gave prominence to those who rejoiced in her death. One report states:

> In Vancouver, it was a party...with Halloween firecrackers, bhangra[17] dances, sweets distribution on the four-block strip on main street, popularly known as Punjabi Market.
>
> About 150 Sikhs handed out sweets while other chanted songs and then observed a moment of silence—not in memory of Gandhi, but for those killed in the Golden Temple attack (Gune 1984a).

All was not animosity. In Los Angeles, 300 Sikhs gathered at the Hollywood gurdwara to maintain communal harmony; and Manmohan Singh, a retired government of India employees stated, "Gandhi was not killed by Sikhs but by two individuals..."(Gune 1984a).

Canada is considered the major off-shore base of the Khalistan movement. Vancouver Sikhs had borne the initial burnt of Western racism and have been the centre of agitation for their rights. In fact, the present roots of Sikh extremism run deeper in Canada than anywhere else outside the Punjab (Barbar 1986:13). Presently, the region has 60,000 of Canada's 200,000 Sikhs. Although Sikhs commanded a monopoly of immigration from South Asia, they now comprise two thirds of the stream. Sikh politics has been faction-ridden and influenced by their homeland, but the Golden Temple operation brought a degree of unity not previously present.

The Khalistan Movement: Current Overseas Effort

Since the attack on the Golden Temple, three political processes have dominated overseas reactions: militant action, diplomatic politics, and Indian Government interference. The *militant action* is centred in but not limited to Vancouver. One prominent revolutionary leader is Talwinder Singh Parmar, a Canadian citizen and leader of the 50 member Babar Khalsa (Tigers of the True Faith), a militant Sikh group demanding the creation of Khalistan. They claim responsibility for 40 murders in Punjab between 1979 and 1981. Another leader is Lakhbir Singh Brar a nephew of the late Bhindranwale, who heads the International Sikh Youth Federation (ISYF) with 150 members in Canada. His coordinator in the United States is Dr. Arjinderpal Singh Khalsa, director of the cardiopulmonary unit of Good Samaritan Hospital in Mount Vernon, Illinois.

Violent reactions seem to have started in Vancouver. When Acting Indian High Commissioner in Canada, K.P. Fabian, visited Winnipeg, Manitoba on July 18, 1984, he was pelted with eggs and attacked, although he was not seriously injured (Abeyesekera 1984). The Indian Independence Day celebrations of 1984 in New York, Toronto, and Vancouver, where disrupted by Sikh secessionist demonstrators while in Washington, Chicago, Los Angeles, San Francisco and Ottawa, protest were more peaceful (Gune 1948:1, 9).

In May, 1985 when Haryana's Chief Minister Bhajan Lal was in the States for medical treatment, five Sikhs plotted to kill him. He was particularly hated because he had worked against the Sikhs as minister of the state neighbouring Punjab. One of the Sikhs accused was Gurpartap Singh Birk, who in March 1986, was convicted of violating America's neutrality laws. Birk, along with other conspirators from New York and Jatinder Singh Ahluwalia of New Orleans, were accused, but not convicted, of planning to assassinate Rajiv Gandhi during the Prime Minister's visit to the States. These Sikhs had also selected a site for a guerrilla training camp in Columbia, New Jersey. The World Sikh Organisation disclaimed knowledge or compliancy with the actions of these men, but did not discredit their behaviour and maintained that Sikhs would look after their defense (Hudson, Haniffa and Gune, 1985).

Birk and his accomplices has attended the Merc School which offered a course in guerrilla warfare for mercenary soldiers. Frank Camper, who runs the school, and his assistant testified that Sikhs were openly trying to learn about terrorism for "they wanted to kill thousands with a single blow" (Hudson 1985). The Indian Government objected to the operation of mercenary training camps; however, U.S. authorities did not find them illegal as long as they did not promote revolution (Haniffa 1985a; Hudson and Haniffa 1985). Although, there was no relationship established between this group and the 1985 Air India crash, links were reported between Birk and Talwinder Singh Parmar of the Babar Khalsa in Vancouver, showing the international character of the networks of the Sikh emigrant revolutionary movement (Hudson 1986a).

When Prime Minister Rajiv Gandhi visited England in October 1985, a plot by 15 Sikhs and Kashmiris to assassinate him was foiled, leading to the conviction of two Sikhs in December 1986 (*India Abroad* 1986a).

Talwinder Singh Parmar of Burnaby, leader and founder of the Babar Khalsa, and Inderjit Singh Reyat were arrested for suspected involvement with the June 23, 1985 crash of Air India Flight 182 and a bomb explosion in Tokyo from luggage off a Canadian Pacific airplane. Parmar was also wanted in India in connection with the killings of two police officers in Punjab in 1982 and had spent over a year in jail in West Germany. The raid to capture Parmar and his associates was conducted on six houses and a gurdwara in Vancouver (Santana 1985a). This action of the Royal Canadian Mounted Police (RCMP) touched off protests in Toronto where 400 rallied at Nathan Philips Square to condemn the raid on a Sikh place of worship (K.A. 1985). After being captured, the pair were set free on bail. In this case, members of the Sikh community resented news reports that "two Sikhs" were arrested. They did not like being singled out as a religious community. As they put it, "you do not hear of a protestant or catholic being arrested, why should they label Sikhs?" (Hudson 1986b, 1986c, 1986d; Sanatana 1985b).

On May 25, 1986, Punjab Planning Minister Malkiat Singh Sidhu, who entered Canada to attend his nephew's wedding was shot four times in the chest at Campbell River, a town on Vancouver Island. Jasbar Singh Atwal, Jaspal Singh Atwal, Sukhdial Singh Gil, and Amarjit singh Dhindsa were charged with and convicted of the attempted murder. The incident shows the efficiency of the Sikh intelligence network since even the Canadian government was not aware or informed of Sidhu's visit and therefore had not afforded him protection (*India Abroad* 1986b; Glavin 1987).

Five Sikhs who were arrested in May 1985, for the intent to cause an explosion, possibly the Air India disaster, were denied bail in Canada, even though the Sikh community was willing to put up two million dollars in cash and property as bail guarantee (Staff Writer 1986).

On June 14, 1986, seven Sikhs were arrested in a plot to blow up Parliament House in New Delhi, trains, oil refineries in various part of India and to kidnap a child of an Indian member of Parliament. These arrests followed the charging of five Montreal Sikhs in an alleged plot to bomb an Air India jumbo jet in flight from New York to India. Talwinder Singh Parmar, who was free on bail in relation to the Air-India Flight 182 was one of those arrested. In February, 1987, two members of the Babar Khalsa were convicted of "plotting to murder by blowing up an aircraft". Which plane was to be bombed, however, was never specified (Drouin 1987).

After the Indian army attacked the Golden Temple premises, support and money for the revolutionary cause increased dramatically among emigrants. Gurdwaras in the United States, England and Canada gave thousands of dollars a week to support the revolutionary movement in Punjab (Chandran 1985), and Manbir Singh, Chaheru, chief of the Khalistan Commando Force in Punjab confessed that he received more than $60,000 from Sikh organisations in Britain and Canada. He also claimed links with the Canada-based Babar Khalsa. One revolutionary put it very well when he said, "all we have to do is commit a violent act and the money for our cause increases drastically" (Ray 1986). Indian authorities also maintain that Tejinder Singh and Rampal Singh Dillon, who were among seven Sikhs arrested and charged in Canada with planning terrorist attacks in India, were Manbir's associates, again illustrating the international character of Sikh revolutionary networks (Ray 1986).

On October 26, 1986, at a dinner and parade held in New York City by the International Immigrant Foundation (IIF), 25 Sikhs, said to be supporters of the World Sikh Organisation (WSO), insisted that the Khalistan flag be placed on the platform. Indian delegates protested the move, but the Pakistani contingent sided with the Sikhs. The Federation of Indian Associations (FIA) condemned the actions.

Diplomatic efforts have been made primarily through the 17,000 strong World Sikh Organisation (Baber 1986). In July 28, 1984, 3,000 Sikhs gathered in Madison Square Garden, New York City, and resolved to establish "Khalistan, and independent sovereign country of the Sikh Nation encompassing the present Punjab and the Sikh majority areas of India". It was the first convention of the newly formed World Sikh Organisation, and representatives from all over the world spoke and/or attended. Speakers included a former representative from California, James C. Corman (Democrat), and John Nicas, assistant on ethnic affairs to Governor Mario Como of New York. Although Chauhan was given some credit for the Khalistan movement, no resolution mentioned him. However, a Secretariat of the WSO was established—to be headed by Major General Jaswant Singh Bhullar, who retired from the Indian Army in 1977. It concluded 40 members, 10 each from the U.S., Britain and Canada and 10 from other countries (Chhabra and Gune 1984). Although some of the speeches called for revenge, violent tactics were not supported by the WSO leadership. The movement for Khalistan was to be developed along diplomatic channels. In fact, the WSO condemned the massacre of 22 Hindus in December 1986 by stating "no Sikh would kill innocent people". The WSO plans to raise funds for Khalistan and WSO of Canada plans to pressure the Canadian government to investigate atrocities against Sikhs in Punjab (Santana 1985c).

In December, 1986, office holders of the WSO met in New York and reaffirmed their commitment to achieve Khalistan, a separate homeland for Sikhs. The WSO-USA president Sandhu stated that they would attempt to achieve their goal through diplomatic channels. They would hire former Senator Vance Hartke of Indiana as a lobbyist and obtain help from Congress-men they had supported. Members of the Pakistani and Afghani communities were also present, along with Bill Qureshi, a former Congressional candidate from California. The slogans incorporated the ideology of Sikhs fighting Communism and communalism, and they pledged to join the Pakistanis and Afghanis against Russian encroachment (Sikri 1986).

The Sikh community in America was able to exert pressure on the U.S. Government to intervene in the situation. Responding to Sikhs in his consistency, Representative Robert J. Mrazek of Long Island wrote in March, 1985 to Representative Stephen Solarz (Democrat of New York), Chairman of the House Subcommittee on Asian and Pacific Affairs, requesting an investigation of "the validity of reported human rights violations which transpired in the days following the tragic slaying of Prime Minister Indira Gandhi". The letter was consigned by 16 other representatives. This increased pressure on Rajiv Gandhi, who agreed to hold a public inquiry into the slayings (Haniffa 1985b). Maneuvering in Congress did not stop, however. As a response to the Sikh lobby, 15 Congressmen on June 2, 1987 condemned India for her disregard of basic human rights in Punjab. Six of the speakers were from California, where many Sikhs reside[18]. It was the first time that so many had spoken on the Punjab situation at such length. According to one source, the treatment of Sikhs also played a role in the discussion in the House of Representatives Foreign Affairs Committee to cut fifteen million dollars in aid to India (Anand 1987)[19].

In the meantime, Major General Jaswant Singh Bhullar, Secretary General of the World Sikh Organisation, presented his views before the Cambridge Club, which was formed by former Indian students and faculty of Harvard University and the Massachusetts Institute of Technology. He gave as causes of the Punjab problem the broken promises by Prime Minister Jawahar Lal Nehru, Indira Gandhi and now Rajiv Gandhi (Venateshwaran 1986).

The *Indian Government response* to the activities of overseas Sikhs started as early as the late 1970s when Mrs. Gandhi made public statements about problems created by the Sikhs in Vancouver. In 1981, soon after some Sikhs hijacked a Indian Airline Boeing to Lahore, Pakistan, the Indian Government pressured the United States, Canada and Britain to oust Khalistan leaders or at least counter their activities (Nayar 1981).

The reaction to the Khalistan movement has had a subtle effect on India's international relations. When the Washington-based Human Rights Internet and the Minority Rights Group of New York in association with the Congressional Human Rights Caucus held hearings in the House Annex building, protest cries were raised in the Indian Parliament, despite the fact that this was not an official government inquiry (Haniffa 1985c). The Indian government also tried to persuade the United States to close the mercenary training camps that were being used by Sikhs. And, the Indian government wanted the Canadian government to close the Eagle Academy near Vancouver. India maintained the camp was being used to train Sikhs, but Canada argued that it was an ordinary martial arts training school.

When Mrs. Thatcher visited India in April, 1985, she gained Indian government support by warning Sikh extremists that they would not be allowed to abuse British hospitality. The Indian government felt that Britain's attitude toward Sikh militants in England was not satisfactory. She assured India's Prime Minister that her government would take all measures within its power to deal with the activities of some Sikh groups in Britain (News Dispatches 1985).

During his October 14, 1985 visit, Rajiv Gandhi pressed Prime Minister Thatcher to do more about the Sikhs in England who allegedly were plotting terrorism, collecting weapons and sowing tension among Indians. Thatcher promised to extend Britain's Prevention of Terrorism Act to facilitate extradition of certain Indians even if their acts were not political (Reuter 1985). Britain's Foreign Secretary, Sir Geoffery Howe named a Minister, Timothy Renton, to deal with India on the issue of

Sikh militants in Britain. Britain refused to heed India's request for a bilateral treaty which the latter judged necessary. India responded that Britain did not give the Irish revolutionaries the same freedom in the U.K. as provided Khalistan advocates (Kerry 1986).

Britain's treatment of Sikh immigrants has both economic and diplomatic effects on Anglo-Indian relations. During the ten week trial in England of three Sikhs accused of plotting to kill Rajiv Gandhi, the defense charged that there were political reasons to convict his clients because of pending contracts, specifically one that India had with the Westland Helicopter Company of Britain (Special to *India Abroad* 1986). Two of the three Sikhs were subsequently convicted. Also, during the meetings in India between Britain's Foreign Office Minister, Timothy Renton, and Indian Minister of State for External Affairs, Natwar Singh, the two agreed that the Sikh issue had placed a strain on British-Indian relations and was a major point of contention. India continued to demand an extradition treaty which Britain maintained was unnecessary. However, credit for the talks going as smoothly as they did was due to the extradition of Amanullah Khan, a Jammu and Kashmiri Libration Front Advocate[20]. He was sent back despite the objections of some members of Parliament who had fought his return to India. British officials had also filed charges against militant Sikhs who were accused of murdering or attempting to murder moderate Sikhs. Furthermore, the leadership of the Conservative Party was distancing itself from the Anglo-Asian Association, an arm of the Conservative Party that had come under the control of militant Sikhs.

One week after the Renton-Singh meetings in Delhi, the Indian Defense Ministry cleared the purchase of combat tractors from Britain. The contract had been negotiated earlier but was held up due to the strained relations. It was the first major defense order by India to Britain in twenty years. Newspaper reports argued that improved relations, brought about by the prosecution or extradition of militants immigrants, would lead to Indian defense, power and steel contracts with Britain.

The situation even influenced India's relations with her neighbour, Pakistan. Since men and materials have been entering Punjab via Pakistan, India has just concluded a pact with Pakistan not to back terrorist acts. Specifically, Pakistan agreed for the first time not to support any terrorist activity directed against New Delhi, Punjab, or elsewhere (Press Trust of India 1986).

Although Indian government efforts are visible on the diplomatic level, they are also present elsewhere. The Toronto *Globe and Mail* reported that Indian agents were operating in Canada to create division in the Sikh community. The article brought denials and threats from the Indian constitute and some Canadian officials, but the *Globe and Mail* stood firmly behind the story (Santana 1985d).

Canada's Secretary of State, Joe Clark, during a visit to India in February 1987, said that Canada would no longer be a safe haven for extremists or financial swindlers from India. On February 6, 1987, he signed an extradition treaty which Canada had previously resisted. At the same time, the countries signed an agreement of collaboration in industry, air service and an economic development package which enabled India to obtain nearly four billion dollars in development assistance. The press reported that the extradition treaty was a crucial factor in the new relationship between the two countries (Basu 1987). Afterward, Clark refused to meet with Sikh groups advocating Khalistan (Santana and Jain, 1987).

Reactions in the West to the Sikh situation tend to stereotype Sikhs as a rebellious and barbaric people. When Mrs. Gandhi was assassinated, Sikh in the United States were shown on television rejoicing and drinking champagne, acts seen by some Americans as barbaric. Sikh are countering this image through their weekly newspaper *Sikh News*, the distribution of information through the Sikh Religion and Educational Trust publications and other organisations. They are also attempting to establish chairs of Sikh studies at various universities. Their endeavours at the University of British Columbia in Vancouver were approved then stopped in December of 1986. Finally, approval was granted in 1987, Canada's Ministry of Interior was blamed for causing the delay.

The Sikhs in North America have an efficient communication network. They attend academic conferences, publish material, talk to political figures, and help finance conferences on Sikh studies. Telephone networks enable them to communicate throughout the world. However, the militant rhetoric, and emphasis by the media on Sikh violence has hampered their publicity efforts. Support for the Khalistan movement is still very strong, but it does not have the unanimous backing of emigrant Sikhs. Possibly only a small minority are hard core supporters.

Why Emigrants are Involved in India's Sikh Politics

Emigrant Sikh are divided over the Khalistan issue as are Sikhs in India. The militant faction obtains the greatest publicity because the drama sells papers. The issue, however, still remains: why is the violent struggle in India carried to the shores of the United States and Canada? If one were to ask an overseas Sky why he is concerned about India's treatment of his people, he would reply like many have already, "because of the injustices committed there". However, injustices are committed all over the world, so the question still remains.

All immigrants are concerned about their homeland. Polish, Irish, and Jewish people are good examples. In the United States, remittances and political pressure are exerted to help those in their land of origin; and, this is the case for those that have been in the States for generations. Thus, arguments like "crisis of identity" are not convincing explanations for Sikh emigrant behaviour. However, immigrants tend to hold to the values and beliefs of their place of origin[21]. Thus many Sikhs are more Sikh abroad than they were in India. Abroad, they feel the threat of extinction. In India, Sikhs fear being absorbed by Hindus. Sikhs in North America have the same fears that their brothers in India have, but to a greater degree. Also society in North America is free, and immigrants are quick to take advantage of the absence of restrictions. As Inderjit Singh, editor of the British *Sikh Messenger*, stated "Canada is looked up to, like Britain, as a place where we can voice things which in India would be an offense and punishable by life sentences". Arup Das supports this view. He says, "Khalistan only exists here. In India it is only a dream. Here, it exists because people have more freedom". Thus, accentuating the home culture, fear of survival and freedom are contributing factors fostering the extreme faction of the Sikh emigrant political wing.

There are other factors causing emigrant Sikh concern for the situation in Punjab. The Indian government has not been open and honest concerning affairs in Punjab. News reports are periodically censored and reporters, especially foreign ones, are sometimes barred from the region. Also, exaggerated stories are told. This is illustrated by one visitor to U.S. in the summer of 1987. She told everyone "We are a marked family by the Sikhs to be killed". Since her family had no apparent political prominence, an Indian pressed her for the basis for the statement. She replied, "We are Hindus and all Hindu families are marked by the Sikhs for slaughter". Claims like these help fan the fires of animosity. It is hard for the emigrant to know what to believe. Thus, people believe rumor and accusations since the official Indian account has been discredited in the past[22].

Next, the news concerning Punjab focuses on violence. As one visitor put it, "When I went to Punjab, I expected it to be a fortress; but no one ever asked for my visa and things seemed calm". Where this individual was, things were calm, but that part of the story is seldom told because it does not sell newspapers. Thus emigrant Sikhs hear about persecution against their fellow Sikhs. Hearing only violence, it is understandable that they contribute money and lives for their cause in India[23].

Also, life in North America is one stressing individualism and anonymity leaving the South Asian immigrant lonely and lost. As one Indian stated, "I am a good heart surgeon; but, when I walk down the street in New York, no one knows who I am. When I go back to India, they all know me". Coming from a close knit society of family and friends, it is not surprising that an Indian looks homeward, and his tactic for gaining a meaningful life lies with the evaluation of those in his home region who adhere to a cultural system that is familiar. It is within the Indian framework that he, as an emigrant, feels that he can gain prestige and recognition, both factors which are crucial in maintaining *izzat* or honour for oneself and the family group. This is not the only thing. Sikhs, like other South Asians, think in terms of the group rather than the individual. Thus, harm to the group, whether it be family or religious body, is a concern of all members, and action has to be taken. Thus, identity is corporate is that group perceptions and situations are just as important as those of the individual. Since Sikhs perceived themselves as being attacked, it is the duty of one and all to do what is possible to aid those harmed.

For Sikhs abroad, there is another factor. They can support terrorism and gain meaning in the tradition of self sacrifice without risk to themselves as long as they do not violate the laws of their place of residence. In India, the militants have to pay a price because they will be prosecuted by the Central Government. Those in Canada or the United States can advocate separation without risk to themselves. They can support revolutionary activity in India without recriminations.

Another factor has to do with the organisation of the Sikhs. Communal life centres on the gurdwara. The gurdwara is the political, social and religious centre of the community. The church also had that function for many European immigrants to the United States as did the synagogue for the Jews. Sikhs attend the gurdwara because it is the only place where Sikh values are upheld in a land of alien culture. Sikh leaders can effectively communicate, and influence social trends as a result of this organisation[24]. It is fort these reasons that Sikhs take a strong interest in the Punjab, for they interpret the events there as determining what will happen everywhere. Whether they live or die, survive or be absorbed—the answer lies in Punjab.

Conclusions

The overseas Sikh community has played a significant role in the internal and external affairs of India. Like the Ghadar conspiracy early in the century, the Khalistan movement initially was an expatriate venture. Since 1981, the emigrants have brought Sikh issues to world attention by militant and diplomatic means. Acts of violence, arrests and accusations have brought world attention to the Khalistan cause. Emigrant Sikhs also have used diplomatic means to pressure governments in their countries of residence. This is particularly the case in the United States where senators and government officials have used their influence because of Sikh constituents who have given monetary support to their election campaigns. Also, it is emigrant Sikhs who have raised issues before the United Nations.

Emigrant behaviour has influenced the way India has related to Britain, Canada and the United States. In the case of Britain reporters, insinuated that defense contracts were awarded to British firms after a revolutionary was sent back to India. India's Parliament raised a cry of concern when U.S. Government facilities were used to hold an inquiry into the situation of Sikhs in India. Furthermore, the behaviour of emigrant Sikhs has been an important issue in the international relationship India has with Britain, Canada and the United States. They have pressured these governments to prosecute or extradite Sikh militants. India has used her influence to stop or inhibit the activities of pro-Khalilstani Sikhs in the West. The activity of militant Sikhs in the West has been a thorn in the relationships between these countries and India.

As is true of the Sikh community in India, not all emigrant Sikh support Khalistan. Khalistan sympathizers may not even be a majority, but the behaviour of Sikhs abroad has had a definite impact on the Khalistan movement. As the efficiency of international communications develops and the politically sophisticated become an increasing part of the migration stream, the Sikh situation may become more and more indicative of how expatriate communities influence local and international affairs of their land of origin. Thus, India and countries with overseas Sikh populations should develop policies that work on the psychological and cultural framework of the overseas community rather than resorting only to subversive activity and legal action. Such policies could be developed with the cooperation of individuals who understand the thinking patterns and group processes of the overseas Sikh Community.

—A.W. Helweg

NOTES

1. He was heavily guarded by Indians in cricket sweaters and/or sports jackets with pants pressed to razor sharp creases.
2. There is no official way to determine remittances. It is generally a percentage of the Private Transfer Payments set forth in the Government of India's Reports on Currency and Finance. Those are the figures used here.
3. In 1981, land in Punjab was round Rs. 40,000 per acres. In 1985, it was Rs. 60,000 per acre.
4. Sikh place of worship.
5. Such a situation is being faced by American farmers today where cheap loans and government aid enabled them to mechanize and now that such easy credit is not available, they are losing their farms because they were not economically competitive.
6. Gujarat is India's second most prosperous state next to Punjab. It is also a high emigration area, comparatively wealthy and is experiencing social strife.
7. During this time, all Asian groups were the object of resentment by the wider community in California.
8. This situation was repeated in 1986 when Gurpartap Singh Birk was tried and convicted for violating United States neutrality laws. It is discussed in greater detail later in this article.
9. The necessity of a Sikh homeland for survival is a prominent part of their tradition. Currently, the debate is whether that has to be an independent country. In the past, and many currently feel, that a Sikh homeland can be achieved without being independent of India.
10. He was also asked to "retire" because of corruption charges.

11. The Akali Dal is the Sikh political party in Punjab. They have established branches abroad, hence the term "Akali Dal U.K." (this is the Akali Dal party in Britain).

12. This was a symbolic gesture since the range of the transmitter was only 1500 meters (Jeffrey 1986:76).

13. Canadian immigration law permits refugees, and it was under that clause that many sikh entered the country.

14. Some senators never confirmed their support, in fact, some claimed they had never heard of the organisation.

15. The unit administering historical Sikh gurdwaras in Punjab.

16. Organisations represented were, Akali Dal, Longowal faction, Shri Nankan Sahib Foundation, Sikh Youth Federation of North America, International Council of Sikhs, Federation of Sikh Societies in Canada, Sikh Cultural Society of New York, and Garden State Sikh Association (Louis 1983).

17. The Punjabi harvest dance, joyful and robust.

18. Dr. Gurmit Singh Aulakh, president of the International Sikh Organisation, was a strong factor in this process. It was remarked by Congressman Morella that he visited every Congressional office several times.

19. None of these lawmakers have supported the formation of Khalistan, but they condemn the violence in India.

20. He was found innocent of making explosives for improper purposes.

21. Immigrants are selective in what retain from their old society and adopt from their new abode. Some Sikhs may appear to be thoroughly westernized, but they perceived of themselves as living according to the dictates of Sikhism as they remember it to be in their home region of Punjab. If they are not living according to the ideals, there is guilt. As a result, this leads to a conservatism among overseas Sikhs that may not be present in their place of origin. Again, this conservatism may not be readily manifest in their outward behaviour, although in places like Yuba City, California, London and Vancouver, much of this homeward orientation is manifest.

22. India has a tradition of an open and fees press, but there are reasons for misinformation besides government censorship. Reporters have not always been free to move in and out of Punjab. Also, some foreign correspondents do not fully understand the region they are writing about. India is a complex culture that can not be understood in a short time, and in a causal way. Some do not make the effort. They sit in Delhi and write their stories by gleaning the Indian press. They do not have a first-hand knowledge of the country to properly analyze the events.

23. It must be kept in mind that ancestry does not determine knowledge. Just because a person is from India does not mean they are knowledgeable about events there.

24. Hindus have temples abroad, but they are not politicized to the degrees of Sikh gurdwaras.

REFERENCES

Abeyesekera, Kirthie, 1984. "Indian Envoy Attacked by Sikhs in Winnipeg". *India Abroad* XIV 3:1.

Akbar, M.J. 1985. *India: The Siege Within: Challenge to A Nation's Unity.* Middlesex: Penguin Books.

Anand, Rajen. 1987, "U.S. Congress Increasingly Adopting Anti-India Posture". *India West XII* 3:18.

Barber, John. 1986. A Troubled Community". *Macleans* ICIX, 25: 19-23.

Basu, Tarun. 1987. "Clark Rules Out Canada As Extremists 'Haven'. "*India Abroad.* XVII 20:1, 20.

Chhabra, Aseem. 1984. "Thousands of Sikhs Protest". *India Abroad*. XIV 37:1, 14.

Chhabra, Aseem and Ramesh Gune. 1984. "3,000 Sikhs in N.Y. Meeting Demand 'Khalistan" Creation". *India Abroad*. XIV 4:1, 5.

Chandran, Ramesh. 1985. "United Kingdom: Tackling Terrorism". *India Today*. X 22:28, 29.

Chopra, Pran. 1985. "A Turning Point for the Sikhs." In *Punjab in Indian Politics: Issues and Trends*, ed. by Amrik Singh, pp. 331-352. Delhi Ajanta Publications.

Drouin, Linda. 1987. "2 in Canada Sentenced to Life for Plotting to Blow Up Plane". *India Abroad* XVII 19:1, 8.

Glavin, Terry. 1987". "4 in Canada Found Guilty in Attempt on Punjab Official". *India Abroad*. XVII 23:1, 17.

Gujral, I.K. 1985. "The Economic Dimension". In *Punjab in Indian Politics: Issues and Trends,* ed. by. Amrik Singh, pp. 42-53. Delhi Ajanta Publications.

Gune, Ramesh. 1984a. "Jubilation Sweeps Sikhs in U.S. and Canada. "*India Abroad.* XIV 37:1, 14.

—. 1984b. "Peaceful and Unruly Protests Mar India Day Celebration". *India Abroad.* XIV 47:1, 9.

—. 1986, "Sikh Unit in New Setup Averts Split". *India Abroad*. XVI 21:1, 20.

Haniffa, Aziz, 1985a. "Attorney General is asked to Probe Mercenary Camps". *India Abroad*. XV. 45:1, 4.

—. 1985b. "Gandhi Riot Inquiry Pleases Mrazek, Who Asked For It". *India Abroad* XV 34:1, 6.

—. 1985c. "Delhi Assails Sikh Hearing in U.S." *India Abroad,* XV 30:1, 1.

—. 1986. "Friend of India Backs Helms". *India Abroad*. XV 30:1, 1.

—. 1986. "Friend of India Backs Helms". XXII 13:6.

Halweg, Arthur. 1983. "Emigrant Remittances: Their Nature and Impact on a Punjabi Village". *New Community*. X: 435-443.

—.1986. *Sikhs in England*. Delhi Bombay, Calcutta, Madras: Oxford University Press.

Hudson, Lynn. 1981. "Head of Khalistan Drive Seeks U.N. Status. "*India Abroad* XII. 11:19.

—. 1985. "Sikhs Received Training In Terrorist Acts in Alabama". *India Abroad* XV 40:1, 12.

—. 1986a. "Birk Sentenced to 7 years in Plots: Arms Plan Alleged". *India Abroad*. XIV 35:1, 22.

—.1986b. "Birk Acquitted in Plot to Kill Gandhi: Guilty on 2 Counts". *India Abroad*. XVI. 26:1, 16.

—. 1986c, "Summations Presented In Brik Conspiracy Case". *India Abroad*. XVI 25:1, 18.

—. 1986d. "Brik In Interview Is Jubilant Over Acquittal by Jury". *India Abroad*. XVI 28:23.

Hudson, Lynn and Azia Haniffa. 1985. "FBI Calls Mercenary Camps Legal". *India Abroad*. 2:1, 6.

Hudson, Lynn, Aziz Hanifa and Ramesh Gune. 1985". 5 Are Denied Bail in Reported Post to Kill Bhajan Lal". *India Abroad*. XV 3:2, 6.

—. 1984. "Khalistan Head Asks Akalis to Declard Sovereign State". *India Abroad* XIV 14:1, 18.

—. 1986a. "2 in Britain Sentenced in Plot to Kill Gandhi". *India Abroad*. XVII 13:1, 11.

—. 1986b. "Punjab Planning Minister Shot in Vancouver: 4 Seized". *India Abroad*. XVI. 35:1, 22.

Jain, Suresh, 1981a. "Canada Requires Visas of Indians". *India Abroad*. XII 4:1, 20.

—. 1981b. "Canadian Visa Difficulties Arise". *India Abroad*. XII 6:1, 17.

— 1982. "Pro-Khalistan Sikhs Pelt Envoy". *India Abroad*. XII 33:1.

Jeffrey, Robin. 1986. *What's Happening in India? Punjab, Ethnic Conflicts, Mrs. Gandhi's Death and the Test for Federalism*. Hampshire and London. Macmillan Press Ltd.

K.A.,1985. "400 in Toronto Protest Over Raids". *India Abroad*. XVI 7:26.

Kabra, K.N. 1976. *Political Economy of Brain Drain*. New Delhi: Arnold-Heninemann.

Kamath, M.V. 1976. *The United States and India 1776-1976*. Washington: The Embassy of India.

Kerry, Francis. 1986. "Britain Names Officials for Deals on Militants". *India Abroad*. XVI 28:1, 8.

Keshavan, Narayan, 1982. "U.S. Bars Entry to "Sikh Leader". *India Abroad* XII 18:1, 7.

Leaf, Murray, 1985. "The Punjab Crisis". *Asian Survey* XXV 5: 475-498.

Louis, Arul B. 1983. "Sikh groups Display Unity in U.N. Protest". *India Abroad* XIII, 30:1, 10.

Nayar, Kuldip. 1981. "Nations Refuse to Oust Khalistan's Supporters". *India Abroad*. XII 3:1, 6.

Nayar, Kuldip and Khushwant Singh, 1984. *Tragedy of Punjab: Operation Baluster and After*. New Delhi: Vision Books.

News Dispatches. 1985. "Thatcher Warns Sikh Extremists". *India Abroad*. XV 29:1.

Press Trust of India. 1986. "Pakistan in India Pact Agrees Not to Back Terrorist Acts". *India Abroad*. XVII 13:1, 24.

Ray, Shantanu. 1986. "Militant Chief Admits Canada Ties". *India Abroad*. XVI 49:1, 5.

Reuter. 1985. "England Charges Four in Plot to Kill Gandhi". *India Abroad*. XVI 4:1. 10.

Santana, Ron. 1985a. "Birk Sentenced to 7 Years in Plots: Arms Plan Alleged". *India Abroad*. XIV 7:1, 26.

—. 1985b. '2 Sikhs Freed on Bail in Inquiry on Jet Crash". *India Abroad*. XVI. 8:1, 26.

—. 1985c. "Sikh Nation: Political Solution Urged". *India Abroad*. XV 23:20.

—. 1985d. "Mounty Official Says 3 Didn't Reboard Plan: Delhi Role Alleged". *India Abroad*. XVI 9:1, 21.

Santana, Ron and Ajit Ajain. 1987. "Clerk Says he Wants to Aid Moderate Sikhs". *India Abroad* XVII 21:1, 10.

Sikri, A. 1986. "WSO Vows 'Khalistan Goal". *India Abroad*. XVII 12:9.

Singh, Amrik. 1985. *Punjab in Indian Politics: Issues and Trends*. Delhi: Ajanta Publications.

Singh, Iqbal. 1986. *Punjab Under Siege: A Critical Analysis*. New York. London. Sydney: Allen, Macmillan and Enderson.

Singh, Khushwant. 1966. *A History of the Sikhs, Volume 2, 1839-1964*. Princeton, New Jersey: Princeton University Press.

Singh, Patwant and Hirji Malik, eds. 1985. *Punjab: The Fatal Miscalculation*. New Delhi: Patwant Singh.

Special to India Abroad. 1986. "Trial of 3 in Britain Nearing End". *India Abroad*. XVII 12:9.

Staff Writer. 1986. "5 in Montreal Denied Bail in Explosive Case". *India Abroad*. XVI 37:1, 4.

Tinkar, Hugh. 1974. *A New System of Slavery: The Export of Indian Labour Overseas 1839-1920.* London: Oxford University Press for the Institute of Race Relation.

—. 1976. *Separate and Unequal*. London: C. Hurst.

Venateshwaran, S. 1986. "Bhullar Calls Khalistan Upto Hindus". *India Abroad*. XVI 24:22.

Wallace, Paul. 1986. "The Sikhs as a 'Minority in A Sikh Majority States". *Asian Survey*. XXVI 3: 363-377.

Unity of God—The Sikh Point of View

I. Introductory

The term 'God' is sufficiently universalized and every religious tradition has got used to finding its own meanings and connotations in the term. Yet, to use an alien term, howsoever diffused and naturalized, in the context of another tradition is to confound the basic issue altogether. Though, for convenience, the term 'God' will be employed frequently in this essay too, it will be preferable and safer to substitute the same with the accepted terms of the Sikh Tradition. The accepted authenticated terms for God in the Sikh Tradition are *Ekoamkar, Wahiguru, Akal Purakh* and even *Nām* or *Satinām*. Such terms of other Indian religious traditions, particularly of the Brahiminical and Yogic as Parabrahm, Brahm (Brahman), Isvara, Parmeshvar, Paramatman, Prabhu, Niranjan, Ram, Narain, Deva, etc. have been employed uninhibitedly in the *Guru Granth*, the Scripture of Sikhism, and the *Dasam Granth*, yet in popular Sikh parlance the above cited terms have the currency and they, in their very connotation, imply unity of godhead. The Sikh terms for God are definitive and point towards the one absolute.

The object of this essay is not to give the total conception of the *Wahigaru* or the *Akal Purakh* as in the Sikh Tradition, but to concentrate of defining the Unity aspect of the Supreme Reality in accordance with the Sikh Scripture and the process of thought.

The Unity of god implies the one and only one God, the one without a second, the one without any other co-eternal, entity, the one of complete supremacy, the one unrivalled and unopposed, the one unequalled, the one unchallenged, the one who is omnipotent, the one whose authority and sovereignty are not questioned, the one who is ever the same, the one uncontradicted internally or externally, and the one who is absolute in all respects. The Unity of god is expressive of the oneness, uniqueness, individuality, particularity, singularity, indivisibility, uniformity, continuity, power, authority, strength and homogeneity. The Unity of God is the unity of infiniteness which is invariable and external. It is the unity or oneness of being, of spirit, of reality of consciousness and of bliss. None or nothing else is God's equal in supremacy, authority, power, knowledge, wisdom, creativity, magnificence, benevolence, etc. No god or *avtara* (incarnation) or man is His equal.

II. Conception of the Unity of God in the Mulmantra

The fundamental doctrine of Sikhism, called the *Mulmantra*, in each of its seven parts, includes one aspect of the transcendental God and one aspect of the Immanent god, both the transcendent and immanent being the two aspects of the same reality. The transcendent aspects enlisted therein are such as indicate that the *Akal Purakh* can never be broken, split or divided. To count them, in the order in which they occur in the *Mulmantra*, they are *(i) ek*, one, *(ii) sati*, truth (real), *(iii) purakh*, person or being, *(iv) nirbhau,* unrivalled, *(v) akal,* timeless, *(vi) saibhang*, self-created, and *(vii) gur*, light or enlightenment. All these terms are absolute and point towards the one which is indivisible infinite. Similarly, the doctrine includes seven aspects of God which are related and immanent but not as eternal as God to whose order or will they come into play. These related aspects of God are: *(i) oamkar*, the one who is the creator, preserver and destroyer, *(ii) nam*, the one who takes any form, appearance or manifestation, *(iii) karta*, creator, *(iv) nirvair*, the one who has no malice towards any other, *(v) murti*, who has a form or entity, *(vi) ajuni*, who is not born and *(vii) parsad*, who is sweet and graceful. These seven terms are related to the phenomenon or appearance which is real or true, but not eternal.

III. Conception of the Unity of God in the Japu of Guru Nanak Dev

Dod has been conceived as *sach*, truth, *niranjan*, transcendent, and *nirankar*, formless in the *Japu* of Guru Nanak Dev. The *sach*, Truth, as conceived there is the one who existed when 'time' was non-existent, when time came to exist and its count into *yugas* or aeons began, the one who exists now in the present and shall continue to exist in all future, even when time shall be no more in count. The being of God has further been conceived as the one who has never been set up by any other entity, that is, the one who derives His power and authority from none other and is not supported by an external force—He is the one, all-alone, all-powerful and all-enduring. God has been described as *sati*, truth, *sohan*, beauty, and *chau*, bliss. His *tan,* strength, *rūp*, form (beauty), *dāt,* bounty are beyond measure. He is the *ādi*, beginning, *anil* unchanged, *ānad*, without a beginning, *anahat*, undying and *ek vais*, ever the same in form or appearance through all ages. In that unrivalled stanza of artistic beauty and conceptual height, the *sodar*. The Gate, His Unity has been thus stressed:

> *He, He alone remains ever the same, the true Master of the true Name.*
>
> *He who erected this frame exists, and even though the whole creation depart, He shall endure ever.*
>
> *He who made Nature, consisting of things of different colours, orders and species.*
>
> *Watches over His handiwork according to His own great purpose.*
>
> *He does just what pleases Him, and none can say what He should do.*
>
> *He is the king of kings, Nanak, and ours is only to live according to His will.*
>
> *(Stanza XXVII)*

Further, the *Japu* holds that God is the ordainer and His Will is supreme (stanza 1, 2), the ordainer continues this process of the world by His will (3), He is all in all (5), He is Himself Maya, the Primal Word and Brahma (21), He alone knows when the world was made (21), and He the Formless dwells in the region of truth (37). So, *Akal Purakh*, Timeless Being is the supreme reality whose *hukam*, command, and *raza*, will, are absolute.

IV. Conception of the Unity of God in the Japu of Guru Gobind Singh

The *Dasam Granth* of Guru Gobind Singh opens with the Japu. The verses below make Guru Gobind Singh's conception of God transparent:

I bow to the sun of suns.

I bow to the moon of moons;

I bow to the king of kings.

I bow to the Lord of Indras;

I bow to the unknown Darkness,

I bow to the Light of lights;

I bow to the greatest of the great.

I bow to the Seed of seeds. (185)

Thou art in all ugliness,

Thou art the Spirit of Beauty;

Thou art the Hope of all hopes,

Thou art the Grace of all elegance;

Thou art immortal, incorporeal and Nameless.

And the destroyer of the three words in the three periods;

Thou art bodiless and desireless. (188)

All superficial and temporary contradictions resolve in Him; He is uncaused, immovable, imperishable, all-pervading (190), ineffaceable, indestructible, incomprehensible (191), immortal, merciful, fateless, garbless (192), nameless, desireless, fathomless, boundless (193). He is all darkness, He is all light; He is all ugliness, he is all beauty, He is all spirit, He is all modes. He is the one absolute who has no marks, symbols, caste, class, lineage, form, hue, shape or garb.

But, He is immanent too. Guru Gobind Singh has sung about this all-pervading aspect of the Lord too:

Lo, ever visible is Thy splendour,

Everywhere resplendent is Thy presence;

Thou art eternal peace,

Thou art universal scripture. (150).

Lo, Thou art the cosmic mind,

Thou art the lamp of beauty;

Thou art perfect and merciful,

Thou art the gracious sustainer. (151)

Lo, Thou art the giver of daily bread,

Thou art the provider and saviour;

Thou art supreme in mercy,

Thy beauty is resplendent. (152).

V. Conceptions of the Gurmat and Unity of God

Four basic conceptions of the Sikh philosophy and thought are noted below. They all emerge from the conception of the fundamental unity of the *Akal Purkah*.

Akal Purakh

The one absolute is infinite and thus beyond comprehension, description and full accountability. He has no features, coloures, clans, castes, forms, categories, garbs, etc. He is Omnipotent and omnipresent. He, as One, is the creator, preserver and destroyer of all the phenomenal existence. As the One Absolute, He is eternal, continuing from infinity to infinity timeless. He is formless, He has no body, He is unborn, indestructible, unbreakable, He cannot be given any name, He is not confined to any place. He does not incarnate Himself as an *avtara* or in any other form. No gods or *avtaras* of mythology share his attributes of power, creation, omniscience. Yet, He is present everywhere. All eyes, ears, noses and feet belong to Him. All see because His light shines in all eyes.

He is One infinite but real, holy and true.

Jiva

Man, as a self or soul which has God's light or spark in it, approaches nearest to God, yet remains too far below. *Jiva,* human soul, and for that matter almost all forms of life, share some of the attributes of God, yet it is far imperfect. God, or the cosmic consciousness is perfect, absolutely perfect and full, without any impediment or flaw, while human soul, howsoever evolved, remains imperfect and lacking, qualitatively as well as quantitatively. God is *pūra*, complete, perfect and full, man is *ūrā*, incomplete, lacking and wanting. Man, howsoever near perfection, cannot be *ek*, one, absolute one in the sense in which god is, nor can he be *oankar, viz*, creator, preserver and destroyer, with the magnitude that God wields, nor can he be *satinamy*, true to all descriptions and attributes, nor can he be *karta purakh*, to be a creator and also to pervade the created, nor can he be *akal*, above time or timeless, nor is he *ajuni*, unborn, or *saibhang*, self-born, nor can he be *gurparsadi*, light and grace, absolute. A *jiva* is a created entity, God is not. Even after salvation or liberation a *jiva* is to stand and wait for the will of the Lord. For that matter, gods, *avtaras, siddhas*, fire, water, *akash,* earth, Indra, yogis, time and space are *jivas,* created beings. God is their creator. Nothing is co-eternal with Him. Nothing else is co-omniscient or omnipotent with Him.

Jagat

Phenomenal creation is not co-eternal with God, the creator, rather it takes form and evolves as willed by God. The will of the ordainer creates the phenomenon. The *Guru Granth* speaks of the infinitely long time, aeons, when nothing but God existed, rather when time itself did not exist. All possibilities and potentialities of creation lay in God. The creation emanates or emerges from God, and after interval of aeons or myriads of aeons, relapses into God. Several times this has happened—creation emanated and returned into Him. Sikhism does not subscribe to the *purusa-prakriti* or *maya-Brahm* relationships in cause and effect of the creation, only the will of God is the cause and He Himself, in the form of creation, is the effect. Sikhism does not subscribe to any theories or conjectures regarding the time, cause, form, dimensions of the creation or its relapse into the creator. The phenomenal creation cosmos or cosmic nature is beyond any accountability. It is his name aspect, the immanent aspect, and is as vast Has He is. It is not an illusion, dream, fabrication of imagination or mountain of smoke—it is real and true, as far as it is there, as willed by the creator. The so-called evil, suffering, sin, or whatever is apparently opposed to the divine nature, is there as willed by God and all this to promote the total evolution of the creation, there is nothing negative or in opposition to the divine purpose, nothing can go against the divine will or purpose.

Salvation

Akal Purakh, jiva and *jagat* meet in the salvation of man, even if they do not get merged or identified. Meditation on the name, which is completely identified with God, under Guru's instruction, gives salvation. The Guru, again, is God's own instrument, appointed by God Himself, for the salvation of man. The Guru receives the divine revelation to broadcast to man, the Guru sets the highest example of living in accordance with the will, and inspires the man to submit to the will and live in accordance with it. Whatever the path chosen for salvation and whatsoever the revelation or Guru followed, all true *sadhaks*, endeavourers in the path of salvation, meet at the *Sodar*, God's Presence (see stanza XXVII of the *Japu* of Guru Nanak Dev). That is the path designed and laid down by God Himself, none else could design the process and work it out.

VI. Conclusions

The Sikh terms for God are *Ekoamkar, Wahiguru, Akal Purakh* which, unambiguously and definitely stand for the unity of God. The *Guru Granth* starts with the numeral one (1). No other philosophical system or doctrine expresses itself so unequivocally on the point of unity.

The transcendent and immanent aspects of the Supreme reality do not undermine its unity.

The one is self-created. He cannot be made or set up. He does not incarnate Himself. No gods, goddesses, *avtaras* share His functions or authority. No Satan or Devil can undermine His power, functioning or authority. He does not stand in need of any advice or consultation from anyone. He is full, complete and perfect. All else is imperfect and incomplete. Nothing can stand as a rival to God.

Maya, duality, doubt and ignorance are admitted in the *Guru Granth*, but they are His creation and designs for the working out of His own schemes and projects. He alone can set these forces on any man to delude him. He alone can rid a man of their onslaught when He is so pleased.

Nothing created will ever comprehend, even on salvation, the Creator, or His ways fully. He will is ever supreme. Man, even when liberated, from transmigration, stands in blissfulness to obey His will and serve Him.

The unity of God whose light shines in all, gives, unity to mankind and one divine purpose to cosmos and nature, His creation. His unity makes all men equal and humanity indivisible by man-made distinctions of castes, creeds, colours, countries, *varnas, ashramas*, evil, good, heaven, hell, etc. God is one, all mankind is one.

Loving meditation and contemplation of the one leads mankind to unity, truth, creativity (dynamism), fearlessness, love, beauty, freedom, sovereignty, light and sweetness. All these attributes are implied in the *Mulmantra* of the Sikh faith.

The doctrine of unity of God is fundamental and basic to Sikhism. But in minute details and in all its aspects, Sikhism in neither Hinduism nor Islam. It is not the same as monism or monotheism, nor is its unity of Godhead identical with the *tauḥīd* of Islam, in all details. The *nirguna* and the *sarguna* go together in Sikhism; *jiva* is the divine spark; he is present in all His creation and pervades it. It is not so in *tauḥīd* or monism or monotheism.

—Taran Singh

Sikh Saints

Bhai Mardana (1459 to 1520)

Bhai Mardana was the lifelong companion and first disciple of Guru Nanak. Bhai Mardana was born in 1459 at Nankara Sahib to Muslim parents Bhai Badre and Mai Lakho. He belonged to a caste of musicians which sang and danced at festivals and weddings. Bhai Mardana became friends with Guru Nanak when they were both children, Mardana being 10 years older than Guru Nanak. Bhai Mardana accompanied Guru Nanak on most of his great journeys, he would play the rebeck (a string instrument) while Guru nanak would be signing and composing his hymns. Three of Bhai Mardana's hymns are included in the Guru Granth Sahib. Bhai Mardana passed away in 1520 on the banks of the river Khuram in Afghanistan. He was returning with Guru Nanak on the Gurus fourth and last great journey to Mecca and Medina. Guru Nanak personally performed the last rites of Bhai Mardana. Bhai Mardana is considered the founder of the musical tradition of the Sikhs.

Baba Buddha (1506 to 1631)

Baba Buddha was the great Sikh saint who had the pleasure of serving under the first six Gurus, Baba Buddha was born in 1506 in the village of Kathu Nangal. When he was a young boy herding cattle in the fields when he met Guru Nanak who was visiting the village. The boy served the Guru milk and Guru Nanak exclaimed that though young in age, he was a Buddha (old man) in terms of his understanding and wisdom. Baba Buddha converted to the path of Sikhism and became an exemplary disciple of the Gurus. Baba Buddha was responsible for the guruship ceremony of the next five Gurus from Guru Angad to Guru Hargobind. Under Guru Arjan Dev, Baba Buddha was appointed the first custodian (granthi) of the Guru Granth Sahib in the Golden Temple in 1604. Baba Buddha was also responsible for the early education of Guru Hargobind as a child and helped to personally construct the Akal Takht. Baba Buddha passed away in 1631 at village Ramdas and had his last rites personally performed by Guru Hargobind.

Bhai Gurdas (1560 to 1629)

Bhai Gurdas was a great Sikh scholar who was the scribe of the original copy of the Guru Granth Sahib under the guidance of Guru Arjan Dev. Bhai Gurdas was born around 1560 at Goindwal and was the son of Datar Chand, the younger brother of Guru Amar Das. Bhai Gurdas learned Sikhism from his uncle Guru Amar Das and upon the Gurus death was sent by Guru Ram Das as a missionary to preach Sikhism at Agra. Under the guidance of Guru Arjan Dev, Bhai Gurdas spent a year with the Guru at Amritsar and helped to scribe the original copy of the Guru Granth Sahib. Bhai Gurdas also met the mughal emperor Akbar and convinced him that the Guru Granth Sahib was not derogatory to Islam. Bhai Gurdas was also a great writer and provides the best information that we have about the early days of Sikhism. He composes 40 vars (ballads) and 556 kabits (couplets) which Guru Arjan Dev blessed as being "the key to the Guru Granth Sahib". Out of his humility Bhai Gurdas did not have any of his compositions included in the Guru Granth Sahib, but they are part of the writings outside the Guru Granth Sahib that are approved for recital by Sikhs. While Guru Hargobind was imprisoned at Gwalior. Fort, Bhai Gurdas along with Baba Buddha were in charge of running the affairs of the Sikh community. Bhai Gurdas also helped to construct the Akal Takht. Bhai Gurdas died in 1629 at Goindwal and had his last rites personally performed by Guru Hargobind.

Bhai Nand Lal (1633 to 1715)

Bhai Nand Lal was a great poet and close associate of Guru Gobind Singh. Bhai Nand Lal was born in 1633 at Ghazni where his father was a high government official. Bhai Nand Lal became an accomplished poet and was fluent in Persian and Arabic. He married a Sikh girl and eventually became a disciple of Guru Gobind Singh. He lived in close association with the Guru from 1697 onwards. Bhai Nand Lal personally accompanied Guru Gobind Singh to Deccan where the Guru was assassinated. Bhai Nand Lal produced a number of works about the teaching of Guru Gobind Singh and the code of conduct he laid down. The works of Bhai Nand Lal are given equal respect as those of Bhai Gurdas and are read in gurdwaras. Bhai Nand Lal died in 1715 at Multan.

The Panj Piaras (The Five Beloved Ones)

The Panj Piaras were the first five Sikhs to be initiated into the Khalsa brotherhood by Guru Gobind Singh on Baisakhi day in 1699. A very large gathering of sikhs had arrived at Anandpur Sahib on that day as per the gurus instructions. After prayers Guru Gobind Singh stood up with his sword and asked the large congregation, "is there anyone here ready to lay down his life at my call? This sword of mine is crying for the blood of a dear Sikh of mine". The congregation was shocked and afraid, the third time Guru Gobind Singh repeat his call, Daya Ram stood up and offered his head. Guru Gobind Singh took him into a tent. The sound of a sword cutting a body was heard and blood trickled out of the tent. Guru Gobind Singh emerged from the tent and asked for another Sikh. Dharam Das stood up and volunteered. Again the same episode was repeated. Three more Sikhs offered their heads to the Guru in the same way, Mukham Chand, Himmat Rai and Sahib Chand. After some time Guru Gobind Singh brought the five Sikhs before the congregation dressed in new clothes and revealed to the congregation that he had really slaughtered five goats inside the tent. Guru Gobind Singh then baptized them with amrit (sweetened water) stirred with his Khanda. The Guru called them his Beloved Ones and gave them the last name 'Singh' which means Lion. Guru Gobind Singh then humbly bowed before the Five Beloved Ones and asked them to initiate Him into the Khalsa Brotherhood. All of the Five Beloved ones remained with Guru Gobind Singh for the rest of their lives and they are remembered every day in Ardas (the common prayer).

Bhai Daya Singh (1669 to 1708)

The first Beloved One, Bhai Daya Singh was born to Khatri parents in Lahore in 1669. He attended Guru Gobind Singh in leaving Chamkaur Sahib during the famous battle in 1704. Bhai Daya Singh also personally delivered Guru Gobind Singh's letter Zafarnama to emperor Aurangzeb in the Deccan. Bhai Daya Singh accompanied Guru Gobind Singh to Nander and died there in 1708.

Bhai Dharam Singh (1666 to 1708?)

The second Beloved One, Bhai Dharam Singh was born to Jat parents at Hastinapur or Delhi in 1666. Bhai Dharam Singh was also assigned to look after Guru Gobind Singh's personal safety during the battle of Chamkaur in 1704. It is unclear whether he died fighting in the battle or accompanied Guru Gobind Singh to Nanader and died there in 1708.

Bhai Mukham Singh (1663 to 1704)

The third beloved one, Bhai Mukham Chand was born in 1663 to a weatherman of Dwarka. He died fighting in the battle of Chairman in 1704.

Bhai Sahib Singh (1662 to 1704)

The fourth Beloved One, Bhai Sahib Singh was born to a barber family in 1662. He died fighting in the battle of Chamkaur in 1704.

Bhai Himmat Singh (1661 to 1704)

The fifth Beloved One, Bhai Himmat Singh was born to a water carrier in 1661. He died fighting in the battle of Chamkaur in 1704.

Bhai Mani Singh (1670 to 1737)

Bhai Mani Singh was a great Sikh scholar and martyr who was the scribe of the final version of the Guru Granth Sahib under the guidance of Guru Gobind Singh and was compiled the Dasham Granth following the death of Guru Gobind Singh. Bhai Mani Singh was born to Jat parents at the village of Sunam in 1670. He was the younger brother of Bhai Dyala who was martyred along with Guru Tegh Bahadur in 1675. Bhai Mani Singh was raised from a young age with Guru Gobind Singh by the Gurus mother Mata Gujri. Bhai Mani Singh became a great preacher of Sikhism and spent almost a year with Guru Gobind Singh at Damdama Sahib compiling the final and current version of the Guru Granth Sahib in 1705. After the death of Guru Gobind Singh, Bhai Mani Singh was installed as the head granthi at the Golden Temple in 1721. Here he produced many works on Sikhism and under the insistence of Guru Gobind Singh's widow Mata Sundri compiled the works of Guru Gobind Singh and produced the Dasam Granth. In 1737 Bhai Mani Singh took permission from the Muslim governor of Lahore for the Sikhs to celebrate

Diwali at the Golden Temple on the payment of Rs. 5,000 as tax, a practice which had been banned. Not enough people attended Diwali that year because they were afraid of the Muslim authorities and as a result not enough money was collected. The Muslim authorities arrested Bhai Mani Singh and publicly executed him in Lahore.

Bhai Singh Bahadur (1670 to 1715)

The great Sikh soldier and martyr who avenged the death of Guru Gobind Singh's two younger sons. He was born as Lachhman Das in 1670 at Rajouri in Jammu to Rajput parents. He spent many years in Hindu monasteries in central India and established a ashram at Nanded in Maharashtra where he lived for fifteen years before meeting Guru Gobind Singh. He was given the name "Banda" meaning slave of the Guru and became a Khalsa. His name was changed to Gurbax Singh but he was popularly known as Banda. When Guru Gobind Singh was in the south at Deccan he sent Banda to Punjab to punish the enemies of the Khalsa. He attacked Samana in 1709 and captured Sirhind in 1710. The killer of Guru Gobind Singh's two sons Wazir Khan the ruler of Sirhind was also killed. Banda Singh Bahadur became the leader of the Khalsa following the death of Guru Gobind Singh and struck coins in the name of Guru Gobind singh. In 1712 Banda conquered the Lohgarh Fort. A huge army of 20,000 mean amassed by the Muslim governor of Lahore besieged Banda for eight months at a fort in Gurdaspur in 1715. Banda Singh Bahadur along with 600 Sikhs were finally captured and brought to Delhi where they were all tortured to death for refusing to convert to Islam.

Baba Deep Singh (1680? to 1762)

Baba Deep Singh was a great Sikh scholar who became a soldier and martyr for the defense of Sikhism. Not much is known about his early life but when he visited Anandpur Sahib in 1700, he became a Khalsa and decided to stay. There he learned Gurmukhi from Bhai Mani Singh along with horse riding, archery as well as other arms training. Baba Deep Singh met Guru Gobind Singh at Damdama Sahib where Guru Gobind Singh told him to start preaching the message of Sikhism. Between 1715 and 1728 Baba Deep Singh and Bhai Mani Singh produced a number of hand written copies of the Guru Granth Sahib for distribution among the Sikhs. When Bhai Mani Singh became the head granthi at the Golden Temple, Baba Deep Singh stayed on as the head at Damdama

Sahib. In 1710 Baba Deep Singh joined Bana Singh Bahadur in the battle of Sirhind. Baba Deep Singh was also a survivor of the Chotta Ghalughara (Small Holocaust) in 1755 when 10,000 Sikhs were killed. In 1762 Ahmed Shah Abdhali the Afghan invader ordered the Golden Temple blown up and the sacred pool filled in with refuse. Baba Deep Singh came out of scholarly retirement at Damdama Sahib and asked Sikhs to march with him to Amritsar to avenge the desecration. Along the way to Amritsar 5,000 Sikhs joined Baba Deep Singh. On the outskirts of Amritsar Baba Deep Singh and the heavily outnumbered Sikh fought two fierce battles against a mughal force of 20,000. In the second engagement Baba Deep Singh was fatally wounded in the neck but had vowed to die in the precincts of the Golden Temple. Although mortally wounded Baba Deep Singh was able to continue fighting until he was able to make his way to the Sacred Pool of the Golden Temple where he finally expired.

The Sahibzadas

These were the four sons of Guru Gobind Singh who bravely sacrificed their lives for Sikhism and are remembered every day in Ardas (the common prayer).

Baba Ajit Singh (1687 to 1704) and Baba Jujhar Singh (1689 to 1704)

Baba Ajit Singh was the oldest son of Guru Gobind Singh and was born on January 7, 1687 at Anandpur Sahib. Baba Jujhar Singh the Gurus second son was born in March 1689. Both brothers received religious education as well as training in the weapons of war. During the battle of Chamkaur in 1704 in which the Guru and 40 Sikh fought against overwhelming odds, both brothers died in battle. During the battle Baba Ajit Singh asked his fathers permission to go out of the fort and fight the enemy. He said, "Dear father, my name is Ajit or Unconquerable. I will not be conquered. And if conquered, I will not flee or come back alive. Permit me to go, dear father". Guru Gobind Singh hugged and kissed his beloved son before sending him into battle where he fought heroically until his last breath. Baba Jujhar Singh having watched his brother fight, asked Guru Gobind Singh, "Permit me, dear father to go where my brother has gone. Don't say that I am too young. I am your son. I am a Singh or Lion of yours. I shall prove worthy of you. I shall die fighting, with my face towards the enemy, with God and the Guru on my lips and in my heart". Guru Gobind Singh embraced him and said, "Go my son and wed life-giving Death. We have been here for a while. Now we shall return to our real home. Go and wait for me there. Your grandfather and elder brother are already waiting for you". Thus the Guru watched his two sons achieve eternal peace through martyrdom.

Baba Zorawar Singh (1696 to 1704) and Baba Fateh Singh (1698 to 1704)

The two youngest sons of Guru Gobind Singh, Baba Zorawar Singh was the third son and was born in 1696 while Baba Fateh Singh was the youngest son and was born in 1698. During the crossing of the river Sarsa following the departure of the Guru and his family from Anandpur Sahib, the Sikhs were attacked by the treacherous mughals who had guaranteed them safe passage. During the ensuring battle and confusion, both sons along with Mata Gujri, Guru Gobind Singh's mother, were separated from the others. Eventually through the treachery of a Brahmin named Gangu they fell into the hands of Nawab Wazir Khan the governor of Sirhind. The Nawab gave the two young brothers a choice of either converting to Islam or being put to death. Baba Zorawar Singh said to his little brother, "My brother the time to sacrifice our lives has arrived. What do you think? What should be our reply?" Baba Fateh Singh his younger brother replied, "Brother dear, our grandfather, Guru Tegh Bahadur parted with his head; he stoutly refused to part with his religion. We should follow his example. We have received the baptism of the spirit and the sword. We are the Guru's lions. Why should we fear death? It is best that we should give up our lives for the sake of our religion. I am prepared to die". Baba Zorawar Singh replied, "That is good, indeed. The blood of Guru Arjan, Guru Hargobind, Guru Tegh Bahadur and Guru Gobind Singh runs in our veins. We are their descendants. We cannot do anything unworthy of our family". Both sons were bricked up in a wall and had their heads cut off but they steadfastly refused to convert to Islam.

Sikhism and Other Religions

"Of all the religions, the best religion is to repeat God's Name and to do pious deeds. Of all the religious rites, the best rite is to remove the filth of evil intellect by association with the saints". (Guru Arjan Dev, Ashtpadi, pg. 266) Sikhism was founded by Guru Nanak who shaped a new, unique and distinct religion during his life time. Under the stewardship of the Ten Gurus Sikhism was able to gather many followers from other religions. Although the Gurus were critical of other religions they very strongly believed in religious freedom. They also emphasized that the most important thing was not which faith one followed but the remembrance of God at all time and the leading of a decent and honourable life. Due to it's relatively young nature Sikhism is sometimes misunderstood to be only a reform movement or branch of older existing religions. This is certainly not the case, like all religions there are some similarities as well as differences.

HINDUISM

Like Hinduism Sikhism believes in the transmigration of the soul. There are countless cycles of births and deaths. One only breaks this cycle when they achieve mukhti (merger with God).

Karma

Karma regulates the reincarnation and transmigration of the soul, Sikhism links Karma with the doctrine of grace.

"Mortals obtain a human body as a result of good deeds but he reaches the gate of salvation with God's kind grace". (Guru Nanak, Japji)

Maya

The world is just an illusion and some get enchanted with this illusion and forget God.

Differences

Sikhism rejects polytheism and accepts monotheism. Whereas Sikhism starts with one God and universalizes him, Hinduism starts with many Gods and occasionally gives glimpses of 'one'.

"I do not accept Ganesha as important. I do not meditate on Krishna, neither on Vishnu. I do not hear them and do not recognize them. My love is with the lotus feet of God. He is my protector, the Supreme Lord. I am dust of his Lotus feet". (Guru Gobind Singh, Krishna Avatar)

Authority of the Vedas and the belief that the truth revealed in them is absolute and that reading them one can realize perfection.

"I have read all the Vedas, but my mind's separation from God is not removed and the fife demons of my house (body) are stilled not even for an instant". (Guru Arjan Dev, Ashtpadis, pg. 687).

Sikhism does not recognize any priestly class.

"Kabir, the Brahman may be the Guru of the world, but he is not the Guru of the saints. He rots to death in the perplexities of the four Vedas" (Bhagat Kabir, Salok, pg. 1377).

Rejection of the Ashrama Dharma theory of dividing man's life into four stages. Instead the Gurus emphasized living the householders life. Rejection of the Varna distinction of division of human society into higher and lower castes.

"There are four castes of the literates, warriors, cultivators and menials and the four stages of life. He who meditates on the Lord is the most distinguished amongst men". (Guru Ram Das, Gond, pg. 861)

"The Lord asks not mortals caste and birth, so find thou out the Lord's true home (truth). That alone is man's caste and that his glory, as are the deeds which he does." (Guru Nanak, Parbhati, pg. 1330)

The Gurus rejected the Avtara theory of the incarnations of God. The Gurus not only exposed the mortality of these gods but used stories to illustrate moral values, such as 'pride leads to a fall' illustrated by the story of Harnakhash, untouchability becoming superior through devotion to god by Krishna stories and stories where Brahma, Vishnu and Shiva are shown to be ordinary mortals. The Gurus stressed that there is only one God and that these gods and goddesses were not true.

"In every age, the Lord creates the kings, who are sung of as His incarnations. Even they have not found His limits". (Guru Amar Das, Ashtpadis, pg. 423).

"Millions of incarnations of Vishnu and Shiv, with matted hair Desire Thee, O Kind Lord, with endless longing of their mind and body. Infinite and Inaccessible is Lord, the World Sustainer, and He is the Omnipresent wealthy Master. The gods, perfect persons, heavenly heralds and celestial singers contemplate on thee. The greater gods and heavenly dancers utter Thine praises. Myriads of kings, gods and many super human beings remember the Lord and Hail him". (Guru Arjan Dev, Chhant, pg. 455)

Worship of Idols and Images

"The blind ignorant ones stray in doubt and so deluded, deluded they pluck followers for worship. They worship the lifeless stones and adore tombs. Their service all goes in vain". (Guru Ram Das, Malar, pg. 1264).

"They who say the stone is a god; in vain is their service. He who falls at the feet of the stone; vain goes his labour. My Lord ever speaks. The Lord gives gifts to all the living beings. The lord is within, but the blind one knows not. Deluded by doubt, he is caught in a noose. The stone speaks not, nor gives anything. In vain are the ceremonies of the idolater, and fruitless his service". (Guru Arjan Dev, Bhairo, pg. 1160).

The Gita and Vedanta goal of a Mukt. Once he achieves salvation he does not live for the community. In Sikhism the Gurmukh achieving salvation lives to save others.

"Abandon lust, wrath, avarice and worldly love. Thus be rid of both birth and death. Distress and darkness shall depart from thy home, when, within thee, the Guru implants wisdom and lights the divine lamp. He, who serves the Lord crosses the sea of life. Through the Guru, O Slave Nanak, the entire world is saved". (Guru Arjan Dev, Gauri, pg. 241).

Belief that reading of the six Shastras and their mastery will bring salvation. "The greatly volumnous Simirtis and Shastras stretch out the extension of worldly love. The fools read them, but know not their Lord. Some rare one knows him by the Guru's grace. Of himself, the creator does and makes others do. By means of the True Bani, he implants truth within the mortal". (Guru Amar Das, Maru, pg. 1053).

"Many Shastras and many Simirtis have I seen and searched them all. Nanak, they equal not Lord God's invaluable Name". (Guru Arjan Dev, Gauri, pg. 265). Rejection of Sanskrit or any language as being sacred.

ISLAM

Fatherhood of God

Gurus believed that not only is God our Father, but he is Mother, Brother, Husband and Friend.

"Thou art my father, Thou art my mother, Thou art my kinsman, and Thou art my brother. In all the places Thou art my protector. Then why should I feel fear and anxiety?" (Guru Arjan Dev, Majh, pg. 103)

Bismillah of the Quran and the Mul Mantra of the Guru Granth Sahib are both dedicated to One Merciful God and are placed at the beginning of every new chapter. In both the nature of God transcends all concepts of time.

"God is one. His name is True. He is the Creator. His is without fear. He is inimical to none. His existence, is unlimited by time. He is beyond the cycles of birth and death, self existent and can be realized through the grace of the Guru". (Guru Nanak)

Emphasis on the Will of God in Quran is similar to the idea of Hukam in Guru Granth Sahib.

"Everyone is under the Hukam of the Lord; there is none outside it". (Guru Nanak, Japji)

Theory of creation of the world by the mere Will of God.

"The night and day, the Lord created, for the world to do the deeds. Through the Guru's instruction, the mind is illuminated and the darkness is dispelled. In His Guru's instruction, the mind is illuminated and the darkness is dispelled. In His Will, He creates all and pervades all the woods and grass blades". (Guru Amar Das, pg. 948)

Encouragement of alms for the needy and poor

Condemnation of idol worship.

Condemnation of asceticism.

Concept of Holy War, but in Sikhism it is only limited to fighting injustice

Differences

Sikhism does not believe that any Holy Book takes precedence over all others or any religions prophet is the final messenger of God.

"Say not that the vedas and Muslim books are false. False is he, who reflects not on them". (Bhagat Kabir, Parbhati, pg. 1350)

"The followers of the Vedas, the Bible and the Koran, standing at Your door, meditate on you. Uncounted are those who fall at Your Door". (Guru Arjan Dev, pg. 518)

"And many have been orthodox amongst the Muslims, and men of miracles, and Ashvini Kumaras, and the part-incarnations of Vishnu, all O all went the way of death. And many were the prophets and spiritual guides, yea, countless were they: they sprang from the dust and to dust they returned". (Guru Gobind Singh, Akal Ustati)

Purpose of the Holy Book

"Thus we have revealed the Koran in the Arabic tongue and proclaimed in it warnings and threats so that they may take heed and guard themselves against evil". (20:114 Quran)

"Upon this Plate, three things have been placed: Truth, Contentment and Contemplation. The Ambrosial nectar of the Naam, the name of our Lord and Master, has been placed upon it as well; it is the support of all. One who eats it and enjoys it shall be saved. This thing can never be forsaken; keep this always and forever in your mind. The dark world-ocean is crossed over, by grasping the feet of the lord; O Nanak, it is all the extension of God". (Guru Arjan Dev, Mundavanee, pg. 1429).

Sikhism believes that people of different religions are equally capable of achieving salvation while still following their own religion.

"Believes, take neither Jews nor Christians for your friends. They are friends with one another. Whoever of you seek their friendship shall become one of their number. Allah does not guide the wrongdoers". (5:49, Quran)

"Mohmmed is Allah's apostle. Those who follow him are ruthless to the unbelievers but merciful to one another". (48:29, Quran)

"When the sacred months are over slay the idolaters wherever you find them. Arrest them, besiege them, and lie in ambush everywhere for them. If they repent and take to prayer and pay the alms-tax, let them go their way. Allah is forgiving and merciful". (9:4, Quran)

"There is a garden, in which so many plants have grown. They bear the Ambrosial Nectar of the Naam as their fruit. Consider this, O wise one, by which you may attain the state of Nirvaanaa. All around this garden are pools of poison, but within it is the Ambrosial Nectar, O Siblings of Destiny. There is only one gardener who tends it. He takes care of every leaf and branch. He brings all sorts of plants and plants them there. They all bear fruit—none is without fruit". (Guru Arjan Dev, Asa, pg. 385).

"The temple or the mosque are the same, the Hindu worship or the Musalman prayer are the same; all men are the same; it is through error they appear different. Deities, demons, Yakshas, heavenly singers, Musalmans and Hindus adopt the customary dress of their different countries. All men have the same eyes, the same ears, the same body, the same build, a compound of earth, air, fire, and water. Allah and Abhekh are the same, the Purans and the Quran are the same; they are all alike; it is the one God who created all. The Hindu God and the Muhammadan God are the same; let no man even by mistake suppose there is a difference". (Guru Gobind Singh, Akal Ustat, pg. 275).

Sri Guru Granth Sahib places greater emphasis on love of God as the main motivation for man rather than fear of God.

"Truly, none will take heed but the wise: those who keep faith with Allah and do not break their pledge; who join together what He has bidden to be united; who fear their Lord and dread the terrors of Judgement-day; who for the sake of Allah endure with fortitude…" (13:18, Quran)

"Allah's reward is great. Therefore fear Him with all your hearts and be attentive, obedient, and charitable. That will be best for you". (64:13, Quran)

"Within my heart, I sing the Glorious praises of the Lord, and celebrate the Word of the Lord's Shabad. The Lord Himself is pervading and permeating the world; so fall I love with him!" (Guru Nanak Dev, pg. 790)

"Remembering Him in meditation, one abides in peace; one becomes happy, and suffering is ended. Celebrate, make merry, and sing God's Glories. Forever and ever, surrender to the True Guru". (Guru Arjan Dev, Asa, pg. 386).

Sikhism does not believe in the idea of Gods name being only those authorized in a religious tradition or Holy Book.

"Many are Thy Names and infinite Thine forms and it cannot be told how many merits Thou hast". (Guru Nanak, Asa, pg. 358).

Non-Sikhs are allowed to visit and enter the most sacred shrine of the religion, the Golden Temple.

"Believers, know that the idolaters are unclean. Let them not approach the Sacred Mosque after this year is ended" (9:26, Quran)

"Blessed is the place, and blessed are those who dwell there, where God's Name is meditated upon. The sermons and songs of God's praises are sung there and there in nothing but peace, poise and tranquillity". (Guru Arjan Dev, Raga Bilaval, pg. 816).

"If the Lord Allah lives only in the mosque, then to whom does the rest of the world belong?...The God of the Hindus lives in the southern lands, and the God of the Muslims lives in the west. So search in your heart—look deep into your heart of hearts; this is the home and the place where God lives". (Bhagat Kabir, pg. 1349)

Attitude towards women. Sikh women are allowed to lead congregations of men at the temple or administer all religious ceremonies involving either men or women.

"Men have authority over women because Allah has made the one superior to the other, and because they spend their wealth to maintain them. Good women are obedient. They guard their unseen parts because Allah has guarded them. As for those from whom you fear disobedience, admonish them and send them to beds apart and beat them". (4:34, Quran)

"We are born of woman, we are conceived in the womb of woman, we are engaged and married to woman. We make friendship with woman and the lineage continued because of woman. When one woman dies, we take another one, we are bound with the world through woman. Why should we talk ill of her, who gives birth to kings? The woman is born from woman; there is nssone without her. Only the One true lord is without woman" (Guru Nanak Dev, Var Asa, pg. 473)

Sikhism does not believe in women wearing veils.

"Stay, stay, O daughter-in-law-do not cover your face with a veil. In the end, this shall not bring you even half a shell". (Bhagat Kabir, Asa, pg. 484)

Sikhism does not believe in fasting or pilgrimages.

"The mind is not softened by fasting or austerities. Nothing else is equal to worship of the Lord's Name". (Guru Nanak Dev, Ramkali, pg. 905).

"The pilgrimage to shrines, fasting, cleanliness and self-mortification are not of any avail, nor are the rituals, religious ceremonies and hollow adoration's. Deliverance, O! Nanak! is in the devotional service of God. Through duality the mortal is engrossed in worldliness. (Guru Nanak, Sri Rag, pg. 75)

Sikhism rejects the killing of any animal evoking a prayer or by slow death. Muslim Halal meat is forbidden for Sikhs.

"Yet holding the knife, the world they butcher. Wearing blue the rulers approval they seek; With money derived from mlechhas the Puranas they worship. Goats slaughtered over the unapproved Muslims texts they eat". (Guru Nanak, Raga Asa, pg. 472).

Sikhism rejects the idea of circumcision.

"Because of the love of woman, circumcision is done; I don't believe in it, O Siblings of Destiny. If God wished me to be a Muslim, it would be cut off by itself.

If circumcision makes one a Muslim, then what about a woman?" (Bhagat Kabir, Asa, pg. 477).

JUDAISM, CHRISTIANITY

Although no direct references are made these two religions, there are references to the holy books of the Sematic religions and their scriptures referred to in the Guru Granth Sahib as 'Kateb' (Taurat: The Book of Moses, Zabur: the Book of David, Injil: New Testament and Quran). It is likely that Guru Nanak met Christian and Jewish missionaries during his extensive travels to the west. Christian missionaries were also active in the southern parts of India visited by Guru Nanak. Because the Sikh Gurus were involved in extensive missionary work to convert people to Sikhism, they concentrated on the dominant religions of the masses at that time, which did not include Christianity and Judaism in the east.

Similarities

Submission to the will of God, Hukam.

Khalsa brotherhood and sacrament.

Brotherhood of man.

Fatherhood of God and salvation by grace.

Jewish emphasis on 'The Name'.

Differences

Salvation for the 'chosen people'. Sikhism believes anyone can achieve salvation irrespective of the religion that they follow if they endear God in their heart and daily actions.

Christian concept of Jesus as son of God. Sikhism regards all as the children of God.

Infant baptism. In Sikhism child baptism into the Khalsa brotherhood is discouraged. One should only become a Khalsa when they are able to fully understand the duties and responsibilities.

Special day for worship. There is no special day like Sunday or Sabbath for worship.

Heaven and hell as physical entities. In Sikhism there are no such physical places. Hell is equivalent to the cycles of birth and deaths and heaven is equivalent to the soul merging with God.

Priests. Guru Gobind Singh abolished the priestly class making Sikhism free from their weaknesses and egos, the only priest is the Living Guru, the Guru Granth Sahib which contains all the knowledge and which is available for reading by any Sikh.

BUDDHISM

Buddha tried to abolish the caste system and believed in the idea of brotherhood.

Complete disregard for forms and rituals and emphasis on purity of the heart and sincerity in our dealings with others.

Buddha preached in the spoken language of the people and did not believe in the sanctity of any one language.

Differences

Buddhism does not believe in the need for God, in that sense Buddhist doctrine is absolutely atheistic.

"By forgetting the Supreme Lord, all the aliments cling to the man. The non-believers in the Omnipresent Lord suffer separation from Him, birth after birth". (Guru Arjan Dev, Majh, pg. 135)

Buddhist belief that to live is to suffer.

"But rare is such a slave and serf of the Lord, who understands the Reality of the union with Him. He (the follower) has no pain, but all comforts and with his eyes, he sees only the One Lord". (Guru Arjan Dev, Kanra, pg. 1302).

"There is joy, bliss and happiness in my home. I sing the praise of the name, reflect on the Name and the Name is the support of my vital breath". (Guru Arjan Dev Kanra, pg. 1302)

The end of life is Nirvana, which is complete extinction. The Guru's idea of Nirvana was eternal bliss as the soul merges with God.

"He who is devoted towards the Lord in his mind, he gets eternal bliss and realises the Lord and the state of Nirvana" (Guru Ram Das, Asa, pg. 444)

Sikhism does not have any order of monks or nuns.

YOGA

Yogis did not recognise the caste system.

They had no scruples about the impurity of certain foods and some were non-vegetarian.

Some yogis led married lives.

Free kitchen, many in western India operate free kitchens open to all twice a day.

Differences

The practice of Yoga is more or less physical in nature, through chanting, breathing and other exercises one tries to achieve physical mastery over the body. The Gurus rejected this because it does not help the yogi to get rid of egoism, selfishness and does not help in the process of building up moral character or interaction with others, so essential for householders life.

"One may be the knower of six schools of philosophy, He may do the work of inhaling, exhaling and holding the breath. He may practice, Divine knowledge, meditation, pilgrimages, and ablutions. He may cook his own food, touch not others and abide in wilderness, if in his heart, he bears not live with the Lord's name, then all that he does, that is perishable. Superior to him, thou the lowest pariah, O Nanak, in whose heart God, the Nurser of the Universe abides". (Guru Arjan Dev, Pauri, pg. 253)

JAINISM

Jainism was completely rejected by the Gurus. It preaches a life of the ascetic combined with extreme Ahinsa (non injury to any living being) as well as a very unhygienic lifestyle.

"They have their heads plucked, drink dirty water and repeatedly beg and eat other's leavings. They spread out ordure, with their mouths, suck its ordure and dread to look at water. With hands smeared with ashes, they have their heads plucked like sheep. The daily routine of their mothers and fathers they give up, and their kith and kin bewail loudl;. For them none gives barley rolls and food on leaves, nor performs last rites, nor lights earthern lamp. After death where shall they be cast? The sixty-eight places of pilgrimage grant them no refuge, and Pandits eat not their food. They ever remain filthy day and night, and bear not sacrificial marks on their brow. They ever sit in groups, as if mourning and go not into the True Court. With begging bowls slung round their loins and a clew in their hands, they walk in single file. They are neither disciples of Gorakh nor adorers of Shiva, nor Muslim Qazis and Mullah's". (Guru Nanak, Solk, pg. 149).

SUFISM

Emphasis on music and singing the praises of God.

"All the comforts lie in the meditation of the one Name. All the religions are contained in singing God's praises". (Guru Arjan Dev, Asa, pg. 392).

Emphasis on inner worth instead of external rituals.

"Easy is it to utter and cause to utter. But difficult it is to accept Thy Will". (Guru Arjan Dev, Sri Rag, pg. 51).

"They who perform many religious rites, but meditate not on the Creator and in their mind have no Divine discrimination, suffer transmigration and wander in many existence's. Guru Arjan Dev, Pauri, pg. 297).

Respect for all religions and prophets and a general tolerance for the convictions of others.

Free community kitchen.

Differences

Belief in poverty and asceticism. Gurus believed one should lead the life of a householder.

"To be a householder, who at least gives to some is better than this wearing deceptive robes (of the recluse)" (Guru Amar Das, Slok, pg. 587).

The final stage of the Sufi is renunciation away from family and community. There is no need to renounce these in Sikhism.

Belief that life is misery and the world nothing but an embodiment of pain.

"Ever meditate within thy mind on Him, by whose kindness thou dwellest comfortably in thy palace. By whose kindness, thou abidest in comfort with thy family, rapeat thou His name with thy tongue for all the eight watches. Nanak, constantly meditate on Him, who is worthy of meditation and by whose favour thou enjoyest love and pleasures". (Guru Arjan Dev, Ashtpadi, pg. 269).

BHAKTI MOVEMENT

The Sikh Gurus and the Bhakti movement shared many similarities as well as a number of differences. Sikhism should not be looked at as simply an extension of the Bhakti movement but as a new movement entirely. While the Bhagat's shared some of the same beliefs as those expressed by the Gurus, the Bhagats were not able to make a clear break from their religious heritage. The Sikh Gurus on the other hand were able to make that clean break to form a new religion which grew and has survived the test of time, unlike many of the Bhakti reform movements which did not. Sikhs consider the works of the various Bhagats in Sri Guru Granth Sahib as being equal to the writings of the Gurus themselves and as such, deserving of the same respect and reverence.

Similarities

Outspoken criticism of the caste system.

Stern condemnation of idol worship.

Harsh attacks on the hyprocrisy of the priestly class and ritualization of religion.

Differences

Bhagat Kabir regarded the world and life as suffering and welcomed death as the beginning of the blissful existence. The Gurus believed you can achieve blissful mukhti while alive and do not have to wait for death.

Bhagat Kabir believed that either one should become a householder and do good actions or he should become a Vairagi and renounce the world. Guru Nanak believed only in the path of the householder.

Kabir was a strict vegetarian and strongly believed in the doctrine of Ahinsa, non destruction of any life; man, animal or even a flower. The Sikh Guru's did not believe in this Hindu practice.

Bhagat Ravi Das believed in a physical heaven, while the Sikh Gurus did not believe in a physical concept of heaven. The Sikh heaven is to merge and become one with God.

Sikhism in the 21st Century

"In the golden age of Satjug, everyone spoke the Truth. In each and every home, devotional worship was performed by the people, according to the Guru's Teachings. In that Golden Age, religion had four feet. How rare are those people who, as Gurmukh, contemplate this and understand. In all four ages, the Naam, the Name of the Lord, is glory and greatness. One who holds tight to the Naam is liberated; without the Guru, no one obtains the Naam. In the Silver Age of Traytai, one leg was removed. Hypocrisy became prevalent, and people thought that the Lord was far away. The Gurmukhs still understood and realized; the Naam abided deep within them, and they were at peace. In the Brass age of Dwaapur, duality and double-mindedness arose. Deluded by doubt, they knew duality. In this Brass age, religion was left, with only two feet. Those who became Gurmukh implanted the Naam deep within. In the Iron age of Kaljug, religion was left with only one power. It walks on just one foot; love and emotional attachment to Maya have increased. Lord and emotional attachment to Maya bring total darkness. If someone meets the True Guru, he is saved, through the Naam, the name of the Lord. Throughout, the ages, there is only the One True Lord. Among all, is the true Lord; there is no other at all. Praising the True Lord, there is no other at all. Praising the True Lord, true peace is attained. How rare are those, who as Gurmukh, chant the Naam. Throughout all the ages, the Naam is the ultimate, the most sublime. How rare are those, who as Gurmukh, understand this. One who meditates on the Lord's Name is a humble devotee. O Nanak, in each and every age, the Naam is glory and greatness." (Guru Amar Das, pg. 880). Here we are in the age of Kaljug, the age of darkness. Where do Sikhs find themselves as a religion and a people and where are they going as the next millennia approaches? Today Sikhs face a host of problems and issues, but instead of focusing on those problems as has been done countless times before, this paper will instead try to highlight some of the key issues and challenges that Sikhs will have to deal with in the very near future.

At this time the Sikh religion is firmly, in control of the older generations from Punjab and it's religious institutions around the world are run as virtual extensions of Punjab and the Punjabi mentality. Many issues are not dealt with because they never had to be dealt with in the past and it is always easier to maintain the status quo rather than try to find new answers. What will happened ten or fifteen years down the road when the Sikh religious institutions around the world are run by a new generation which were not born in Punjab or have very little contact with Punjab? A lot of these potential problems that Sikhs will be faced are still in their infancy right now. Either Sikhs can choose to ignore them today as they have been to a large extent, which means that they will become major crises for the religious tomorrow, or they can start planning and trying to develop solutions. We are approaching a major crossroads as a religion which will either see Sikhism become truly a major world religion as the Gurus wished or we will see it wither away and become extinct over time. The choice is clearly in our own hands. Karl Marx, the father of communism once said, "if God manifests in the research institute, then only shall I believe in His existence". There is an increasing belief in the world today that the ideas of "faith" are blind and that "faith" is equivalent to "being blind". The question which should be asked is that does society not also place blind faith in science? Who Has Seen or touched an electron? Scientists have never actually seen a black hole in outer space, but only theorize its existence based on the bending of light waves of neighbouring stars and galaxies.

Can science convey the beauty of a sunset or the small of a rose or the value of a person? No it can not. All that science can do is to quantify these by breaking them down into various analysis that do not necessarily add up to describe the substance of the whole. A human being is much more than water, minerals and trace elements that make up our bodies. The smell of a rose is much more than the quantity and type of molecules that it releases into the air. God and religion can not be understood by blindly applying the scientific method. "God is not found by intellectual devices; His is unknowable and unseen". (Guru Arjan Dev, pg. 1098) "He is not obtained by intellectual recitation or great cleaverness; only by love does the mind obtain him". (Guru Nanak Dev, pg. 436)

As science pushes back the frontiers of the known universe can science and logic be used to explain the entire universe?

"So many worlds beyond this world, O, so very many! What power holds them, and supports their weight? The names and the colours of the assorted species of beings were all inscribed by the ever-flowing Pen of God. Who knows how to write this account? Just imagine what a huge scroll it would take! What power! What fascinating beauty! And what gifts! Who can know their extent? You created the vast expanse of the universe with one word! Hundred of thousands of rivers began to flow. How can your creative potency be described?" (Guru Nanak Dev, Japji Sahib)

When Guru Arjan Dev and his scribe Bhai Gurdas finished compiling Sri Guru Granth Sahib in 1604, the technology of the time was limited to paper. Now 400 years later technology has advanced at a blinding pace and its advancement is continuing at an exponential rate. How Sikhs deal with these advancement will be critical to their survival.

How can technology affect something as timeless and immortal as Sri Guru Granth Sahib? Well the definition of what exactly is our Guru is causing controversy in itself. Do we as Sikhs worships the teachings of our Gurus as our living Shabad Guru today, or do we worship the technology of that message, i.e. the physical "book"? Sikh are very quick to point out to the unfamiliar outsider that may visit a Gurdwara that 'no we are not idol worshippers' because of the way we treat Sri Guru Granth Sahib in the Gurdwara. The standard Sikh response is that we worship and show utmost respect to the wisdom of our Gurus enshrined in the book and are not worshipping the book itself. If we truly worship the message and not the messenger then why is there so much confusion starting to develop over what exactly is the Shabad Guru? Some say that the Guru can only be in book form in its original Gurmukhi form. That the Guru can only be in the one volume, not two or 8 volumes. How do we deal with translations of Sri Guru Granth Sahib into different languages? How do we deal with a CD containing the original Gurmukhi and a English translation of Sri Guru Granth Sahib? How do we deal with Gurmukhi and English versions of Sri Guru Granth Sahib being transmitted across the Internet?

What is our Guru? A good starting place to start in searching for answers can be found at the very end of Sri Guru Granth Sahib itself in Mundaavanee. Here Guru Arjan Dev Ji writes:

"Upon this plate, three things have been placed: Truth, Contentment and Contemplation. The Ambrosial Nectar of the Naam, the name of our Lord and Master, has been placed upon it as well; it is the support of all. One who eats it and enjoys it shall be saved. This thing can never be forsaken; keep this always and forever in your mind. The dark world-ocean is crossed over, by grasping the Feet of the Lord; O Nanak, it is all the extension of God". (Guru Arjan Dev, Mundaavanee, pg. 1429).

Are Truth, Contentment and Contemplation not contained in two volumes, or on a Gurbani CD or a translation in another language or possibly transmitted across the Internet?

"The Ambrosial Word of Gurbani proclaims the essence of reality. Spiritual wisdom and meditation are contained within it. The Gurmukhs chant it, and the Gurmukhs realize it. Intuitively aware, they meditate on it". (Guru Angad Dev, pg. 1243).

Are spiritual wisdom, meditation and the essence of reality not contained in two volumes, or on a Gurbani CD or transmitted across the Internet or translated into another language?

The Gurus undertook missions to spread their teachings in the native languages of the people they came into contact with. They never believed in the exclusivity of their teachings or in an intellectual elite with a 'sacred' language.

"All the sources of creation, and all languages meditate on Him, forever and ever". (Guru Arjan Dev, pg. 456) "Now, you are an Arab, now a Persian, now a Turk. Now the utterer of Pehlavi, now of Pashtu, now of Sanskrit, now of the peoples tongue, now of the language of the gods". (Guru Gobind Singh, Akal Ustati).

Guru Amar Das, the Guru which helped to turn Sikhism into an organised institutional religion by sending Sikh missionaries to the various parts of Asia wrote:

"Enshrine the Lord's name within your heart. The Word of the Guru's Bani prevails throughout the world; through this Bani, the Lord's Name is obtained". (Guru Amar Das, pg. 1066).

How could Guru's Bani prevail throughout the world unless Guru Amar Das meant that the message of the house of Nanak as found in Sri Guru Granth Sahib transcends all cultural and linguistic boundaries.

Unlike the sematic religions (Judaism, Christianity, Islam), Sikhism does not believe in the idea of a "chosen people" yet we continue to propagate our religion for the most part solely through inheritance. How can Sikhism ever become a major world religion if we stick to this "ghetto mentality"? The Gurus had a true world view of humanity as opposed to a "Punjabi-centric" view that most Sikhs hold today.

"The True Guru, the Primal Being, is kind and compassionate; all are alike to Him. He looks upon all impartially; with pure faith in the mind, He is obtained". (Guru Ram Das, pg. 300).

"The same eyes have they, the same ears, the same body, the same habits, a get-together of earth, air, water and fire. Allah is no different from Abhekha, the Puranas no different from the Quran. All men are made alike. They appear no different to me". (Guru Gobind Singh, Kabitas 71-90, Akal Ustati)

Only by returning to our missionary roots and realizing and accepting that Sikhism must be propagated based on it's virtues and principals as opposed to inheritance can we break free of this "ghetto mentality" which is seriously inhibiting the growth and global propagation of Sikhism.

Like most world religions today, we can see a divergence taking place. On one side you have people who have totally abandoned Sikhism or treat religion like a part time hobby. On the other end of the spectrum you have the development of hard-core fundamentalists with their "exclusive club" mentality, intolerance and attempts at distorting our religious heritage and history to accommodate their own views. Which is the more dangerous and destructive element? Narrow mindedness and intolerance is just as bad or worse than having no religion at all. Religion is not about showing others how devoted and religious a person one is, but actually living by the principles and teachings of the Gurus for ones own sake rather than for the sake of others. "Whosoever assumes a religious garb pleases not God even a bit. O ye men, understand this clearly in your minds, that God is attained not through showmanship. They who practice deceit, attain not Deliverance in the hereafter. They do so only to accomplish the affairs of the world and even the kings worship them for their appearance! But through showmanship, God is attained not, howsoever one searches. He who subdues his mind alone recognizes the Transcendent God". (Guru Gobind Singh, Chaupai 53-55, Chapter 6, Vachitra Natak).

The 5K's and physical distinctiveness of the Khalsa are a cornerstone of Sikhism and this will never change, nor should it. What has changed though is the shift in emphasis to the ritualization of our religion as opposed to understanding and applying the spiritual teachings of the Gurus. Sri Guru Granth Sahib has become something only accessible and understood by an elite minority. The majority are happy just to go to the Gurdwara and listen to the hymns and show respect to the "book" without understanding what they hear or read. The shift in emphasis has occurred over time because of a lack of religious education, both on the institutional level as well as the family level. Unless this disturbing trend is reversed Sikhism will become nothing but a religion of empty rituals.

"Kabeer, the paper is the prison, and the ink of rituals are the bars on the windows". (Bhagat Kabir, pg. 1371). With a shift in emphasis to rituals, religion itself becomes a marketable commodity. We can see this in it's advanced stages in the Christian religion, but Sikhism is starting to follow this same trend. The religious experience itself is being exploited as a financial commodity and a money making scheme. This is clearly unacceptable according to the Sikh doctrine. "Cursed are the lives of those who read and write the Lord's name to sell it". (Guru Nanak Dev, pg. 1245). The name of the Lord o this alone is my wealth. I do not tie it up to hide it, nor do I sell it to make my living". (Bhagat Kabir, pg. 1157).

To help clearly define what a Sikh is and how a Sikh individual should lead their daily life in accordance with the spiritual principles of Sri Guru Granth Sahib, the Rehit Maryada was developed. A tremendous amount of work and effort went into creating the Rehit Maryada and it has been ratified and accepted by the entire Sikh people as their one and only official Sikh Code of Conduct and Conventions. It must be realized that unlike Sri Guru Granth Sahib, the Rehit Maryada is a dynamic document of Panthic consensus. As such it must be fully representative of the changes in society and take into account the Sikh Diaspora. The current Rehit Maryada contains such comments as:

"A Sikh daughter must be married to a Sikh" (Chapter 11, Article 18) and "A baptized Sikh ought to get his wife baptized".

What does this mean? Does this mean that a Sikh's son may freely marry a non-Sikh? Does this mean that a baptized Sikh's wife should not encourage her husband to also become a Khalsa?

"Nor must a lit lamp be placed beside or a cow got bestowed in donation" (Funeral Ceremonies, Article 19). How realistic is such a scenario ever occurring outside of rural Punjab? Not very likely.

Because of it's dynamic nature and because the framework has already been laid, the Rehit Maryada needs to be constantly reviewed and updated to reflect current social realities. The Rehit Maryada is the document which every Sikh can turn to as a guide on how the universal spiritual principles of the Gurus found in Sri Guru Granth Sahib can be applied to their daily lives in order to be considered a Sikh and a member of the Sikh community at large. The fact that we have such a document for maintaining uniformity in Sikh practices around the world is a great accomplishment. But we can not rest on our laurels for having completed this great task. Instead the Rehit Maryada must be constantly updated to avoid it's obsolescence. It must be gender neutral, it must be geographically neutral and it must be a source of answers to new social issues and concerns which develop as society changes.

What is the Sikh view on homosexuality? What is the Sikh view of abortion? What is the Sikh view on divorce? What is the Sikh view on abortion? What is the Sikh view on euthanasia? What is the Sikh view on contraception and birth control? The current Rehit Maryada does not contain any answers to any of these questions. Answers to such questions can be found in the Living Guru, Sri Guru Granth Sahib, but every Sikh currently has their own interpretations and views on these topics. It is precisely to avoid such a plurality of views and to foster Panthic uniformity as per the Sikh doctrine that we must rely on the Rehit Maryada to provide us with the answers.

Sikhs always like to talk and complain about what is wrong with other Sikhs, how they do not follow the vision of our Gurus and what they should be doing. There have been plenty of papers such as this which have clearly defined what problems we face or will face and what we should be doing. There is no shortage in that regard. The problem exists in having the collective willpower to enact the necessary solutions.

"Easy is it to utter and cause to utter. But difficult is it to accept Thy Will". (Guru Arjan Dev, pg. 51)

In conclusion it is my firm belief that the solutions to any challenges that Sikhs may face as a religion in the next millennia can only come about if we first start to make changes to our own way of thinking and acting on the individual level. The wisdom of the Gurus and their teachings are something too priceless which we cannot afford to loose due to our own shortsightedness or lack of vision.

Appendix—I

Sikh Calendar

Starting in 1999 all religious holidays will be observed according to the newly modified Nanakshahi Calendar. The years of the Nanakshahi calendar start with the birth of Guru Nanak Dev in 1469, 1998 is considered Nanakshahi 530. The modification is that now the calendar is based on the length of the tropical solar year, instead of the lunar cycle, meaning that dates will not fluctuate from year to year as they did previously. The Sikh new year begins with Chet 1 which in the Common Era calendar in March 14, in 1999 and it will be the year 531 Nanakshahi.

Sikh Month	*Common era date for beginning of month*
Chet	March 14
Vaisakh	April 14
Jeth	May 15
Harh	June 15
Sawan	July 16
Bhadon	August 16
Asu	September 15
Katik	October 15
Maghar	November 14
Poh	December 14
Magh	January 13
Phagan	February 12

Gurpurbs

Guru	*Parkash (Birth)*	*Gur Ghaddhi (Guruship)*	*Jyoti Jot (Death)*
			Asu 8
Guru Nanak Dev	Katik Pooranmashi*	from Parkash	Asu 8 September 22
	Vaisakh 5	Asu 4	Vaisakh 3
Guru Angad Dev	April 18	September 18	April 16

(Contd...)

Guru Amar Das	Jeth 9	Vaisakh 3	Asu 2
	May 23	April 16	September 16
Guru Ram Das	Asu 25	Asu 2	Asu 2
	October 9	September 16	September 16
Guru Arjan Dev	Vaisakh 19	Asu 2	Harh 2
	May 2	September 16	June 16
Guru Har Gobind	Harh 21	Jeth 28	Chet 6
	July 5	June 11	March 19
Guru Har Rai	Magh 19	Chet 1	Katik 6
	January 31	March 14	October 20
Guru Harkrishan	Sawan 8	Katik 6	Vaisakh 3
	July 23	October 20	April 16
Guru Tegh Bahadur	Vaisakh 5	Vaisakh 3	Maghar 11
	April 18	April 16	November 24
Guru Gobind Singh	Poh 23	Maghar 11	Katik 7
	January 5	November 24	October 21
Guru Granth Sahib	Bhadon 17	Katik 6	
	September 1 Installation in Golden Temple by Guru Arjan Dev	October 20	

* Guru Nanak's birthday has been traditionally celebrated on Katik Poornamashi. Although the correct birth date has been established as Vaisakh 1 (April 14), it will continue to be celebrated on Katik Poornamashi until such time as it is changed to Vaisakh 1. Katik Pooranmashi in 1999 is on November 23 and in 2000 is on November 11.

Other Religious Observances

Event	*Date*
Creation of the Khalsa	Vaisakh 1
Vaisakhi	April 14
Martyrdom of Guru	Poh 8
Gobind Singh's Elder Sons	December 21
Martyrdom of Guru	Poh 13
Gobind Singh Younger Sons	December 26

1998 Dates

Events in 1998 will still be marked by the old lunar calendar. The remaining events include:

Installation of Guru Granth Sahib as Eternal Guru—October 22, 1998

Birthday of Guru Nanak Dev—November 4, 1998

Death of Guru Tegh Behadur—November 24, 1998

Sikh Festivals

There are numerous Sikh fairs and festivals. Some are of local importance as Maghi of Muktsar and Hola Mohalla of Anandpur. The most important festivals are observed by the Sikhs wherever they are. On such occasions the whole Sikh families of a particular place gather in a gurudwara. It is properly decorated and illuminated. The Granth is read constantly. Hymns are sung in chorus or by professional Sikh singers. Prayer is said. Sweet pudding (karah prasad) is distributed in the whole congregation. In hot weather sweetened and ice water is served at various places. Houses are lighted in the evening. A free langar at the main gurudwara is a must for every fair and festival.

Gurupurab

Literally festivals, Gurupurabs are anniversaries associated with the lives of the Sikh Gurus. The Sikhs celebrate 10 Gurupurabs in a year. At each of these festivals, one of the ten gurus of the Khalsa Pantha is honoured. Of these the important ones are the birthdays of Guru Nanak and Guru Gobind Singh and the martyrdom days of Guru Arjun Dev and Guru Teg Bahadur.

Guru Nanak's jayanti falls in the month of Kartik (October/November). The Sikhs believes that Guru Nanak brought enlightenment to the world, hence the festival is also called Prakash Utsav, the festival of light. The Tenth Guru Gobind Singh, was born on 2 December 1666 in Patna. The martyrdom day of the fifth Guru, Arjun Dev falls in the months of May and June and that of the ninth Guru, Tegh Bahadur, in November.

Prabhat Phersis, the early morning religious procession that goes around the localities singing shabads (hymns) start three weeks before the festival. Devotees offer sweets and tea when the procession passes by their homes. Gurupurabs mark the culmination of Prabhat Pheris.

The Guru Granth Sahib (the holy book of the Sikhs) is read continuously from beginning to end without a break for three days. This is known as akhand path. It is concluded on the day of the festival. The Granth Sahib is also carried in procession on a float decorated with flowers. Five armed guards, was represent the Panj Pyares, head the procession carrying Nishan Sahibs (the Sikh flag). Local bands play religious music and marching schoolchildren form a special part of the procession.

Sweets and community lunches are also offered to everyone irrespective of religious faith. It is served with a spirit of seva (service) and bhakti (devotion). Sikhs visit gurdwaras where special programmes are arranged and (religious songs) sung. Houses and gurudwaras are lit up to add to the festivities. On the martyrdom of Guru Arjun Dev sweetened milk is offered to the thirsty passers-by to commemorate the death of the Guru.

Guru Nanak, the founder of the Sikh faith, was born in a Punjabi village (presently in Pakistan) in 1469. Always secular in his outlook, he even organised a canteen where Muslims and Hindus of all castes could come and eat together. It is believed that he had a vision from god, in Sultanpur, directing him to preach to mankind.

Guru Gobind Singh forged the distinctive identity of the Sikhs and called them Khalsa (the pure) and made it mandatory for them to have the five Ks—Kesh (hair), Kripan (dagger), Kada (bracelet), Kangha (comb) and Kachcha (underwear). Guru Arjun Dev was burnt alive at the stake in the hot months of May and June and Guru Teg Bahadur was beheaded in Delhi.

Gurpurbs are part and parcel of Sikhism. In history we see that the Sikhs have to sacrifice even their lives in order to celebrate the Gurpurbs. Whether it is DEWALI (Bandi Chhor Diwas), VAISAKHI (Khalsa Sajna Diwas), or Martyrdom day of Guru Arjan Sahib (Sahidi Diwas), Sikhs gather and remember their Gurus and pay homage to the great Martyrs. All the Gurpurbs are celebrated with great fervour and enthusiasm by the Sikhs throughout the world. We are giving the account of the main and widely celebrated Gurpurbs.

The birthday celebrations and Gurpurbs of Guru Sahibs usually last for three days.

Generally before the birthday-date Akhand Path is held in the Gurdwara. A large procession (Nagarkirtan) is organised one day before the birthday. This is led by the Panj Piyaras (Five beloved ones) and the Palki (Palanquin) of Shri Guru Granth Sahib and followed by groups of kirtani Jatha, various schools bands and students, eminent citizens, Gatka parties (displaying mock-battle with the traditional weapons), and devotees singing hymns from Guru Granth Sahib in chorus. The passage of the nagarkirtan is decorated with flags, flowers, religious posters decorated gates and banners depicting various aspects of Sikhism. On the Gurpurab day, the Divan begins early in morning at about 4 or 5 a.m. with the singing of Asa-di-var and hymns from Guru Granth Sahib. Sometimes it is followed by katha (discourse), religious and Sikh Historical lectures and recitation of poems in praise of the Guru. Kirtan-Darbars and Amrit Sanchar ceremonies are also held in the Gurdwara hall. After Ardas and distribution of Karah Parshad (sweet pudding) the Langar (food) is served to one and all and there is kirtan till late in the night, the distribution of langer continues to the end of the programme.

Birthday of Guru Nanak Sahib

Guru Nanak Sahib (the First Nanak, the founder of Sikhism) was born on 20th October, 1469 at Rai-Bhoi-di Talwandi in the present district of Shekhupura (Pakistan), now Nankana Sahib. The Birthday of Guru Nanak Sahib falls on Kartik Puranmashi i.e., full moon day of the month Kartik. On this day the Birthday is celebrated every year. The Shrine (Gurdwara) representing the home of Baba Kalu (Father) and Mata Tripta (Mother) is called Gurdwara Janam Asthan, situated at Rai-Bhoi-di-Talwandi in the present district of Shekhupura (now Nanakana Sahib in Pakistani). The Sikh from all over the world gather here and celebrate the Gurupurab every year with great devotion and enthusiasm.

Birthday of Guru Gobind Singh Sahib

Guru Gobind Singh Sahib, the tenth Nanak was born at Patna Sahib on 22nd December 1666, (Poh Sudi Saptmi). His birthday generally falls in December or January or sometimes twice within a year as it is calculated according to Hindu Bikrami Calendar based on moon-year. S.Pal Singh Purewal of Canada prepared a new calender which is called "Nanakshahi Calendar" based on sun-year. According to this calendar the birthday of Guru Gobind Singh Sahib falls only once in a year i.e. on 5th January (every year). But the implementation of Nanakshahi Calendar is yet postponed.

Guru Arjan's Martyrdom Day

Guru Arjan's martyrdom day falls towards the close of May or beginning of June. In Lahore before partition almost every Hindu and Sikh was out to visit the Guru's samadhi or tomb. At short intervals there were sabils where sweetened and iced milk-water was served to every passer-by. The number of visitors was in lakh, not in thousands. Arrangements were so perfect that the parents of a lost child could be traced in no time. At numerous places there were parties of singers singing hymns, lecturers, sermons and kathas or narration of stories from sacred scriptures. Nowadays this day is celebrated everywhere in gurdwaras and by leading processions and serving cold drinks free.

Guru Tegh Bahadur's Martyrdom Day

Guru Tegh Bahadur's martyrdom day falls in November-December. The day is celebrated by organising processions, singing hymns in gurd varas, and by organising lecturers, sermons, kirtans, etc.

Baisakhi

Baisakhi is new year's day in Punjab. It falls on the month of Vaisakh. This festival marks in ripening of the Rabi harvest. The day coincides with the solar equinox on the 13th of April. It was on this day that the tenth Sikh Guru, Guru Gobind Singh, founded the Khalsa (the Sikh brotherhood) in 1699. For Sikhs, this is as a collective birthday. It is celebrated on April 13, though once in 36 years it occurs on 14th April.

The tenth guru, Guru Gobind Singh selected the auspicious day of Baisakhi to form the order of the Khalsa. On the 13th of April of 1699, at a meeting in Anandpur in Punjab, the guru called upon his people to come forward to sacrifice themselves for the good of the clan. Initially there were no response from the audience. However, after several calls from the guru five persons— Daya Ram Khatri, Dharm Das, Mokham Chand, Sahib Chand and Himmat Rai—were ready to offer themselves. Guru took each of them to the tent nearby and every time he returned alone with his bloodied sword. Then the guru went to the tent yet again, this time for a long time. He reappeared followed by the five men, clad in saffron-coloured garments. They sat on the dais while the guru prepared water to bless them. It an iron vessel, he stirred the batasha that his wife, Mata Jitoji had put into water, with a sword called Khanda Sahib. The water was not considered the sacred nectar of immortality called amrita. It was first given to the five volunteers, then drunk by the guru and later distributed to the crowd. All present, irrespective of caste or creed, became members of the Khalsa Pantha. Those five men were christened the Panch Pyare. He discontinued the tradition of gurus and asked all Sikhs to accept the Grantha Sahib as their eternal guide. The suffix Singh derived from the Sanskrit word singha meaning 'lion', was added to the name of all male Sikhs, while the women were to call themselves Kaur, assistants to the Singh.

To pay tribute to this event, prayer meetings are organised in gurdwaras across the country. The main celebration however, takes place in the gurdwara at Anandpur Sahib, where the order was formed. The Guru Grantha Sahib is ceremonially taken out, symbolically bathed with milk and water and placed on its throne. Priests called the Panch Pyare then chant the verses that were recited by the original Panch Pyare when the order was created. While the 'Panch Bani are being chanted, amrita is prepared in an iron vessel and distributed. Devotees sip the amrita five times and vow to work for the Khalsa Panth.

People visit gurdwaras and listen to kirtans (religious songs) and discourses. The holy scriptures known as the Grantha are read, and the book is then carried in a procession led by five leaders of the congregation, carrying drawn swords. After the prayer, sweetened semolinai is served to the congregation. The function ends with the community lunches. The traditional folk dances of Punjab, called the Gidda and Bhangra, are performed with great enthusiasm. Processions include mock duels and bands playing religious tunes.

On this memorable Baisakhi day (March, 30 of A.D. 1699), Guru Gobind Singh Sahib called a big meeting at Kesgarh Sahib near the city of Anandpur Sahib. Between fifty and eighty thousand Sikhs attended this meeting. When all were expecting to hear words of comfort and consolation from the lips of their Guru, they were perturbed to see him with a drawn sword in his hand and cried'. Is there anyone here who would lay down his life for Dharam?' There was a big silence, but the Guru went on repeating his demand. At the third call Daya Ram, A Khatri of Lahore, rose from his seat and offered himself. The Guru took him into an adjoining enclosure…(and soon after) came out with the (blood) dripping…(sword in hand) and flourishing it before the gathering, asked again, 'Is there any other Sikh here who will offer himself as a sacrifice (for the cause of Dharam)? At this Daram Das, a Jat of Delhi (Haryana side) came forward and was taken into the enclosure…(The Guru again came out with the blood-stained sword, and made his previous demand). In the same way three other men stood up, one after another, and offered themselves for the sacrifice. One was Mohkam Chand, a washerman of Dwarka (Gujarat State); another was Himmat, a cook of Jagannath (Orissa State); and the third was Sahib Chand, a barber of Bidar (Karnataka State). The Guru, after dressing the five in handsome clothes, brought them to the assembly. These five were then administered 'Khande di Pahul' (the double-edged Sword Amrit). They were then knighted as Singhs, as the Five beloved ones, the first members of the order of the Khalsa. The Guru then asked them to administer the Pahul to him in the same manner in which he had given the Pahul to them, and it was done so.

With the creation of Khalsa, the Khalsa created history and since the birth of Khalsa, the history of Punjab has been the history of Sikhs. Baisakhi played a significant role in this regard. In 1762, Ahmed Shah Abdali, with the sole purpose to destroy the entire Sikh nation, declared 'Jehad' (holy-war) against the Sikh and all the Muslims of the Punjab rallied under this slogan. The Sikhs were surrounded near the village Kup in Ludhiana District. Chronicles mention that about twenty thousand sikhs were martyred in a single day. This event is known in the history of the Sikhs as "Ghallughara" (Bloody Carnage). After this, Ahmed Shah Abdali thought that he had crushed the entire Sikh nation, but was greatly disillusioned when after a few months heard that the Sikhs in large number are celebrating Baisakhi at Amritsar. In due course of time Baisakhi reminds every Sikh of his cultural and religious heritage. On Baisakhi day all the Sikhs used to assemble at Amritsar and decide their problems relating to politics and religion. This convention still goes on.

The celebrations of Baisakhi are similar to the three-day schedule of the celebrations of other Gurpurabs. It is generally celebrated on 13th April every year.

Holla Mohalla

Holla Mohalla is a Sikh festival celebrated in the month of Phalguna, a day after Holi. An annual festival held at Anandpur Sahib in Punjab, Hola Mohalla was started by the tenth Sikh Guru, Gobind Singh, as a gathering of Sikhs for military exercises and mock battles on the day following the festival of Holi. It reminds the people of valour and defence preparedness, concepts dear to the Tenth Guru who was at that time battling the Mughal empire. On this three-day festival mock battles are held followed by music and poetry competitions. The Nihand Singhs (members of the Sikh army that was founded by Guru Gobind Singh) carry on the martial tradition with mock battles and displays of swordsmanship and horse riding. They perform daring feats, such as Gatka (mock encounters), tent pegging, bareback horse-riding and standing erect on two speeding horses.

There are also a number of durbars where Sri Guru Sahib is present and kirtan and religious lectures take place. Sporting shining swords, long spears, conical turbans, the Nihangs present a fierce picture as they gallop past on horseback spraying colours on people. On the last day a long procession, led by Panj Pyaras, starts from takth Keshgarh Sahib, one of the five Sikh religious seats, and passes through various important gurdwaras like Qila Anandgarh, Lohgarh Sahib, Mata Jitoji and terminates at the Takth.

For people visiting Anandpur Sahib, langars (voluntary community kitchens) are organised by the local people as a part of sewa (community service). Raw materials like wheat flour, rice, vegetables, milk and sugar is provided by the villagers living nearby. Women volunteer to cook and others take part in cleaning the utensils. Traditional cuisine is served to the pilgrim who eat while sitting in rows on the ground.

The tenth guru Gobind Singh felt that Holi, has lost its original meaning over the years. It was no longer a celebration to reaffirm fraternity and brotherhood. In 1757 AD he decided to revive the spirit of Holi and weave its essence into a festival created in the Khalsa traditions. Holla Mohalla is celebrated in the month of Phalguna a day after Holi.

Early morning prayers at the gurdwaras mark the beginning of the festival. The Guru Grantha Sahib is brought out with ceremony and placed on the dais. It is given a symbolic bath with milk and water. Akhandapathas, Kar seva, Shabads and Kirtans are performed the Karah Prasad is distributed to the congregation, after it has been consecrated by the guru. At noon, men and women from all castes and creed eat together at the guru ka langar.

Stories are narrated about the bravery of Guru Gobind Singh in prose and verse. Tribute is also accorded to Guru Har Gobind, who led his army to free 52 captive kings from the Gwalior jail in 1612 AD.

Colourful processions are ogranised on Hola Mohalla. Sikhs, especially the Nihangs, dressed in their traditional martial costumes, display their skills in archery, sword fencing, horse-riding and shooting. Battles are enacted and ancient canons fired to focus on the training required for war. Holla Mohalla is an occasion for the Sikhs to reaffirm their commitment to the Khalsa Pantha.

Maghi

Maghi, Makara Sankranti, the first day of the month of Magh. The eve of Maghi is the common Indian festival of Lohri when bonfires are lit in Hindu homes to greet the birth of sons in the families and alms are distributed. In the morning, people go out for an early-hour dip in nearby tanks. For Sikhs, Maghi means primarily the festival at Muktsar, a district town of the Punjab, in commemoration of the heroic fight of the Chali Mukte, literally, the Forty Liberated Ones, who laid down their lives warding off an attack by an imperial army marching in pursuit of Guru Gobind Singh.

The action took place near a pool of water, Khidrane di Dhab, on 29 December 1705. The bodies were cremated the following day, the first of Magh (hence the name of the festival), which now falls usually on the 13th of January. Following the custom of the Sikhs to observe their anniversaries of happy and tragic events alike, Maghi is celebrated with end-to-end recital of the Guru Granth Sahib and religious divans in almost all gurdwaras. The largest assembly, however, takes place at Muktsar in the form of a big fair during which pilgrims take a dip in the sacred sarovar and visit several shrines connected with the historic battle. A malala or big march of pilgrims from the main shrine to gurdwara Tibbi Sahib, sacred to Guru Gobind Singh, marks the conclusion of the three-day celebration.

Bandi-Chhorh Divas (Diwali)

The Sikh celebration of the return of the sixth Nanak from detention in the Gwalior Fort coincides with Hindu festival of Diwali. This coincidence has resulted in similarity of celebration amongst Sikhs and Hindus.

The Sikhs celebrate this day as Bandi Chhorh Divas i.e., "the day of release of detainees", because the sixth Nanak had agreed to his release on the condition that the other fifty-two detainees would also be released. These other fifty-two detainees were the vassal kings who had done something to annoy the emperor.

Emperor Jahangir had imprisoned the sixth Nanak because he was afraid of the Gurus's growing following and power. The Sikh on this

Appendix—II

Chronology of Gurus

	Name	Date of birth Place of birth	Age	Date of Martydom Place	Wife
1.	Shri Guru Nanak Dev ji Listen in Real Audio®	October 20, 1469 Nankara Sahib	70	September 22, 1539 Kartarpur	Sulakhni ji
2.	Shri Guru Angad Dev ji Listen in Real Audio®	March 31, 1504 Amritsar	48	March 1, 1552 Khadur	Khivi ji
3.	Shri Guru Amar Das ji Listen in Real Audio®	May 5, 1479 Amritsar	95	September 1, 1574 Goindwal	Mansa ji
4.	Shri Guru Ram Das ji Listen in Real Audio®	September 24, 1534 Lahore	47	November 2, 1581 Goindwal	Bhani ji
5.	Shri Guru Arjan Dev ji Listen in Real Audio®	April 15, 1563 Goindwal	43	May 30, 1606 Lahore	Ganga ji
6.	Shri Guru Hargobind ji Listen in Real Audio®	June 19, 1595 Amritsar	49	March 3, 1644 Kiratpur	Damdori Nanaki ji
7.	Shri Guru Har Rai ji Listen in Real Audio®	January 16, 1630 Kiratpur	32	October 6, 1661 Kiratpur	Krishna ji

(Contd...)

	Name	Date of birth Place of birth	Age	Date of Martydom Place	Wife
8.	Shri Guru Har Krishan ji Listen in Real Audio®	July 7, 1656 Amritsar	8	March 30, 1664 Delhi	N/A
9.	Shri Guru Teg Bhadur ji Listen in Real Audio®	April 1, 1621 Amritsar	54	November 11, 1675 Delhi	Gujri ji
10.	Shri Guru Gobind Singh ji Listen in Real Audio®	December 22, 1666 Patna Sahib	42	October 7, 1708 Nanded	Ajit Kaur (Sundri ji)
11.	Shri Guru Granth Sahib ji Listen in Real Audio®	Everlasting Guru—Guru Gadi Day—October 7, 1708, Pages 1430 Shabbads—5,871 in 31 Raags			

day, which generally falls in October-November, hold a one-day celebrations in the Gurdwaras. So in the evening, illuminations are done with Deewe (earthen oil lamps) or candles and fireworks. The celebrations are held both in the Gurdwaras and in homes.

SIKHISM GLOSSARY

A

Adi Granth

Adi means first, Adi Granth is the first edition of the Guru Granth Sahib as was compiled by Guru Arjun in 1604.

Akal Purukh

It means Timeless one, or The Being Beyond Time and is applied as a name of God.

Akhand Path

An uninterrupted continuous reading of the Guru Granth Sahib. It is undertaken by a team of readers and takes approximately 48 hours.

Amrit

It means nectar. It is sugar water which is used during the Khalsa initiation ceremony.

Amrit Bani

A term applied to the Sikh Scriptures, meaning the words are as sweet as nectar (amrit).

Amrit Vaila

The early morning hours of dawn. This is considered an auspicious time for meditation and prayer as stressed by Guru Nanak.

Amritdhari

A Sikh who has undergone the Khalsa initiation ceremony.

Amritsanskar

The rite of initiation into the Khalsa brotherhood.

Anand

A state of bliss which defies description. It is also the name of a composition by Guru Amar Das found on pg. 917 of the Guru Granth Sahib.

Anand Karaj

The Sikh wedding ceremony.

Anand Sahib

Composition by Guru Amar Das found on page 917 of the Guru Granth Sahib. Parts of it are used in a number of Sikh ceremonies.

Anbhav Prakash

The enlightened perception of reality which is enjoyed by a person who has become a gurmukh.

Antim Ardas

The last of the Sikh funeral rites.

Artha

Wealth, it is acceptable to acquire wealth, but it should not become an end to itself.

Asa Di Var

A collection of hymns meant to be sung at dawn.

Atma

The soul which is considered immortal.

B

Babur Bani

References to the invasion of India by the Mughal emperor Babur found in the Guru Granth Sahib. God is said to have sent Babur as deaths messenger.

Baisakhi

The celebration which takes place every April 13th. Guru Amardas initiated the annual gathering of Sikhs at Goindwal in 1567. In 1699 Guru Gobind Singh founded the Khalsa order on this day.

Barhmaha

Compositions about the twelve months. By Guru Arjun in Raga Majh, by Guru Nanak in Raga Tukhari and by Guru Gobind Singh in Krishavtar.

Bani

An abbreviation of Gurbani, applied to any of the writings which appear in the Guru Granth Sahib.

Benati

An appeal for assistance made to Sikhs world wide.

Bhagat Bani

Any of the writings which appear in the Guru Granth Sahib which were not written by the Gurus.

Bhog

The ceremony marking the conclusion of a Path.

Bole So Nihal

Part of the Sikh salutation meaning "anyone who speaks will be happy".

Buddha Dal

The 'army of veterans' formed by Nawab Kapur Singh in 1733 to look after Sikh holy places, preach and initiate new converts to the Khalsa order.

C

Chandoa

The canopy which is placed over the Guru Granth Sahib.

Chanpada

A poetical composition consisting of four lines in a specified meter.

Charan Pahul

Baptism ceremony involving the drinking of water which the Guru or a member of the Gurus family had dipped their feet in.

Chaupai

A four line stanza form used by some of the Gurus.

Chaur(i)

Yak hair or man-made fiber embedded in a metal placed in a wooden handle. It is ceremonially waved over the Guru Granth Sahib as a symbol of respect.

Chela

A disciple of the guru, used in the Guru Granth Sahib, to refer to Sikhs.

Chola

Clothing of the Gurus. Also applied to the coverings of the nishan sahib at a gurdwara.

D

Dal Khalsa

The Khalsa army set up on Baisakhi day 1748 and divided up into 11 misls.

Dasam Granth

The book of writings of Guru Gobind Singh compiled after his death by Bhai Mani Singh are finished in 1734.

Daswandh

Giving of one-tenth of ones income to charity.

Deg Teg

The dual responsibility of the Panth to provide food and protection for the needy and oppressed.

Dhadi

One who sings the praises of God.

Dharam Yudh

War in the defence of righteousness.

Dharma

Religion or teaching or life-style, as in Sikh Dharma.

Diwali

Indian festival also celebrated by Sikhs. From the time of Guru Amar Das onwards Sikhs annually gathered on this day. In 1577 the foundation stone of the Harmandir Sahib was also laid on this day.

Diwan

Congregational worship where Guru Granth Sahib is present.

Doha

Verse form used commonly by Guru Nanak and Kabir consisting of stanzas of two rhyming lines.

F

Forty Immortals

Forty Sikhs who died in the battle of Muktsar in 1762 and blessed by Guru Gobind Singh.

G

Gaddi

The seat or throne of guruship.

Giani

A person of spiritual knowledge.

Granthi

One who performs the reading of the Guru Granth Sahib at religious occasions, it may be a man or woman.

Gristhi

Sikh ideal is that of being married, having a family, earning ones living by honest socially useful employment, serving ones fellow human beings and worshipping God.

Gurbani

The writings of the Gurus

Gurdwara

Name given to a Sikh temple. It means 'Gateway to the Guru'.

Gurmat

A general term for Sikhism, including the teachings of the Gurus, as well as the Rahit Maryada.

Gurmata

A resolution passed in a council presided over by the Guru or the advice of the Guru.

Gurmukh

Someone who has become God oriented and God filled instead of self centred (manmukh).

Gurmukhi

The written form of Punjabi used in the Sikh scriptures, propagated by Guru Nanak and Guru Angad.

Gursikh

Someone who is deeply and sincerely devoted to the service of the Guru.

Gurpurb

The celebration of the anniversary of the birth or death of a Guru. Also applied to the anniversary of the installation of the Guru Granth Sahib in 1604 or the deaths of the sons of Guru Gobind Singh.

Gutka

Book containing the daily prayers of the Sikhs.

H

Hankar

Pride, one of the weaknesses.

Hazare Shabad

The common name given to 7 Shabads from the Guru Granth Sahib and 10 from the Dasam Granth.

Haumai

Pride and self centerdness.

Hola Mohalla

Annual spring gathering of Sikhs at Anandpur Sahib for sports contests, music and poetry compositions. The annual celebration was initiated by Guru Gobind Singh in 1680.

Hukam

The ordered will of God.

Hukamnama

Instructions issued by the Gurus, or other people in Sikh authority.

I

Ik Onkar

It is found at the beginning of the Mul Mantra meaning their is only One God.

J

Jalous

Outdoor procession led by the Guru Granth Sahib and five Khalsa Sikhs.

Janam Sakhi

A bibliographic account of the life of Guru Nanak, or other Gurus.

Jap

Devout repetition of the divine name of God, or a scripture.

Japu Sahib

A composition of Guru Gobind Singh read by Sikhs as part of their daily prayers.

Jathedar

The appointed head of one of the five Sikh Takhts.

Jhatka Meat

Meat of an animal which has been killed quickly with one stroke. Guru Gobind Singh dictated that Sikhs can eat jhatka meat of any animal but cannot eat Muslim Halal meat, where the animal has been slowly bled to death.

Jivan Mukti

The Sikh belief that a person may achieve spiritual liberation during their lifetime and not necessarily only on their death.

K

Kachha

Drawers or briefs. One of the five physical symbols that a Khalsa Sikh must wear. It is a symbol of self control.

Kalyug

An age in which righteousness and godliness is forgotten.

Kam

Lust, one of the weakness.

Kanga

Comb, one of the five physical symbols that a Khalsa Sikh must wear. It is a symbol of hygiene and discipline.

Kara

Steel bracelet, one of the five physical symbols that a Khalsa Sikh must wear. It is a symbol of restraint and remembrance of God.

Karah Parshad

A standard dish served at religious ceremonies in the presence of the Guru Granth Sahib and sanctified by prayers. It is a symbol of equality of all members of the congregation.

Karma

The reward or punishment of any action of man is given by Gods order according to merit, God may give it or withhold it.

Kaur

Middle or last name of a Sikh female. Mandatory last name for a Khalsa Sikh female.

Kar Seva

Term used to describe any voluntary work carried out for religious purposes, especially the building of gurdwaras. Also used to refer to the removal of silt from the tank surrounding Harmandir Sahib every 50 years.

Karta Purukh

A name of God, the Creator of all.

Katha

A religious lecture of Sikhism.

Kes

Uncut hair, one of the five physical symbols that a Khalsa Sikh must have. It is a symbol of spirituality.

Kesdhari

A Sikh who does not cut their hair, they may or may not be amritdhari.

Keski

Head covering worn between the turban and hair by some Sikhs. Also worn by some boys before they begin wearing turbans.

Kirpan

Sword, one of the five physical symbols that a Khalsa Sikh must wear. It is a symbol of the Sikh fight against injustice and religious oppression.

Kirtan

Musical rendering of Sikh gurbani.

Kirtan Sohila

Collection of 3 hymns by Guru Nanak, 1 by Guru Ram Das and 1 by Guru Arjun. It is recited as part of Nitnem at bed time and also forms part of the funeral rites.

Krodh

Anger, one of the weaknesses.

Kurahts

The vows of abstinence that one takes on becoming a Khalsa. Not to cut your hair, not to eat Muslim halal meat, adultery, intoxicants.

L

Langar

Free community kitchen found in all Sikh Gurdwaras. A cornerstone of the Sikh religion and a symbol of equality, it was instituted by Guru Nanak.

Lawan

Circumventing the Guru Granth Sahib during the Sikh marriage ceremony. Also the name of the four stanza composition by Guru Ram Das found on page 773 of the Guru Granth Sahib.

Lobh

Greed, one of the weaknesses.

M

Maghi

Sikh festival held annually on January 14 to celebrate the memory of the martyrdom of the Forty immortals in battle at Muktsar.

Mahala

Used in the Guru Granth Sahib to indicate the author of a composition by the Gurus. Each Guru used the name Nanak, for example Mahala 5 is Guru Arjun, Mahala 3 is Guru Amardas.

Mahant

Corrupt officials who had control of the gurdwaras prior to the Shromani Gurdwara Parbandhak Committee gaining control in 1925.

Manji

The stool or string bed upon which the Guru Granth Sahib is placed on as a symbol of its sovereignty.

Mala

A wool cord with knots used as an aid to prayer or meditation.

Manmukh

A person who is self-centred and has forgotten God, the opposite of a Gurmukh.

Matta Tekna

Bowing down and touching the floor with your forehead in front of the Guru Granth Sahib as a sign of respect to the Living Guru.

Maya

The dillusion of being wrapped up in the material world and attached to it.

Mela

Any Sikh religious festival other than the birth or death of a Guru.

Miri and Piri

The concept of spiritual and worldly matters. Sikhs are expected to maintain the balance between the two, this idea was introduced by Guru Hargobind and represented by two swords.

Misl

A fighting unit of the Sikh armies of the eighteenth century.

Mukti

Spiritual liberation from the cycles of birth and death.

Mul Mantra

It is the opening lines of the Japji by Guru Nanak and the beginning of the Guru Granth Sahib. It is considered the cornerstone of Sikhism. "God is one. His name is True. He is the Creator. He is without fear. He is inimical to none. His existence is unlimited by time. He is beyond the cycles of birth and death, self existent and can be realized through the grace of the Guru".

Mundavani

The word means seal and refers to the concluding poem by Guru Arjun in the Guru Granth Sahib which describes the spiritual qualities of reading and following the Guru Granth Sahib.

N

Nagara

A kettledrum found in some gurdwaras and introduced by Guru Hargobind to be beaten when langer was ready. It is also a symbol of royal authority.

Nam

Name, name of God. Sikhism places emphasis on the remembrance of God through meditation on Gods name.

Nam Japna, Kirt Karna, Vand Chakna

Mediation on Gods name, honest work and giving to charity. Three fundamental requirements for Sikhs.

Nam Simran

The remembrance of God through meditation.

Nanak Panthi

A follower of Guru Nanak.

Nihang

An order to Sikhs who follow the soldier lifestyle of the time of Guru Gobind Singh. They wear blue robes and reject household comforts.

Nirankar

A name of God meaning the one who has no physical form.

Nirguna

Applied to God meaning one without form on material attributes. God is considered beyond human knowledge and comprehension.

Nitnem

The daily prayers that Sikhs are expected to read. Nitnem consists of reading Japji of Guru Nanak, Jap and Ten Swayyas of Guru Gobind Singh in the morning; Rihiras, a collection of nine hymns by Guru Nanak, Guru Amar Das and Guru Arjan at sunset and Kirtan Sohila, five hymns by the same three Gurus at bedtime.

O

Onkar

God as the Primal Being. Also refers to a composition of Guru Nanak which appears of page 929 of the Guru Granth Sahib.

P

Pada

Division of a hymn in the Guru Granth Sahib, it varies in length from one to four verses.

Palki

The wooden, golden or marble palaquin in which the Guru Granth Sahib is ceremonially installed.

Panj Kakke

The five physical symbols which must be worn at all times by Khalsa Sikhs; kachha (briefs), kangha (comb), kara (steel bracelet), kes (unshorn hair) and kirpan (ceremonial sword).

Panj Piaras

The five beloved ones, referring to the first five Sikhs initiated into the Khalsa order by Guru Gobind Singh. Five Khalsa Sikhs are required for initiation of a new member.

Panth

The entire Sikh community.

Parkarma

The walkway around the sarovar (pool) found at many gurdwaras.

Patit

A Khalsa Sikh who has failed to live upto the vows of the Khalsa order.

Prakash Karna

The early morning ceremony when the Guru Granth Sahib is formally opened and the days worship begins.

Path

A reading of the Guru Granth Sahib.

Paudi

A stanza of the Guru Granth Sahib.

Pauri

Verses in the Guru Granth Sahib, their length and metre are both variable.

Phera

Circling of the Guru Granth Sahib during the wedding ceremony.

Pothi

A book or volume of religious hymns.

R

Rag

A tune or the series of five or more notes upon which it is based.

Rag Mala

The last composition in the Guru Granth Sahib. It is a listing of 84 rags used in Indian music in the early seventeenth century.

Ragi

A musician who sings the hymns of the Guru Granth Sahib in gurdwaras.

Rahiras

A collection of 9 hymns, 4 by Guru Nanak, 3 by Guru Ram Das and 2 by Guru Arjun which are read at sunset as part of Nitnem.

Rahit Maryada

The Sikh Code of conduct conceived by the Shromani Gurdwara Parbandhak Committee.

Rahit Nama

A manual of conduct for Khalsa Sikhs. There are a number of them by various Sikhs dating back to the eighteenth century.

Raj Karega Khalsa

The battle cry of the Sikhs during the rule of Banda Singh Bahadur meaning "The Khalsa shall rule". It is the concluding line of the daily prayer Ardas.

Rumala

The cloth which is used ceremonially to cover the Guru Granth Sahib.

S

Sach Khand

The realm of truth, the final stage of spiritual ascent where the believer becomes one with God.

Sadh Sangat

The Sikh congregation or community.

Sahibzadas

The four sons of Guru Gobind Singh who all died as martyrs to the Sikh faith. Ajit Singh, Jujhar Singh, Zorawar Singh, Fateh Singh.

Sahaj

The state of spiritual peace resulting from the attainment of union with God.

Sahaj Path

A non continuous reading of the entire Guru Granth Sahib over any period of time.

Sahib

Term of respect used for the Sikh Holy Book as well as applied to historical gurdwaras.

Sakhi

Story about a Guru.

Sangat

Holy congregation.

Sangrand

The first day of the month according to the Indian calendar. The reading of the relevant portion of the composition Barhmaha by Guru Nanak or Guru Arjun Dev relating to each month is read out.

Sant

A holy person or saint.

Sarbat Khalsa

A representative meeting of all the Sikhs to consider important matters related to the panth.

Saropa

A gift of honour presented by the Sikh community. Usually a length of cloth for tying a turban or a scarf worn over the shoulders.

Sarovar

The pool for bathing found a many gurdwaras.

Sat Guru

The Supreme Guru, God.

Sat Sri Akal

The Sikh greeting meaning "Immortal God is Truth".

Satyug

An era in which Truth prevails, the opposite of Kalyug.

Seli

A woollen cord worn by Guru Nanak around his turban. It was worn as a symbol of living in the world but not in worldly matters. It was passed on to each successive Guru upto Guru Hargobind who chose to wear the symbol of two swords of meri and peri instead.

Seva

Service to ones fellow beings, a cornerstone of Sikhism.

Seva Panthi

A Sikh whose life is devoted to the service of the Sikh community.

Shabad

The religious hymns contained in Sikh scriptures.

Shaheed

Title used before the name of someone who has died for the Sikh faith as a martyr.

Shlok

Couplet found in the Guru Granth Sahib.

Shiromani Gurdwara Parbandhak Committee (S.G.P.C.)

Committee which oversees the administration of many Gurdwaras in Punjab, Haryana and Himachal Pradesh as well as involved in publication and education related to Sikhism.

Sikhi

Sikh teachings

Sikhia

Advice given to the couple during the Sikh marriage ceremony.

Singh

Lion, the common last or middle name of male Sikhs. It is a compulsory last name for male Khalsa Sikhs.

Sodar

A composition of Guru Nanaks which is read by Sikhs at sunset as part of Rahiras.

Sukh Asan

The ceremony that takes place at the end of the day when the Guru Granth Sahib is formally closed for the night.

Sukhmani Sahib

A major composition of Guru Arjun found on page 262 of the Guru Granth Sahib.

Swayya

A group of hymns composed by Guru Gobind Singh and found in the Dasam Granth.

Takht

A seat of Sikh authority, there are five gurdwaras which are designated as takhts

Thambh Sahib

A pole or tower associated with a Guru.

Tankhaiya

A person who has committed a religious offence meriting punishment.

Z

Zafarnama

The Latter of Victory written by Guru Gobind Singh.

Bibliography

Primary Sources

Dass, Nirmal, Trans. *Songs of the Saints from the Adi Granth*. Albany, NY: State University of New York Press, 2000.

Of Interest because it collects the Poetry of the Non-Sikh Members of the Sikh Canon. Here, Among others, you'll find the surdas of the Sikhs.

Gurbachan, Singh Talib, Trans. *Sri Guru Granth Sahib*. Patiala: Punjabi University, 1984-88.

For the Adventures and Strong (Its a big, heavy book or several books!), here's the whole Adi Granth.

Kaur Singh, Nikky-Gunninder, Trans. *The Name of My Beloved: Verses of the Sikh Gurus*. New York: Harper Collins Publishers, 1995.

Key Sections of the Guru Granth Sahib Translated in the "*Language of Today*". A Book that will make a more accessible approach than a direct dive into the voluminous entire original text.

McLeod, H.W., Trans. *Textual Sources for the Study of Sikhism*. Manchester University Press, 1984.

Includes Portions from the Adi Granth and the Dasam Granth, the works the Janam, Sakhis, of Bhai Gurdas and Nand Lal, the *rahit-namas*, Popular Sikh History, Sectarian texts and Modern Sikh Theologians.

—. *The B-40 Janam Sakhi*. Amritsar, India: Guru Nanak Dev University Press, 1980.

An English Translation of a manuscript from the India Office Library, the oldest extant manuscript in the Punjabi language. With its 57 paintings, it has served as the basis of many popular narratives about Guru Nanak.

—. *Early Sikh Tradition: A Study of the Janam-Sakhis*. Oxford Clarendon Press, 1968.

A detailed study of the origins and content of the traditional accounts of Guru Nanak's life. Basic Work on source materials and crucial issues concerning, Guru Nanak and his Time.

The Sikh Rahit Maryada. Amritsar, India: Shiromani Gurdwara Parbandhak Committee, 1978.

An approved document of Sikh rituals and ceremonies, adopted after many years of deliberation within Sikh committee. It has assumed a status of a standard orthodox text.

General Works on Sikhism and Sikh History

Juergensmyer, Mark and N. Gerald Barrier, eds. *Sikh Studies: Comparative Perspective on a Changing Tradition*. Berkeley: Berkeley Religious Studies Series, 1979. Papers from the Conference on Sikh Studies held in Berkeley in 1976.

Grewal, J.S. *The Sikh of the Punjab*. New York: Cambridge University Press, 1990.

A broad historical introduction to the geography and cultural history of the Punjab, focusing of course on these topics as a back-drop to the Development of Sikhism, Right Up to the Present Day. Also has a somewhat helpful bibliographical essay.

—. *From Guru Nanak to Maharaja Ranjit Singh*. 2nd Revised ed. Amritsar: Guru Nanak University, 1982. (Original, ed., 1972).

Essay on Aspects of Sikh History from the late 15th to mid-19th centuries.

—. "The Sikh Panth: 1500-1800", in David N. Lorenzen, ed., Religious Change and Cultural Domination. Mexico: El Colegio de Mexico, 1981, pp. 193-97.

McLoed, W.H. *The Evolution of the Sikh Community: Five Essay*. Delhi: Oxford University Press, 1975.

Critical Essays on Major Theological and Socio-Religious Issues Concerning the Origin and Development of Sikhim. Outlines the Current State of Research and Suggests New Questions and Approaches.

Reference Works

Kohli, Surindar Singh, *Dictionary of Mythological References in Guru Granth Sahib*. Amritsar: Singh Bros., 1993.

Alphabetical List of Hindu Mythological Names Included in the Adi-Granth with Interpretive Notes. Includes Passages in Gurmukhi. Would be helpful for a consideration of Sikhism's relationship to Hinduism.

Tatla, Darshan Singh and Ian Talbot, eds. Punjab: World Bibliographical Series, Vol. 180. Santa Barbara, CA: Clio Press, 1995.

Though there are several Bibliographies of Sikh Works, this is by far the most up-to-date, comprehensive and well-annotated. Covers Works on topics from Geography to Religion.

The Gurus

Deora, Man Singh. *Guru Gobind Singh: A Literary Survey*. New Delhi, India: Anmol Publications, 1989.

Helpful Bibliography on the Tenth Sikh Guru.

Gil, P.S. *Guru Tegh Bahadur, the Unique Martyr*. Jalandhar: New Academic Publishing, Co., 1975.

Narrates the Life and Times of the Ninth Sikh Guru.

Gandhi, S.S. *History of the Sikh Gurus: A Comprehensive Study*. Delhi: Gur Das Kapur, 1978.

A general account dealing with all ten Gurus and their social milieu.

Grewal, J.S. *Guru Nanak in History*. Chandigarh: Panjab University, 1969. A Study of Guru Nanak's Work as a response to his Political, Social and Religious environment.

—. *Guru Nanak in Western Scholarship*. Shimla: Indian Institute for Advanced Study, 1992.

As the title says. Scholars discussed include W.H. McLeod and W. Owen Cole.

Singh, Harbans. *Guru Tegh Bahadur*. New Delhi: Sterling Publishers, 1982.

An understanding of the Ninth Guru's life which provides a contrast to and a context for the 'militarization' under Bahadur's Son, Gobind Singh.

Kaur Singh, Nikky Gunninder. *The Feminine Principle in the Sikh Vision of the Transcendent*. New York: Cambridge University Press, 1993.

This publication presents a pioneer study of sikh ethics from a feminist perspective. The author examines some of the relevant scriptures and later Sikh literature, especially Vir Singh's writings.

Schomer, Karine and W.H. McLeod, eds., *The Sants: Studies in a Devotional Tradition of India*. Berkeley: Berkeley Religious Studies Series, 1987.

A valuable collection of papers concerning various aspects of the Bhakti Tradition of Northern India. For Sikh studies, two papers are especially noteworthy: McLeod's discussion of the word Panth as used in the Sikh Tradition; and La Breck's report on the influence of Sikh sanits among overseas Sikh immigrants, especially in North America. This Volume is similar to Lorenzen's Bhakti religion in North India (see Shapiro and Oberoi Below). The relationship of the Bhakti Movement with Sikhism is a vexed one and invites further analysis

Singh, Darshan. *Indian Bhakti Tradition and the Sikh Gurus*. Chandigarh: Punjab Publishers, 1968. A Study of traditional Bhakti and the attitudes of the Sikh Gurus towards it.

Shapiro, Michael C. "The Theology of the Locative Case in Sacred Sikh Scripture (Gurabani)," in *Bhakti Religion in North India: Community Identity and Political Action*. ed. David N. Lorenzen. Albany: State University of New York Press, 1995, pp. 145-159.

A careful philosophically-based study of the use of a specific grammatical case in The Adi Granth with reflections on the theological significance of its use.

Recent Developments, Politics and the Construction of Sikh Identity

Kapur, Rajiv. *Sikh Separatism: The Politics of Faith*. London: Allen and Ulwin, 1986.

Describe the evolution of the Sikh Community in the 20th century from an ambiguous relationship with its parent Hindu society, towards a well-defined Khalsa identity. Concludes with a commentary on events up Until 1986.

Kaur, Harminder. *Bluestar Over Amritsar.* New Delhi: Ajanta, 1990.

A detailed Study of the aftermath of the Indian Army's 1984 action in the Golden Temple, code-named Operation Bluestar.

Grewal, J.S., Contesting interpretations of the Sikh tradition. New Delhi: Manohar, 1998.

Deals with the 'insider'/'outsider' debate that has recently focused on McLeod's Scholarship on Sikhism. Highlights the contested nature of Sikh studies itself.

Oberoi, Harjot, "The Making of a Religious Paradox: Sikh, Khalsa, Sahajdhari as Modes of Early Sikh Identity, in *Bhakti Religion in North India: Community Identity and Political Action*. ed. David N. Lorenzen. Albany: State University of New York Press, 1995.

Oberoi challenges modern presentations of Sikh history that follow a neat linear growth model. Such unified presentations may be comforting to present-day Sikh Consciousness, but argues Oberoi, the history of the development of Sikhism in marked by "highly complex ruptures, rapproachments and transitions".

Particularly helpful for anyone dealing with issues related to W.C. Smith's idea of 'crystalization of communities'.

—. *The Construction of Religious Boundaries: Culture, Identity and Diversity in Sikh Tradition*. New Delhi: Oxford University Press, 1994.

Examines the construction of a uniform Sikh identity from an earlier diverse set of beliefs. Pay particular attention to the role of the *Singh Sabha* movement in this process, a revivalist and 'reformist' movement that began at the end of the 19th Century.

O'Connell, Joseph, ed. *Sikh History and Religion in the Twentieth Century*. Toronto: University of Toronto, 1988.

This book is the result of a conference on Sikh Studies at the University of Toronto in 1987. Its four parts are devoted to 'Religion and Culture'; 'History and Politics'; 'The Sikh Diaspora'; and

'Comments' on recent events. The volume constitutes an important work both for its bibliographical material and its array of prominent scholars.

Singh, Darshan. *Western Perspectives on the Sikh Religion*. New Delhi: Sehgal Publishers, 1991.

Gives an overview of Western constructions/interpretations of Sikhism, from E.M. Forster to W.H. McLeod.

Webster, John C. *The Nirankari Sikhs*. Delhi: Macmillan, for the Christian Institute of Sikh Studies, 1979.

Explores the rise and fall of this sect, based on contemporary records. A good specific example of the ways in which the contest over Sikh identity is internal to the community.

Comments on recent works. The volume constitutes an important work both for its bibliographical material and its analysis of prominent scholars.

Singh, Darshan. *Western Perspective on the Sikh Religion*. New Delhi: Sehgal Publishers, 1991.

Gives an overview of Western perceptions and interpretations of Sikhism, from E.M. Forster to W.H. McLeod.

Webster, John. *The Nirankari Sikhs*. Delhi: Macmillan for the Christian Institute of Sikh Studies, 1979.

Explores the rise and fall of this sect based on contemporary records. A good specific example of the way in which the contemporary Sikh identity was formed in the community.